A Dream of Tartary: the origins and misfortunes of Henry P'u Yi.

That Chinese Woman: the life of Sai-chin-hua.

The Modern History of China.

BLACK FLAGS IN VIETNAM

BLACK FLAGS
IN VIETNAM

The Story of a Chinese Intervention

by HENRY McALEAVY

The Macmillan Company, New York

Library of Congress Catalog Card Number: 68-17518

First American Edition

Originally published in Great Britain in 1968 by
George Allen & Unwin Ltd., London

The Macmillan Company, New York
Collier-Macmillan Canada Ltd., Toronto, Ontario

Printed in the United States of America

ACKNOWLEDGEMENTS

The publishers wish to thank the following for permission
to reproduce pictures in this book:
The Radio Times Hulton Picture Library—nos. 5, 7, 13a,
13b, 14a, 16a.
The Trustees of the British Museum—nos. 6b, 8.
The Mansell Collection—nos. 9, 11, 12, 14b.

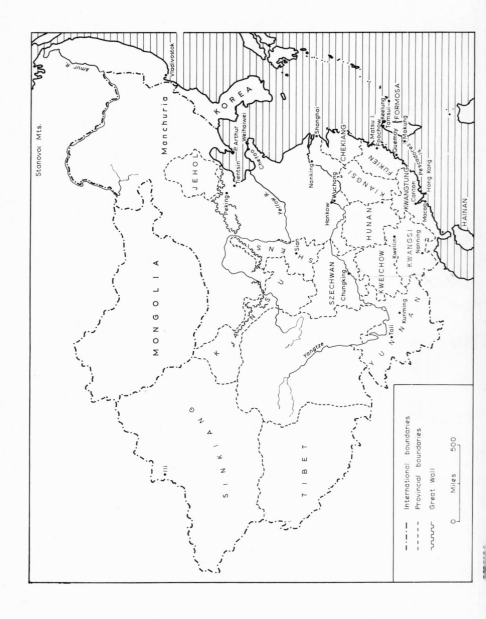

Stanovoi Mts.

Amur R.

Vladivostok

Manchuria

MONGOLIA

JEHOL

KOREA

P. Arthur
Weihaiwei
Tientsin
Peking
Chefoo

Yellow R.

Shanghai

Nanking

CHEKIANG

Matsu I.
Foochow
Tamsui
Quemoy
Keelung
FORMOSA
Makung

Wuchang
Hankow

KIANGSI

FUKIEN

Pescadores Is.

Sian

SHENSI

Hong Kong

Macao
Canton
KWANGTUNG

HAINAN

KANSU

SZECHWAN

Chungking

HUNAN

KWEICHOW

Kweilin

KWANGSI

Nanning

YUNNAN

Kunming

Tali

Yangtze

KANSU

SINKIANG

Ili

TIBET

International boundaries
Provincial boundaries
Great Wall

0   Miles   500

✤ PREFACE

There can be no doubt that the interest and alarm with which the western world is following the war in Vietnam are due almost entirely to the fear that it may lead to a direct clash between China and the United States. It is all the stranger, therefore, that so little attention has been paid to a series of events a couple of lifetimes ago which resulted in a Chinese intervention of the very kind we dread today, especially since the outcome has profoundly influenced the attitude of the Peking government towards the present conflict. This book attempts to tell the story in a manner suitable for the ordinary reader. It is not a history of Vietnam, though it was obviously necessary in the early chapters to sketch the historical background. Nor is it a work for academic specialists: thus, for instance, Chinese names, which invariably give non-sinologues a headache, have been used as sparingly as possible. Reference-notes have been inserted only at those places in the text where otherwise the author might be suspected of exaggeration.

French colonial expansion in the 1880s was by no means restricted to Tongking, yet to have introduced the affairs of Madagascar and Tunis would have added quite intolerable complexity to a tale which even as it is has more than enough ramifications. For the same reason, Sino-Japanese rivalry in Korea, which to some extent influenced Chinese policy towards Vietnam, has been given only the briefest mention.

❧ CONTENTS

✤ ILLUSTRATIONS

MAPS

BLACK FLAGS IN VIETNAM

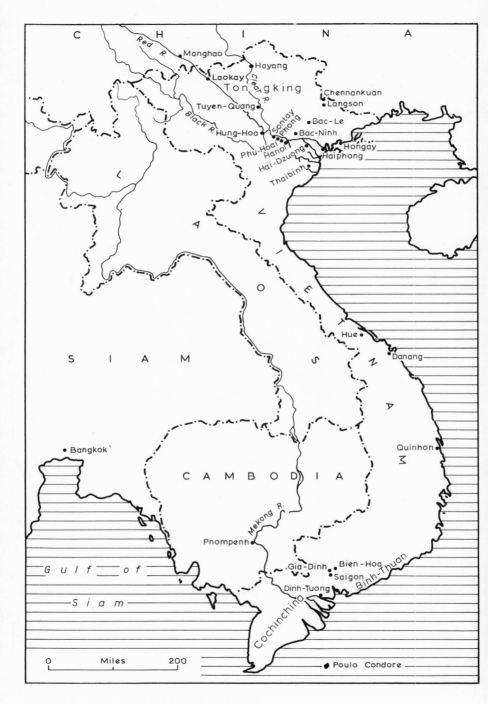

VIETNAM AND SURROUNDING REGIONS

❦ CHAPTER ONE

The Birthpangs of Vietnam

TODAY, in the Peking of Mao Tse-tung and the Red Guards, it would be unreasonable to expect any but a handful of the older citizens to be very knowledgeable on the subject of the Emperor Chia Ch'ing. These survivors of an antediluvian world, if you were to ask them, would probably tell you that the monarch in question was chiefly remarkable for the abominable manner of his death, an event which occurred in September 1820. The heat in the Chinese capital, as it often is at that season, was insupportable, and like a sensible man the Emperor had gone to find coolness a hundred miles to the north in the mountains of Jehol, across the Great Wall, where his predecessors had contrived a sylvan retreat precisely for such occasions. 'I have explored the pine-decked valleys,' his father had written sixty years before. 'Water, stones, mists and flowers make a fairyland. Truly it is like a dwelling in the moon, far from the earth.' In this paradise, time would glide by until with the progress of autumn Peking was livable once again. Then, before the Emperor returned to the Forbidden City, he would say farewell to Jehol by deploying twelve hundred Mongolian beaters in a vast tiger hunt, for at sixty, though rather corpulent, he was still vigorous and well-preserved.

Fate, however, had decided that this imperial programme was not to be realized. Days after Chia Ch'ing had set out on his vacation, word came that he was dead. Other things were reported too, so that when the funeral cortege, moving at a solemn ten miles a day, at last reached the capital, the enormous catafalque made its way through streets buzzing with ribald gossip. The theme of all rumours was the same: the Son of Heaven, in unnatural conjunction with a boy in the Garden of Ten Thousand Trees, had been in an instant frizzled to a cinder by a stroke of lightning. Indeed, they said, there was not enough of him left to be worth burying, so for decency's sake a eunuch of a build resembling his had been strangled in order to occupy his coffin.[1]

Scholars, who are in general enemies of good stories, are unanimous that nothing of this is true and that the Emperor succumbed to a bout of apoplexy brought on by the excessive heat, for in the matter of temperature Jehol had for once proved a disappointment. Nor, it appears, does he deserve to be singled out for special infamy as a sodomite; any partiality he may have had towards the masculine gender was kept within the limits of decorum and would not have excited comment in an English public school. Even with such a claim to distinction, it is unlikely that his memory would have survived outside his own country; without it his name might well, as far as the world at large is concerned, have vanished for ever into the night of time. To be sure, China has assumed a fresh importance in recent years, but it seems a far cry from the moon-gates and pigtails of a century and a half ago to that People's Republic which looms so menacingly in the imagination of western statesmen. Nevertheless, Chia Ch'ing bequeathed one keepsake to posterity, a word grown to such odious familiarity that by 1967 President Lyndon Johnson and his advisers, not to mention newspaper readers and television viewers throughout both hemispheres, must have found it hard to recall that there was an age of innocence, not so long since, when they had never heard the hateful sound of it. For the Manchu Emperor in all his glory on the Dragon Throne invented the name of what has to us become a nightmare.

It was in 1802, the seventh year of his reign, and the occasion was the reception of a tribute mission from one of the vassal states which lay on the borders of the Middle Kingdom from Korea to Nepal. This particular principality, which was called by the name of Annam, had been in a scandalous condition for decades: civil war and anarchy had turned it into a hell on earth, and a rather half-hearted attempt by Peking to restore order had only made the mess worse. Yet at last there had come to pass what, on a larger scale, had happened so often in the history of China herself. From the midst of the chaos a man had emerged to restore peace and government, and had proved his capacity to rule in the most effective way possible, by crushing all his opponents. But victory in the field, though an indispensable preliminary, was still insufficient to establish his title to power: he needed a formal investiture from his suzerain the Emperor of China, and this was what, through his ambassadors, he was now requesting. Nothing could have been more respectful than his profession of loyalty.

'Prostrate upon the ground [he wrote], I hope that Your Majesty will deign to show me pity: I am no more than a tiny tributary of Your Empire and my strongest desire is to be sprinkled by the rain of Your Generosity. While my thoughts fly towards You and the fumes of incense rise in the air in Your Honour, I address this petition to You.'

There were material offerings too: elephants' tusks, rhinoceros horns, fine silks. Everything, or nearly everything, was as it should be. The one exception was the style with which the petitioner proposed to signalize his new regime, and which he used in his letter, for he termed himself 'King of Nanyueh.' Now the word 'nan' in Chinese means 'south', and 'Yueh', the name of an ancient kingdom in south-eastern China, was sometimes applied to various modern Chinese provinces occupying roughly the same area. If the satellite principality should indeed be recognized as 'Southern Yueh', was it not at least conceivable that the expression might be misinterpreted as granting a right to some purely Chinese territory as well? Fortunately the elegant simplicity of the Chinese language provided a handy means of avoiding such an absurdity. All that was necessary was to transpose the syllables 'Nanyueh' to read 'Yuehnan', which instead of the solecism 'Southern Yueh' conveyed the very sensible meaning 'South of Yueh', a name which was particularly apt in the circumstances since the vassal realm was in part bounded on the north by the Chinese provinces of Kwangtung and Kwangsi, to both of which the name 'Yueh' could properly be applied. So Chia Ch'ing decreed that his loyal tributary should in future be known as 'Yuehnan', or as local mouths would pronounce it, 'Vietnam'.[2]

The confusion about names, which had been so neatly resolved, was very pardonable. Two centuries before the Christian era, the feudal states which made up what is now China had been unified by conquest at the hands of one of their number, the principality of Ch'in, whose ruler is in consequence celebrated in history as the First Emperor. From then on the normal condition of China was to be unity under a central government, but the Ch'in empire itself, on the death of its founder, fell apart, to be reamalgamated after a few years under the great dynasty of Han. During the brief period of disunity, a Ch'in general in command of what are now the provinces of Kwangtung and Kwangsi took it upon himself to march further south still into modern North Vietnam. The inhabitants of that region, who were a blend of Indonesian and Mongoloid elements, he incorporated with their northern neighbours to form an independent kingdom, with its capital near what is now the Chinese city of Canton, and bearing the same title— Nanyueh or Namviet—that, as we have just seen, was vainly proposed in 1802. This creation of Namviet seems to have been thoroughly successful: there was no great racial discrepancy between its northern and southern portions. In the latter (the North Vietnam of today), the Indonesian strain would be stronger, whereas the Mongoloid would predominate on the other side of the present Chinese border; but this was merely a question of degree. At any rate Namviet maintained its freedom for nearly a century, until in 111 BC it was absorbed by the overwhelming might of the Han empire. Thenceforward for the next thousand years Vietnam—if for the sake of convenience we may be permitted the anachronism—remained an integral part of China proper. Not only that: for three hundred and fifty years, down to the middle of the third century AD, it did not even constitute a distinct administrative unit, but was included in one region with Kwangsi, Kwangtung and the island of Hainan; and later, when it emerged as a province by itself, its inhabitants were regarded as Chinese on precisely the same terms as, say, the Cantonese.

Already before the conquest, the Vietnamese had been touched to some extent by the influence of Chinese culture, and now of course the process of sinicization was accelerated. The geographical character of North Vietnam was peculiarly suitable for the importation of a Chinese pattern of society. For Chinese civilization was originally a product of the plains traversed by the Yellow River, and it showed its nativity in a hundred ways. Since prehistoric times the farmers of North China, while benefiting from their alluvial soil had been obliged to provide against the danger of floods by an elaborate system of dykes, and it was the maintenance of these public works that was the prime duty of the Chinese state, and the infallible touchstone for determining a government's success or failure. The political organization thus brought into being had expanded across the Yangtze and over the mountains of South China until now it had reached a valley through which flowed a stream similar both in its bounty and in its dangers. For the Red River as, descending from the Chinese province of Yunnan, it runs across North Vietnam to Hanoi and the sea, poses to the cultivator problems of the same urgency as its more famous rival. Here the rich land cried out for Chinese agricultural techniques, and the use of the plough effected a revolution in daily life. The skills acquired throughout centuries of experience in the erection of dykes and embankments were eagerly adopted by a people regularly confronted by the menace of floods. Nor were the innovations only of a material sort. The Chinese written language soon gained among the Vietnamese that supremacy it was not to lose until eighty years ago, and every current of Chinese intellectual life duly made its way to this southernmost part of the Empire.

In the course of this millennium of Chinese rule, Vietnam shared in the vicissitudes of its conquerors. After four centuries of power, the Han Dynasty collapsed in 220 A.D. and its fall ushered in a period of disunity longer than any the Chinese world was to know again. For almost four hundred years, the Empire was parcelled out between warring regimes. To add to the chaos, the nomad tribes of the northern wastes came down through the Great Wall, built to keep them out but effective only so long as it was garrisoned and controlled by a resolute government. The first purpose of these invaders was to plunder, but before long they were settling permanently on the fertile plains of North China, from which a considerable proportion of the original inhabitants had fled southwards. Mixing with what remained of the Chinese population, the barbarians had soon assimilated Chinese institutions and established dynasties to rival the purely native regimes which flourished in the Yangtze Valley and beyond. During all this time Vietnam, as was natural, recognized the authority of whichever of the southern governments was closest at hand, just as did the provinces of Kwangtung or Kwangsi. Indeed, the immediate result of the turmoil was to reinforce the sinicization of Vietnam, for many northern refugees in their flight from the Huns were not content until they had put as great a distance as possible between themselves and the alien intruders, and pressed on as far as the valley of the Red River. In this way the Chinese element in the Vietnamese population was massively increased.

At last, as has been the cast throughout history, anarchy yielded place to order, and unity was restored to the Chinese world. For three hundred years, between the seventh and the tenth centuries, the Dragon Throne was occupied by the house of T'ang, a name which has become synonymous with the most splendid period of Chinese arts and letters. Within this great empire the Vietnamese were perfectly at home, and natives of the southernmost province were found from one end of China to the other engaged in government administration or in private affairs. Then the brilliance faded: the T'ang dynasty went the way of the Han and in 907 came to an end. The subsequent period of confusion was mercifully short, for in 960 another famous dynasty, the Sung, emerged to claim men's obedience, but this time Vietnam did not heed the summons.

The circumstances of this recovery of independence are obscure, but in considering the event there are some facts which ought to be borne in mind. First of all, even during the periods of most effective imperial unity, local risings and disturbances were of frequent occurrence throughout Chinese territory, and when a dynasty had entered on the road to decline such revolts were even more numerous and on a larger scale. It would have been strange if Vietnam had not shared this experience with the rest of the country. Uprisings occurred there more than once during the thousand years of Chinese rule: on one occasion, in the turmoil just before the advent of the T'ang, the insurgents are said to have created a local 'dynasty' on the model of other such petty regimes which had been proliferating in China after the collapse of the Han. It is very doubtful to what extent this 'dynasty'—if it ever deserved such a title—was truly separatist in tendency, and in any case it was of exceedingly short duration. When more than three centuries later, on the downfall of the T'ang, there broke out the revolt which was destined to restore Vietnam's domestic autonomy, its leaders seemed at first merely to have rejected the authority of an ephemeral Chinese regime with its seat at Canton, in favour of another claimant, less troublesome because it was further off. Having succeeded in driving out a Cantonese invasion, they were emboldened to defy the Sung power, too, when the latter appeared on the scene, and against all expectations they contrived in A.D. 981 to rout an expedition sent to reduce them into subjection. What is perhaps still more surprising, the Sung Emperor consented to make peace and grant the status of feudal tributary to the commander who had emerged as the king of the Vietnamese nation.

This apparent lack of resolution on the part of the Chinese to bring Vietnam back under their control may perhaps be explained, as far as the Sung dynasty is concerned, by the serious threat posed by northern invaders which demanded the prior attention of the imperial government. However, when in the thirteenth century the Mongol conquerors of the Sung made no less than three massive attempts to subdue the little country as they had subdued China itself, and were each time driven out with heavy losses, some other reason must be sought for the phenomenon. It is true that after the Mongols had fallen in their turn, their successors, the Chinese house of Ming, seizing in A.D. 1406 an opportunity to intervene in a Vietnamese civil war, once more transformed the satellite into a directly-ruled province; but even this, the final Chinese occupation, lasted only until A.D. 1428, in which year the intruders were again compelled to withdraw.

Our experience in the last two decades is enough to convince anyone of the fighting qualities of the Vietnamese, and in the struggle for independence these were enhanced by the fact that a thousand years of Chinese rule had ensured that the patriotic armies were not much inferior in equipment to the soldiers of their former overlords. But when we think of the vast difference in manpower, it is hard to credit that Vietnamese military excellence would by itself account for what happened. The Chinese historians go to the heart of the matter in describing the prostration of the invading forces by the perpetual heat and malaria. For it is a cardinal fact of history and politics that the dominant part of the Chinese people are accustomed to live in a climate with strongly contrasted seasons. Almost everywhere in China summer is oppressively hot, but as compensation winter in Peking is Siberian in intensity while even in the Yangtze Valley December can be at least as raw as in England. The principal exception is found in the south-eastern corner of the country, along the coast of Fukien and Kwangtung, where winter, especially in Southern Kwangtung, is noticeably warmer. It is from these regions, whose inhabitants are distinct from their fellow-countrymen in speech, temperament and bodily characteristics, that are drawn nearly all the Chinese who live abroad. Americans and Europeans who form an impression of Chinese people in general from the laundrymen and restaurant-keepers they see in their midst are committing a folly as great as if a Japanese tourist, going ashore at Palermo, were to imagine that the Sicilian crowds around him were to all intents and purposes indistinguishable from their brother Europeans in Hamburg or Stockholm. Furthermore, the difference between North and South, during the period of Chinese rule in Vietnam, had become more marked in consequence of the heavy infiltration into northern China of invaders from the other side of the Great Wall, and the process was accelerated in Sung times after Vietnam had achieved independence. Today, a man from the North China plain, physically at any rate, bears less resemblance to a Cantonese—let alone a Vietnamese—than would have been the case, say, fifteen hundred years ago. Also, throughout history the government of a united China has never had its seat further south than the Yangtze Valley, and usually a great deal to the north of that. The main expansion of Chinese political power has, from before the Christian era, been directed towards the north-west, into Central Asia; and from medieval times onwards the tendency has been reinforced by the fact that during two separate periods the whole

Chinese Empire was ruled by northern invaders, by the Mongols for a hundred years in the thirteenth and fourteenth centuries and then by the Manchus between 1644 and 1912. In other words, when a traveller from the West approaches China by the traditional route, and encounters a Chinese community for the first time at such a place as Singapore, he must bear in mind that what he sees is in no way typical of metropolitan China, and that in particular the ancestors of the colonists were not transplanted to the tropics under the aegis of their government but even in many cases left their homes in Fukien or Kwangtung in order to escape from its political control.

On the other hand, if the course of history, in the ten centuries that have passed since Vietnam assumed its independence, has confirmed China in its rôle as a continental nation, aloof from maritime expansion and with its gaze turned away from the sea towards the Asian heartland, Vietnam has been led in the opposite direction. The independence movement was headed by grandees largely Chinese by race and thoroughly imbued with Chinese habits. The only form of administration they could imagine was on purely Chinese lines, and superficially at any rate Vietnam became a China in little. Conflicts between rival chieftains resulted in the emergence of a victor, who founded a dynasty and united the country under a central government. For a while, law and order would prevail; but then, as in China itself, there would appear seemingly inevitable corruption and inefficiency and the machinery of administration would break down. Again there would be chaos, from which a fresh dynasty would arise. The annals and institutional books of these dynasties were written in the Chinese language and modelled on Chinese originals, and their ruling families always claimed Chinese descent. They recognized the Chinese emperor as their necessary suzerain, and were punctilious in paying tribute to the Dragon Throne. In this way Vietnam assumed a function for which China itself showed little taste: it became the spearhead of Chinese cultural influence in South-East Asia, a policy which paradoxically enough was to dilute its own Chinese quality.

No greater piece of nonsense was ever uttered by a statesman than the saying of Pandit Nehru, before his troubles with Peking,

that China and India had set an example to the world by two
thousand years of harmonious coexistence. A glance at the map
will show that the two countries are separated by the most
formidable impediment—the Himalayas—that nature has ever set
in the way of international intercourse. A few hardy Buddhist
missionaries overcame all difficulties to carry their good tidings
to China, and an occasional Chinese pilgrim made a pious journey
to the holy places of his faith, but even this limited activity did not
survive the first centuries of the Christian era, and neither then
nor later was there any direct Sino-Indian confrontation. Where
the two civilizations did meet it was at second hand, through their
cultural colonies in the Indo-Chinese peninsula, and the encounter
was a peculiarly bloody one.

We have already seen that Vietnam during its existence as a
Chinese province was confined to what is now the territory of the
Communist North. Indeed its extent was considerably less, for
on the south it attained only to the eighteenth parallel, whereas
at the present day Hanoi controls down to the seventeenth
parallel. Beyond this lay peoples of the same stock as the Indonesian element among the Vietnamese, but deriving their higher
culture not from China but from India. Southwards down the
coast the immediate neighbour was the indianized kingdom of
Champa, running approximately from the eighteenth to the
thirteenth parallel. Further south still, the Mekong delta, by the
time a separate Vietnam had appeared in the tenth century,
formed part of the dominions of Cambodia. From the first it was a
prime task of an independent Vietnamese regime to overthrow
these states, which seemed alien and barbaric because they were
un-Chinese in culture, and to bring under its control all the land
today reckoned as Vietnamese. This 'drive to the South' was not
merely inspired by dreams of aggrandizement: it was, in the
beginning at least, a measure of self-defence, for Champa had
proved to be an exceedingly dangerous neighbour, constantly
raiding Vietnamese territory, and once, in 1371, actually pillaging
the Vietnamese capital of Hanoi. The resulting wars went on for
centuries. The power of Champa was dealt a mortal blow by the
1470s, and gradually disappeared from the scene, thus opening the
way towards the real South, the Mekong delta. But Saigon was not

taken from the Cambodians till 1691 and the complete occupation of the delta had to wait for the nineteenth century.

These conquests were followed, as might have been expected, by a flood of Vietnamese colonists into the southern regions, whose original inhabitants—at any rate those who had not fled before the invaders—were either gradually absorbed by intermarriage or, in places, remained as racial minorities. Although the conquerors firmly retained their Sino-Vietnamese culture, the geographical conditions of their new surroundings, as well as the increased admixture of fresh blood, must have had the consequence in the long run, of emphasizing still further the non-Chinese element in the national character; though to complicate matters, from the seventeenth century onwards large numbers of Cantonese immigrants began to arrive by sea in the Mekong delta, which offered better hope of settlement than the densely cultivated valley of the Red River.

While Vietnam was assuming little by little its present dimensions, another augury of things to come was manifested in a political phenomenon of which no prototype could be found in China, for it was wholly a product of local circumstances. The great triumphs of the southward advance occurred, appropriately enough, under the most famous of all the native regimes, founded by the hero who expelled the Chinese in 1428, and known to history as the Later Le Dynasty to distinguish it from an earlier house of the same name. The glories of its first few decades have passed into legend as a kind of apogee of Vietnamese culture. But in a matter of eighty years or so, at the beginning of the sixteenth century, the Le were clearly descending the slope, well trodden by their predecessors, towards impotence and decay. By all precedent, Vietnamese or Chinese, it was time for them to be replaced by another dynasty. Strangely, however, this did not happen. There was indeed an attempt at such a substitution, but the usurpers were thwarted not by the Le themselves, but by two grandee clans, acting on their behalf, who on the re-establishment of the dynasty proceeded to divide the kingdom into two satrapies, each one virtually independent, while maintaining the fiction of accepting the authority of the Le sovereign. How this came to pass is a long and involved story for which there is no space here. It is enough for us to note that by the early seventeenth century there existed to all intents and purposes two Vietnamese states, a northern and a southern, which, to complete the resemblance to the situation today, were divided almost at the seventeenth parallel.

Geography was largely instrumental in determining this outcome. Modern Vietnam has been compared in shape to a pair of rice baskets (the Red River basin in the north and the Mekong delta in the south), fastened to opposite ends of a coolie's carrying-pole (the corridor about forty miles wide which forms the centre of the country). Of the territory so delineated, the area of Vietnamese habitation was more restricted still, since they eschewed hilly country and cultivated their rice in the plains. The mountains, which form the country's western frontier and divide it from Laos, as well as the highlands generally, were left to non-Vietnamese tribes. These had various origins. In the centre and south the hill dwellers were and are a people called the Moi, said to spring from a blending of Indonesian stock with a yet earlier population akin to the Australian aborigines. In the north the *montagnards*, to use the French term by which they are generally known, are descendants of Mongoloid immigrations. The most numerous are the Thai, from what is now Yunnan province in south-western China. The last massive incursion of the Thai occurred in the thirteenth century, when their ancestors were driven out of Yunnan by Kublai Khan who for the first time incorporated that province into the Chinese Empire. The mainstream of the refugees went due south to create Siam, but a sizeable portion made their home in north-western Vietnam. These ethnic minorities, forced to stay in the hills by Vietnamese pressure in the lowlands, have throughout the ages been accustomed to look on the dominant race as their natural enemies, and have seized every opportunity of profiting by the latter's domestic troubles.

The two satrapies into which, by the seventeenth century, Vietnam was divided were to outward view very unequally matched. The northern one was ruled by a family named Trinh, who had not merely the theoretical advantage of keeping the legal sovereign, the Le king, under their control at Hanoi (where on state occasions they paraded with him, mounted on ceremonial elephants as splendid as his), but, what was more important, held in dominion the greater part of the population and of the nation's economic wealth. Looked at in this way it was a wonder that the southern satrapy, which became the hereditary possession of a family called Nguyen, was able to retain its identity at all in face of the Trinh hostility; for during the first three-quarters of the seventeenth century, the Trinh launched a series of campaigns to eliminate their rivals. The Nguyen, however, benefited from the narrowness of the coastal strip in the neighbourhood of the seventeenth parallel to erect a pair of fortified walls, which held the Trinh at bay so successfully that at length, in 1672, they consented to make peace. For the next hundred years the Nguyen were at liberty to concentrate on the conquest of the southern lands, but although they had long since ceased to pay tribute to the Le Court at Hanoi, they maintained the fiction that they governed merely as viceroys of the dynasty, and all their official acts were dated with the regnal style of the poor puppet in the North. This was of course a mere outward trapping, but there was behind it a genuine sentiment of national solidarity. Observers from abroad agreed that there was a remarkable degree of cultural uniformity throughout the whole country. The Vietnamese language showed only trifling differences of dialect, and the same method of administration, through a mandarinate recruited as in China by public examination, was found in North and South.

The civil war had had as one of its consequences the multi-plication of taxes. This was specially obnoxious in the weaker South, and in fact the Trinh had been able to contrive some good propaganda on the topic, as for instance by the following manifesto addressed to the subjects of the Nguyen:

'Your leaders dig deep moats, and raise high walls. It is to pay for such things that they crush you beneath the weight of their impositions. They force you to take up the spear and the javelin, to the neglect of the arts of peace. Only by submitting to us will these burdens be eased from your shoulders!'[3]

It is likely that the continual extension of the southern frontier, and the opportunities offered thereby to the active and adven-turous, rather blunted the edge of such appeals, which might equally well have fallen on receptive ears in the North also, where the peasantry had little reason to congratulate themselves on the advantages of their lot. Nevertheless, the incessant wars against Cambodia claimed their toll and it was in the South that the common people at last roused themselves effectively against their exploiters.

The leaders of the revolt were a family of three brothers, natives of a place called Tayson, and in consequence this term is used by historians as a convenient name to denote the revolutionary movement and its adherents. 'Tayson' means 'western mountain', and the home of the insurgent chieftains was a village deep in the hills, originally a penal settlement to which their great-grand-father had been sent when taken prisoner in the civil war. From such an inauspicious beginning, the family had done well, and when it emerges into the light of day was apparently established in commerce. The eldest brother was later said by his enemies to have attained the rank of treasurer in the provincial administration only to be ruined by his passion for gambling. Pursued for mis-appropriation of public funds, according to this account he fled to his native place and gathered around him a crowd of mal-contents of every sort. By 1772 the activities of this oriental Robin Hood had become a household word among the peasantry, but the appeal of the movement went farther, and extended to the merchant class who had an interest in a change of régime and in the restoration of national unity. In 1776 Saigon fell to the Tayson forces, and although the city changed hands several times during the next few years, 1783 saw what looked like a final collapse of the old southern satrapy with the flight of the Nguyen claimant to Siam. On the other side of the dividing wall the Trinh watched with pleasure the destruction of their rivals and made a brief treaty of friendship with the Tayson, but the end of their own power was at hand. Turning against the North, the Tayson entered Hanoi in triumph in 1786 ostensibly to restore the Le dynasty, for two centuries and more a puppet in the hands of the Trinh, to its rightful privileges. The Le King, a decrepit septua-genarian, welcomed his liberators, cementing the alliance by giving his daughter in marriage to the second of the victorious brothers, but the excitement proved too much for him: he died within a matter of weeks, and his grandson and successor was induced by enemies of the new dispensation to flee to the Chinese frontier and invoke the aid of Peking against the Tayson, whom he denounced as rebels.

The Dragon Throne at that time was occupied by the Emperor Ch'ien Lung, one of the greatest of Chinese sovereigns, who ruled over an Empire at the very height of its power and prestige. If we bear this in mind, his attitude towards Vietnam will seem all the more remarkable. For those qualities of nationalism which had gained for the Tayson the support of the great majority of the Vietnamese people both in the North and in the South imparted to their cause a decidedly anti-Chinese colour. This was most strikingly shown on their occupation of Saigon, when they signalized the occasion by the slaughter of Chinese merchants and the destruction of their goods. Such an outrage, occurring in a country which acknowledged itself to be a feudatory of China, must surely, one would have thought, have been resented as an intolerable affront by a monarch whose armies, on much less provocation, reduced to obedience even the distant Gurkhas in their Himalayan fastness. But Ch'ien Lung betrayed not the faintest sign of concern: it was as if he agreed with Lord Palmerston that 'Buccaneers must expect to rough it.' Since these Cantonese adventurers had seen fit to leave their homes in search of profit, they must suffer the consequences of their folly. The imperial dignity was not touched in any way by their fate. However, the appeal from the satellite king in person was another matter. The rulers of the house of Le had always been punctilious in their missions of tribute to Peking, and it would be dishonourable to ignore such a cry for help. Accordingly intervention was decided upon and in 1788 a Chinese army of 200,000 men crossed the border and advanced irresistibly to Hanoi where, in a palace hurriedly vacated by the Tayson, the last of the Le rulers was solemnly installed as a vassal of Peking. Yet the festivity was premature, for the Tayson withdrawal was no more than a feint to gain time. Early in 1789 a surprise attack caught the Chinese in the full relaxation of the lunar New Year. Totally demoralized, they fled in disorder northwards to their own land, leaving thousands dead in their wake. Ch'ien Lung's fury when the news reached Peking was dreadful to behold, and a new expedition was at once organized, charged with the task of vengeance. Then a miracle happened. On the heels of the courier with his message of disaster, there came envoys from the Tayson themselves. Never, they said, had the insurgent chieftains intended for one moment to deny their duty of loyalty to China. The regrettable events which had just occurred had been brought about by the machinations of the wretched Le claimant who, having forfeited by his conduct all right to reign, was bent on involving the Son of Heaven in his miserable intrigues. Destiny had put Vietnam into the hands of the Tayson brothers of whom the eldest now begged to be recognized as king of the country and loyal tributary of Peking. By these words the detestable necessity of another tropical campaign was removed, since the sole object of such a venture—the reduction of a vassal to obedience—was achieved without fighting. Ch'ien Lung graciously assented to the request, the Tayson regime was legitimized, and the unlucky representative of the house of Le, who had fled for safety with the Chinese troops, was pensioned off in Peking, where he died in 1793. To forestall the formation of a court in exile, his principal followers were sent to Manchuria or Central Asia. All historical precedent suggested that an era of peace had dawned for Vietnam. In fact, while the Tayson were celebrating their triumph in the North, the other extremity of the country was witnessing transactions which were destined not only to destroy the new dynasty but in the long run to lead the nation itself under a foreign yoke.

The division of Vietnam into two warring zones coincided very nearly with the arrival of Europeans. First on the scene were the Portuguese merchants, but by the seventeenth century they had been overtaken by the Dutch, and then—a considerable distance behind—by the British. France was a comparative late-comer, and few could have foretold the rôle she was to play.

Neither the Dutch nor the British had any interest in the propagation of the gospel; and even the zealously Catholic Portuguese and Spaniards had in the beginning little time to spare for the evangelization of Vietnam, when China and Japan offered infinitely greater scope for religious activity. It was not until Japan, alarmed by the threat to her national security, had started to shut her doors to foreign missionaries that their endeavours were diverted to this less attractive field. In the year 1615, a group of Jesuits, barred from entering Japan, sailed from the southern Chinese port of Macao, a Portuguese possession since 1556, and disembarked on the coast of Vietnam.

In those days before the Industrial Revolution, westerners would have had little to offer in exchange for the silks and spices of the Orient, had it not been for their mastery of one science which aroused the wonder and enthusiasm of every government in East Asia, namely the manufacture and use of firearms. Gunpowder was certainly a medieval Chinese discovery, and it had been argued that the invention of the gun may be traced to the same source, but it is a plain fact of history that the cannon of the early Portuguese voyagers seemed to the Chinese a miracle of ingenuity, and that the Ming dynasty, which then occupied the Dragon Throne, wlecomed the Jesuit missionaries chiefly because the latter were astute enough to include in their ranks men skilled in casting artillery. The fathers were fond of dedicating their weapons to the honour of some patron saint, and would always send them forth to war with a formal blessing. In the seventeenth century, when the Manchus began their conquest of China, the services of these accomplished technicians were given impartially to the invaders and to the Ming troops, and many of the guns made at that time were to be employed two hundred years later against the British in the Opium War. The result was that the association of Catholic missionaries with the manufacture of cannon was something indelibly printed upon the Chinese mind. To give one instance out of many: as late as 1881, when a Christian community in Kwangtung province came to blows with its pagan neighbours—a frequent occurrence in those days—the latter accused the local priest, a Frenchman, of equipping his parishioners with artillery, and the story, though a complete fabrication, was widely credited.[4]

The war between North and South ensured that Europeans were welcomed to Vietnam, at any rate as importers of firearms; however, as in China itself, the missionaries soon encountered opposition, and for the same reason. The State in Vietnam, as in China, was based on Confucianism, and government was ad-

ministered on behalf of the sovereign by civil servants—
'mandarins' as they were termed by westerners—recruited by
examination in the principles of that philosophy. Confucius, who
lived five hundred years before Christ at a time when China had
not yet achieved unity but was divided between a group of
mutually hostile kingdoms, taught that the prime necessity for
man was to live at peace with his fellows and in harmony with
nature. He seemed to be concerned only with this life, and
resolutely declined any discussion of such problems as the
immortality of the soul. 'The Master did not talk about spirits',
says the classical record of his conversations, and this aversion to
the supernatural was communicated to his followers, with the
result that when, after the unification of the Empire, Confucianism
was accepted as the dominant philosophy of the Chinese State,
the intellectual elite of the country were reared in an atmosphere
of profound scepticism regarding matters of religion. One must
not exaggerate this point. Voltaire and others of the French
Enlightenment, on hearing reports of this remarkable lack of
ecclesiastical dogma, concluded that the Chinese were a nation of
philosophers. In fact, Confucianism is too dry and austere a creed
to satisfy more than an educated minority. The mass of the
Chinese cultivated the supernatural with an almost Mediterranean
exuberance. The basis of the indigenous religion was a form of
animism which saw a divine personality behind natural or man-
made phenomena. Hence, for instance, a god of smallpox would
be asked to show mercy, or the spiritual patron of a city would be
placated with sacrifices in order to ward off fire or flood. Then,
about the beginning of the Christian era, Buddhism was introduced from India, but unlike Christianity, which completely
submerged the old European religion, Buddhism never conquered
China. True, as the centuries passed, its alien origin was almost
forgotten, and it formed part and parcel of the Chinese world,
inspiring much great art and literature, and offering the hope of
survival beyond the grave, a survival in which good deeds would
be rewarded and the penalties incurred by sin could be lessened
by the performances, subsidized by bereaved relatives, of liturgies
of requiem: yet in spite of this, there was always at the centre of
the Chinese world the ideal of the Confucian scholar, watching

1 Pigneau de Béhaine

Prince Canh

2 Chaigneau's house at Hue

the praying and the temple-going at best with amused tolerance, and interfering to suppress charlatanism and superstition wherever they showed signs of getting out of hand. The legacy of this in our own day has been that there does not exist in China any sub-stantial body of educated opinion which finds Marxist atheism unpalatable.

While Confucius ostentatiously eschewed the supernatural, he not only acquiesced in the veneration of ancestors, already ancient in his time, but made it the corner-stone of his social system. Some enlightened missionaries, notably the Jesuits, recognized that this respect for one's forebears was in no way repugnant to Christianity, and that indeed the ritual employed for the purpose had no necessary religious significance at all. One can pay homage to the memory of the dead without even believing in their continued existence, let alone attributing to them quasi-divine powers. But this was too subtle a notion for the majority of theologians, and early in the eighteenth century the 'Chinese rites' were condemned by the Pope, a blow from which the Catholic missions never fully recovered, for from then on the Confucian leaders of Chinese thought, whose rationalist prejudices were in any case shocked by the supernatural content of the foreign doctrine, could brand the Europeans as enemies of society.

Over and above these considerations, which applied in Vietnam with the same force as in China, there was in the former country an added reason for the mandarins' hostility. Finding the educated classes unreceptive to their teaching, the missionaries concentrated their efforts on the peasantry, among whom they recruited an impressive number of converts. For their own convenience, they had devised a method of writing Vietnamese words in Roman letters, as they had done in Japan and China. But whereas the Japanese experiment was cut short by the closing of the country, and the alphabetical script for Chinese was confirmed to diction-aries and textbooks for European students, the foreign system of writing Vietnamese—first printed in a catechism published in Rome in 1650—was soon being encouraged among Christians as a rival to the Chinese characters of the intellectuals. Reasonably enough, the latter saw in this a deliberate attempt to cut off

33

Christian converts from the source of traditional Vietnamese civilization—to create a state within a state.

Notwithstanding the hostility they aroused, the missionaries proved to be more tenacious than the merchants. At the height of the civil war between North and South during the seventeenth century, traders of various nationalities establised themselves in 'factories' along the coast. The longest-lived of these was a Dutch post at Hanoi founded in 1637, for the Dutch from their dominion in Indonesia, had emerged as the principal suppliers of arms to the North, a role which in the South was sustained by the Portuguese from Macao. The British East India Company, too, made its way to Hanoi, but not until 1673, when the civil war, and the consequent demand for weapons, were dying down. Indeed the military stalemate between the two zones in the closing years of the seventeenth century has been alleged as one of the main reasons for the drying up of western trade. Of course there were many other causes: the murderous rivalry between the merchants, the wars in Europe, and the fact that in both parts of Vietnam the authorities were strong enough to intimidate the foreigners from the type of exploitation they could practise in other regions of South-east Asia. At all events, the British withdrew from Hanoi in 1697 and the Dutch followed suit three years later. The Catholic missionaries persisted in their efforts, sometimes tolerated and even favoured by the local rulers for the sake of their technical knowledge, but more often than not hiding from persecution among the poorest of the poor.

One of the first Jesuits to devote himself to the Vietnam mission was a man named Alexandre de Rhodes (1591-1660), a native of Avignon and therefore strictly speaking a papal subject, though thinking of himself primarily as a Frenchman. Expelled from Vietnam after intense activity in both zones, he returned to Europe to win support for a more ambitious programme of evangelization—it was he who supervised the printing of the romanized catechism—and although he never saw Vietnam again, ending his days in Persia, he decisively influenced the fate of the country to which he had given his heart. He wrote a number of works in French, in which, as well as in his conversations with influential people in Paris, he described the wealth in gold, silk and

34

spices to be found in that fortunate land. The result of his eloquence was seen after his death, when in the year 1664, there came into existence both the Paris Society of Foreign Missions and the French East India Company.

From the start the two institutions were intended to complement one another, and this intention was so completely realized that in 1680, on the opening of a French 'factory' near Hanoi, the British and Dutch could scarcely tell whether their rivals were traders or clergymen. The venture soon collapsed, however, and by the beginning of the eighteenth century French commerce, like that of Holland and Britain, had quit Vietnam, and the Company was giving its chief attention to the footholds, such as Pondicherry, which it had acquired in India.

The Society of Foreign Missions, however, never forgot the vision of Alexandre de Rhodes. Naturally, it encountered hostility both locally and at home itself, from the Jesuits, mainly Portuguese and Spaniards, who had been first in the field, but the quarrel was resolved by the decision of the Holy See that the Frenchmen should devote themselves to the South, leaving the North to their competitors. The flow of French missionaries continued, and as the eighteenth century wore on their voices were often heard lamenting the extraordinary pusillanimity of their home government, which seemed to have lost all interest in oriental adventures. Throughout the complaints one theme was reiterated which in future years was to become the great slogan of French empire-builders: hated of England, the secular enemy, who at every step was frustrating French aspirations, and now in the Far East was beginning to take the lion's share of the trade with China. What an admirable thing it would be to have a French stronghold half-way between Canton and Calcutta, from which the shipping lanes could be controlled at will! The only trouble was that whenever war came—and it came all too frequently—the French found it as much as they could do to keep hold of their minute colonies in India, let alone think of extending their sphere of activity. In fact it was an open secret that many important people in Paris were sick and tired of all talk of oriental enterprises, no matter how well argued the projects might be.

One great concern of the Church was the fostering of a native priesthood in the mission lands. Such was the special task allotted to Father Pierre Pigneau (later commonly called Pigneau de Béhaine, from his family's place of origin), who came to the southernmost tip of Vietnam in 1767, at the age of twenty-six. His seminary, which at its largest consisted of forty pupils, was unable in the unsettled conditions of the time to stay long in one place. After having spent a period in prison, Father Pigneau was obliged to retreat to Pondicherry with as many of his students as he could retain, but in 1775 was back once more in his appointed territory, as full of enthusiasm as ever, and with considerably enhanced prestige, for during his absence he had been elevated to the titular See of Adran, an ancient episcopate in Asia Minor.

His return coincided with the revolt of the Tayson against the government of the southern zone, and the fates ordained that after the slaughter of the ruling family the one survivor and claimant to the satrapy, a youth of seventeen named Nguyen Anh, should, while fleeing for his life, be succoured by the Bishop and escorted for safety to an island in the Gulf of Siam. The refugee had will-power and ability far beyond his years, and within a matter of months, profiting from a premature withdrawal of the Tayson forces and the loyalty of some local grandees, he was installed in Saigon and asserting his right to rule the whole of the South.

It was natural that Nguyen Anh should feel an obligation to his foreign benefactor and that Pigneau should try and reap profit for his church from such a remarkable change of fortune. But the relationship between the two far exceeded this. From the start, Pigneau discerned Nguyen's genius for leadership, while the latter revered the older man as a teacher and counsellor. Mission work was tolerated as never before: several prominent mandarins embraced the faith, and even Nguyen himself—though evincing no personal inclination towards Christianity—often attended mass and listened to his friend's sermons, for the Bishop was a fluent speaker of Vietnamese. Under these circumstances, was it strange if Pigneau imagined that a day might come when the land should be the great bastion of Catholicism in the East? However, a long journey lay ahead. Nguyen's position was still precarious: he had only a foothold in the southernmost provinces, and to reconquer the rest of his dominions he stood in need of all the help he could find. Here indeed was an opportunity for France to win friends and allies to counterbalance Britain's success in India. France, though, had her hands full just then with the fight for American independence; nor did Nguyen seem at first convinced of the necessity of foreign aid.

By 1784, however, Pigneau's warnings were justified. Once again Nguyen, driven from the continent, cruised disconsolately from island to island. Now at last he heeded his friend's advice. It was decided that the Bishop would go on an embassy to King Louis XVI, and in token of sincerity would take with him Nguyen's eldest son, a boy of six, named Prince Canh.

The party did not reach France till February 1787, and at first their reception, as had been the case en route at Pondicherry, was frigid in the extreme. The state of the French treasury, on the very eve of the Revolution, was not of a sort to encourage overseas adventures, and besides, Pigneau's enthusiasm had earned him in official quarters the reputation of a crackpot. Fortunately, the day was saved by Prince Canh. Fashionable Paris raved over the urchin, whose exotic appearance inspired coiffeurs and dress-makers to new flights of fancy, and the Court, especially the circle around the Queen, could never see enough of him. Meanwhile, Pigneau showed he was no crank or fanatic: he did not allow his own austere moral standards to prevent him from soliciting the patronage of some of the prelates whose libertine habits were a byword even in that uncensorious age; and whenever he had the occasion to discuss the technical side of his mission, experienced military men were impressed by his grasp of detail. In short it proved impossible for the government to resist the growing pressure, and in November 1787 a treaty was signed at Versailles by the Comte de Montmorrin, Secretary of State for Louis XVI, and the Bishop of Adran as Ambassador of Nguyen Anh.

So familiar had westerners become with the division of Vietnam that the two zones were regarded as legally separate entities. The North was known as the Kingdom of Tongking, a term which in Sino-Vietnamese means 'Eastern Capital' and was at first applied by Chinese merchants to the city of Hanoi. The southern zone acquired among European travellers the name of Cochinchina, an expression whose origins are obscure, and it was as King of

Cochinchina that Nguyen Anh figured in the treaty of 1787.

A preamble declared that King Louis, being convinced of the justice of Nguyen's cause, had decided to grant the latter's request for help in the recovery of his rights. The amount of assistance was then stated: four ships and 1,650 men equipped with artillery. In return, Nguyen ceded to France the harbour of Tourane (now better known as Danang), and the island of Poulo Condore, out in the South China Sea opposite the Mekong delta. French merchants would enjoy full liberty of commerce to the exclusion of other European nations. Curiously enough there was no mention of the Christian missions, though in all his speculations Pigneau foresaw the advancement of religion as surely as the ruin of British trade. 'We shall make the English tremble even as far away as Bengal!' he wrote in a moment of exultation. When, two days after Christmas 1787, he set sail for the East, he had every reason to feel satisfied.

Pigneau had been informed that the command of the expedition would, in the first instance, fall to the Comte de Conway, an officer of Irish birth who had recently been put in charge of the French establishments in India. What the Bishop did not know was that the ship he sailed in carried secret instructions to Conway, which, after telling the latter that it was entirely for him to decide whether the expedition took place or not, went on to give the broadest possible hint, by stressing the condition of the royal purse and the absolute necessity of avoiding all risks, that Paris would be well pleased to hear that the project had been abandoned altogether. In ignorance of this duplicity, all Pigneau could see, on his arrival in Pondicherry in May 1788, was that Conway was gratuitously putting obstacles in his path. The delay was especially infuriating since Nguyen Anh had managed once more to seize a foothold on the southern tip of his 'kingdom' and at that very moment the Chinese invasion in the north was providing the opportunity for him to reach still further up the coast. Conway, however, remained deaf to all appeals: to him the whole project was a piece of folly, and his opinion was accepted by Louis XVI in October 1788: the treaty thus became a dead-letter just eleven months after its conclusion. An exceedingly cold message from Paris conveyed the dismal tidings to the Bishop, and to add insult to injury offered him a free passage back to France, but it is doubtful if he ever received it, for he had decided to take matters into his own hands. Local French merchants, who resented Conway as much as he did, were forthcoming with loans and contributions, and upwards of a hundred men of spirit announced their readiness to serve under the flag of Cochinchina. Two ships were procured, with arms and ammunition, and in July 1789 Pigneau and the young Prince rejoined Nguyen Anh near Saigon.

It is easily understandable that western historians should be inclined to exaggerate the rôle played by Europeans in Far Eastern affairs, particularly when the Europeans in question are their own countrymen. Thus French writers generally maintain that Pigneau was the indispensable architect of Nguyen's victory, and that the latter, without his French allies, could never have prevailed against the Tayson. In fact the expeditionary force, such as it was, melted away in a year or two, either succumbing to the climate or finding the service unrewarding. Nevertheless, the handful of Frenchmen who stayed accomplished some notable things. Using their pair of ships as a nucleus they organized Nguyen's junks into a regular navy, which they strengthened further by vessels made under their direction. By this means a superiority at sea was soon assured. On land, they supervised the construction of fortresses and citadels on the most approved principles of Vauban, first at Saigon, and afterwards in other places of strategic importance.

In the meantime the Tayson regime, which had started as a popular insurrection against feudal oppression, had shed most of its reforming zeal and, reassured by Chinese recognition, was settling down into the familiar dynastic mould, so much so that there was no longer any compelling reason why the peasantry should take sides in the war. Even so the struggle was harder than Pigneau had led his companions to expect, a fact which no doubt caused most of them to abandon the enterprise. The Tayson king had established his court at the city of Hue, formerly the headquarters of the Nguyen satrapy and now making its first appearance in place of Hanoi as the national capital; but the great bulwark of Tayson power was the port of Quinhon, down the coast about halfway between Hue and Saigon. Every summer Nguyen Anh and his French advisors would profit from the monsoon to direct an armada northwards in the hope of capturing the place, but year after year the expeditions failed until even Pigneau began to wonder whether perhaps he had been too sanguine. Nguyen himself, now that he was secure in his brand new fortress in Saigon, clearly thought that he was entitled to indulge in some of the regal privileges he had been so long deprived of, and was spending in his seraglio precious hours which the Bishop felt ought to have been devoted to the planning of the war. At such times Pigneau would talk angrily of returning home and although Nguyen must have suspected his friend was bluffing, for the news of the Reign of Terror had lost nothing in transit from Paris to Saigon and the missionaries went about lamenting that poor France had neither God nor King, nevertheless he was shamed into a sense of duty. To this extent Pigneau may be claimed as the moral inspirer of Nguyen's triumph. In November 1799, the city of Quinhon at last fell to the besiegers, a month too late to gladden the final moments of Pigneau's life. Dysentery and other diseases of the country had taken their toll of him for years, but he had insisted on accompanying the army to the north, and appropriately enough it was in the camp outside Quinhon that he closed his eyes on the world. They took him back to Saigon and buried him with great magnificence in the garden of his house, where he had often said he would like to lie.

Pigneau's compatriots recognize in him the last of the great breed of warrior-prelates, and certainly his exploits at Quinhon put one in mind of Richelieu at La Rochelle. Yet the comparison would be unjust, for in Pigneau's case religion governed every aspect of his life. Providence, by putting Nguyen Anh in his way, had created the possibility of winning a privileged place for Catholicism in Vietnam. True, that could happen only after a bitter fight to set Nguyen on the throne, but even if the country had to swim in blood it was a small price to pay. This indifference to the slaughter and suffering around him was in sharp contrast to his hatred of carnal impurity. Fiercely chaste himself, he imposed chastity on all beneath his roof, and we read that in his later days, when Nguyen had given him a swarm of servants, he would wander round the house at night to frustrate any notions the Devil might be whispering into their ears in the tropical darkness. Yet he was prudent enough to discourage Prince Canh, on whom he pinned his hopes, from offending his father by asking for baptism, and on his death he bequeathed to Nguyen several volumes of the *Encyclopédie*, an unedifying work but one which contained useful information on the art of war.

Quinhon lost, the enemy morale began to crumble. In 1801 Nguyen's army entered Hue, and then sweeping northwards with little opposition took Hanoi in the following summer. The Tayson dynasty had lasted a mere thirteen years, but the central authority it had re-established after centuries of division passed enhanced to its successor. All that remained was that the transfer of power should be ratified by China, hence the embassy to Peking and the transactions described at the beginning of this chapter. As we saw then, all went off satisfactorily. Provided tribute was duly paid to the Dragon Throne, the Emperor Chia Ch'ing showed as little desire as his father, Ch'ien Lung, to interfere with whatever arrangements the vassal state thought fit to make in its domestic affairs. The Tayson regime had been recognized when it was in effective control, but now that it had fallen it was only reasonable that its supplanter, being willing and able to undertake the duties of his new position, should in return benefit from its rights. In 1804 a Chinese mission journeyed south carrying letters patent proclaiming to the world at large that Nguyen Anh was henceforward King of Vietnam and that his reign would bear the style of Gia Long or 'Praiseworthy Excellence'. It is under this title that the founder of the last Vietnamese dynasty is known to history.

CHAPTER TWO

Martyrs and Mandarins

GIA Long took seriously his rôle as the founder of a new dynasty. After so many years of Civil War and disunity, the machinery of government clearly needed an overhaul, and the task was commenced without delay. There was no dispute about the programme to be followed. Modern administration required modern laws, and of these a perfect example was at hand in the system of Manchu China. A Penal Code, almost a word for word replica of that of Peking, was promulgated in 1812 by Gia Long, and was followed in later reigns by a similar reenactment of the main body of Chinese administrative law. In government, at any rate, Vietnam became more than ever before a miniature China. Communications both within the country itself and with the suzerain power were improved by the construction of the so-called 'Mandarin Road', which ran like a spinal column from Saigon, through the capital at Hue, to the Chinese frontier. It was an appropriate symbol of the centralized power which was the most notable achievement of the regime. Local feudalism was given a deathblow by the abolition of excessively large landed estates. The Confucian pattern of organization which had become obscured in the years of turmoil was vigorously reinstated. Under Gia Long and his successors, the ruling class, in accordance with the Chinese ideal, was unquestionably the elite of Confucian scholars from whom the mandarinate or civil service was chosen by competitive examination. As in China, there was no caste of hereditary nobility, since titles of honour diminished by descent, and vanished altogether in a maximum period of five generations.

In some respects the social primacy of Confucian learning was even more assured in Vietnam than in China, for the former lacked altogether the wealthy merchant class which in the latter was more and more buying its way into the mandarinate. Trade whether internal or foreign was poorly developed, and whenever it approached sizeable dimensions was in the hands of Chinese. Agriculture was the basis of society, as by Confucian principles it should be, and a vital part of the administration—again on the Chinese model—lay in organization of public works for dyking and irrigation, while every encouragement was given to the extension of land in cultivation.

Yet, at best, this policy represented a withdrawal behind cultural fortifications erected to keep at bay outside influences and the forces of change. The Confucian learning so lavishly patronized was entirely literary, and the budding administrator was left in ignorance not merely of natural science and technology but even of such vocational branches of knowledge as law or economics. China, secure in her immense size, her still great prestige and her ancient self-sufficiency, may be forgiven for her slowness to recognize the need for reform, but recent experience ought to have convinced the Vietnamese that a mere revival of Confucian ideology and practice would not suffice to ward off the encroachment from the West which was coming steadily closer. Even from a strictly domestic point of view, the country soon began to show the kind of unrest that was endemic in China itself, sometimes provoked by government, sometimes attributable to nature. The peasantry chafed under the taxation and the forced corvees which the programme of reconstruction made necessary; and when calamities like flood and famine added to the misery uprisings were only to be expected, and political dissidents were quick to take advantage of the opportunity. In the North, every now and then, troublemakers appeared with the claim to descent from the old Le kings or from the Tayson chieftains, and we shall read below of a great Catholic-supported revolt in the South during the 1830s.

Meanwhile the Son of Heaven in Peking, as was customary, did not manifest the slightest concern with the affairs of his satellite. The latter's tribute came punctually and was graciously received, and, like Gia Long himself, the three successors of his blood to rule over a free Vietnam were ceremonially installed on the throne by letters patent from their overlord. Yet it is a remarkable fact that although Gia Long at the commencement of his reign established the seat of his authority at Hue, the Court of Peking took no cognizance of this arrangement and sent the letters-patent to the former capital at Hanoi, where the Vietnamese kings were forced to go to receive them. Not until the accession in 1848 of Tu Duc, great-grandson of Gia Long, and destined to be the last of his house to rule an autonomous Vietnam, did the Chinese condescend to address themselves to Hue, and it has been suggested that even then this courtesy had to be extorted from Peking by the threat that the King would rather not receive enfeoffment at all than make the journey to Hanoi for the ceremony. But if this was the case, no hint of ill temper ruffled the welcome extended to the Chinese mission. The 'Celestial Messenger', as the envoy from Peking was termed, was always escorted from the frontier with enormous pomp. The letter from the Son of Heaven was carried in solitary state under a canopy, while in front of it, similarly shielded from the sun, was borne a smoking incense-burner. As the embassy passed along the road, in the midst of an armed escort of Vietnamese troops, preceded by elephants in war paraphernalia, magistrates of all the towns en route welcomed it on their knees. When the mission of 1848 arrived at Hue, it was considered unseemly that a representative of the Court of Peking should enter the citadel through the gates like an ordinary mortal and the envoy and his suite were transported over the walls by means of a ramp erected for the occasion.

Yet in spite of everything, the Chinese diplomats when talking frankly among themselves rarely had a good word to say for their reception. The chief causes of complaint were the heat and the mosquitoes which made day and night misery. The Vietnamese houses, sensibly adapted to such a climate, appeared to Chinese eyes nothing more than beggarly wooden huts thatched with leaves. Whenever a civilized-looking building of brick or stone came into view, inquiries nearly always confirmed that it was the residence of some Chinese colonist. The dress of the ordinary Vietnamese matched their lodgings. Women would stand at the doors of their cabins with their shoulders naked to see the procession go by, and in the streets total nudity was not uncommon. Even officers thought nothing of showing themselves on parade in bare feet. Undoubtedly the King must have believed that he cut a distinguished figure in his robe of yellow silk embroidered with golden dragons and gathered at the waist by a scarlet girdle, but he only succeeded in reminding his visitors of some actor on the Peking stage, and it was all they could do to keep their faces straight while they were in his presence. For in the course of two hundred years of Manchu rule, close-fitting Tartar gowns had become so familiar to Chinese men that the loose robes of their forefathers, which survived in Vietnam, struck them as ridiculous pieces of theatrical property, just as the time-honoured mode of wearing the hair long and wound into a topnot seemed dirty and uncouth when contrasted with their own shaven crowns and pigtails. Neither Hanoi nor Hue, though celebrated as earthly paradises by the Vietnamese, could be mentioned in the same breath either with Peking, or with such cities as Soochow or Nanking. The palace interiors seemed bare and forbidding, and at official entertainments, when one was supposed to squat on a kind of low table, it was torture to Chinese legs which were accustomed to the use of chairs. As for the cuisine, the less said the better. The Chinese have always had the vulgarity to believe that the grand purpose of cooking is to delight the palate but the royal banquests, whether at Hanoi or Hue, abounding as they did with dishes smothered in flowers, deserved the worst criticism that a Chinese can make about food, namely that more attention had been given to pleasing the eye than the taste. The obvious boredom of the imperial ambassadors and their eagerness to get back home is unmistakable, and serves to explain the almost total lack of curiosity which Chinese travellers and storytellers consistently manifested towards their southern neighbours.[5]

Of the French adventurers who attached themselves to Gia Long during the war, only two remained with him throughout his reign. These were a pair of Bretons, a naval officer named Chaigneau, who was a cousin of the great Chateaubriand, and Vannier, a veteran of the War of American Independence. Both of them were treated with notable favour by the King, who appointed them mandarins and members of his Privy Council and they installed themselves with the wives they had chosen from the Vietnamese Catholic community in houses near the palace. Their company was a reminder of the old days of friendship with Pigneau and they were admitted to the royal presence with a surprising lack of formality. Perhaps, indeed, Gia Long was a little too affable, for the Frenchmen, cut off permanently, as it must have seemed, from their own country, had turned for consolation to the religion of their boyhood, and were zealous churchgoers, never missing a Sunday mass and surrounding themselves in their families with all the emblems of simple Catholic piety. To such men, Gia Long continually presented himself in the most revolting aspect. He delighted above all else, remarked an observer, in discussing the physical details of copulation, even going so far on occasion—a disconcerting breach of filial piety in a Confucian—as to speculate on the technique employed by his own parents in begetting him. When Chaigneau's first wife died, leaving him with a son, the King expressed a wish to see the boy, and at once launched into an obscene harangue in praise of the father's handiwork, which more than half a century later, writing in Paris on the eve of the Franco-Prussian war, the object of the criticism still remembered with horror. To make things worse, the author of this perpetual stream of filth had all the appearance of a Confucian sage. At fifty his hair was quite white—a circumstance which can impart a look of shocking senility to a Far Eastern face—and he had grown a long snowy beard of a luxuriance rarely found in his country.[6]

But the Frenchmen stomached the nastiness and hoped that their patience was laying the foundations of a future understanding between Vietnam and their own land. Of course, nothing could be expected so long as the revolutionary and Napoleonic wars dragged on, but at least they were able to frustrate the British, who every now and then would send a ship to ask for trading concessions. In fact, if they had only known, Pigneau and his schemes were far from having been forgotten in Paris. Napoleon in particular manifested a keen interest, but the Russian expedition intervened.

Then at last the day came, in 1817, when a French ship arrived, the first to sail those waters for twenty-five years. Others followed, but the Bordeaux merchants who financed the venture had no idea of the local market, and all the efforts of the two French mandarins did not avail to prevent an embarrassing failure. French naval vessels came too, with instructions to preserve for the time being a discreet silence on the subject of the 1787 Treaty, but with private letters for Chaigneau from the French government, requesting his assistance in establishing commercial relations. To all these visitors, Gia Long showed himself personally very gracious, but at the same time made it plain that he had no intention whatsoever of entering into any commitments. As Chaigneau longed for an opportunity to see France again, he took the opportunity in 1819, with Gia Long's blessing, of returning to Europe with his family. His stay in France was shorter than he had expected, and in 1821 he was back in Hue, bearing the credentials of Consul.

He found an ominous change at the Court, for at the beginning of 1820, his old patron, Gia Long, had died. According to Pigneau's calculations all those years ago, this was the moment which should have ushered in a new era for Vietnam. But Prince Canh, the heir-apparent, in whom such hopes had been placed, had survived Pigneau by less than two years, dying of smallpox in 1801, and the throne passed to another son of Gia Long, who succeeded under the style of Minh Mang. The new ruler was aware that there were people both at Court and in the country who regretted the loss of his elder brother, and the knowledge turned him against all those who had been associated with Canh. This by itself would have sufficed to make him hate the missionaries and foreigners in general, but in addition he had imbibed all the Confucian scholar's prejudices against Christianity —prejudices which for that matter were almost as strong in the mind of Gia Long, though in the latter's case kept in check by gratitude towards Pigneau. Then again, quite apart from the distaste with which a disciple of Confucius viewed what he took to be superstition, there were plenty of examples, not too remote in space or time, of what happened to nations which engaged in traffic with the West. The Philippines and Indonesia were only a few days journey away. The British exploits in India were somewhat further off, but the conquerors were creeping nearer all the time, and since 1819 had been in Singapore.

Here it must be conceded that the French committed a most egregious blunder, for in the catalogue of presents which Chaigneau carried from Paris for the King one item was a set of sixteen engravings to illustrate the famous military victories of Napoleon— an odd choice, one might have thought, by the government of Louis XVIII. However this gift was intended, it certainly made a profound impression on Minh Mang, who hastily summoned Chaigneau's son to explain the meaning of the battle scenes, while the Court scribes ransacked their brains to find suitable Chinese characters for such barbarous names as Soult and Kleber. The King listened like one fascinated but when the audience was over, a chamberlain said to young Chaigneau, on the way out, that he must have taken leave of his senses to tell His Majesty in so many words that his army was nothing compared with that of France. 'What, do you want me to lie?' exclaimed the young man. 'Certainly,' replied the mandarin, 'rather than give offence.'[7]

The history of the Far East contained a striking example which Minh Mang believed worthy of imitation. For two hundred years, since the beginning of the seventeenth century, Japan, once the favourite goal of the European missions, had succeeded in keeping its doors locked against all foreign intrusion. As we have seen, it was this policy which had in the first place deflected the efforts of the church towards Vietnam itself, and it would be no more than proper, in the King's opinion, if he employed identical methods to ward off the same unwholesome influence. At the very outset of his reign, therefore, rather to the surprise of his courtiers, he plunged into a study of Japanese policy, from which he emerged with his convictions reinforced. It was soon clear to the two foreign mandarins that they no longer enjoyed the privileged position given to them by Gia Long, so much so that they decided to abandon the scene of their past importance and resume the drab anonymity of life among their own people. They left for France in 1825; and on their arrival, Chaigneau, in a final report to the government, declared that armed force alone would wrest from Vietnam the concessions Paris hoped for.

With their departure, the only westerners remaining in the country were the Catholic missionaries, whose situation reverted to what it had been before the advent of Gia Long, that is to say of official prohibition—not very effective, if we consider the number of priests still active throughout the countryside—varied

48

MARTYRE DU B^{EUX} MARCHAND COCHINCHINE 1835

3   The martyrdom of Father Marchand

4 Jean Dupuis in Chinese clothing

at times by the employment of some of them at Court as translators or informants. This state of affairs, unsatisfactory for the Church, but still far from intolerable, was altered abruptly by a dramatic turn of events in Saigon and the Mekong delta.

That part of the country had until recently been administered by one of the most illustrious of the followers of Gia Long, Marshal Le Van Duyet, who had in his time been a great friend of Pigneau, and in consequence was a patron and pro-protector of Christians. Minh Mang had a special cause to hate him, for he had been prominent among those who had opposed the King's nomination as Heir Apparent in place of Prince Canh, but his services to the dynasty had been so outstanding that vengeance during his lifetime was out of the question. When he died in 1831, however, his territorial administration, which had assumed the appearance of a satrapy, was not allowed to pass to his adopted son, as the latter had expected, but was abolished altogether, and the region brought under the direct control of the central government. The disappointed claimant launched a revolt at Saigon in 1833, and a large area in the South threw off the authority of Hue. From the start, Khoi, the Marshal's adopted son, looked for help to the Christians, both converts and Europeans, and they justified his trust. Western help did not seem impossible, but that would take time and the urgency was pressing. An appeal was made to Siam, which responded promptly by sending an army in through Cambodia. Among the messengers dispatched to Bangkok were native Catholics with a letter to a French missionary. This was intercepted, and became proof positive to Minh Mang of Christian treason. He reacted with extreme speed. A large army hurried South, defeated the Siamese and surrounded Saigon. But the citadel, built forty years earlier by a French engineer, proved a tough nut to crack, and the siege lingered on for more than twelve months. When the place at last fell, Khoi, the leader, was dead, but among the prisoners there was a real prize, a French priest named Marchand. Most of the garrison were slaughtered out of hand, but Marchand was one of the few men of importance taken to Hue. The fate reserved for him merits attention, for it was to have far-reaching consequences.

One of the legacies bequeathed to us by the nineteenth century is the notion that the Chinese, and indeed the Yellow Race generally, are distinguished from the rest of mankind by their delight in cruelty. The 'black legend', for that is what it amounts to, was unknown to our ancestors in earlier times, but about the period we are now describing, that is to say from the 1830s onwards, it began to take hold of the western imagination, and it would be useless to pretend that it does not still influence men's minds in Europe and America.

In 1802, when Gia Long at last gained possession of his capital of Hue, the founder of the Tayson power was already in his grave, and the titular head of the regime was a mere boy. His youth, however, did not save him from a horrible punishment. As an overture, the remains of the dead chieftain and his wife were exhumed and tumbled into a basket, which Gia Long's army thereupon proceeded to treat as a urinal. Then the poor captive, who had been forced to watch this transaction, was tied to four elephants, and torn limb from limb.

What vileness, we say to ourselves, where even innocent animals are made the instruments of human iniquity! And if we confine ourselves to that statement, we are, of course, perfectly right. If we go further, however, and see in the atrocity a proof of oriental barbarism, we only reveal our ignorance of our own past. For just forty-five years before the execution at Hue, a man who had inflicted a trifling wound upon King Louis XV with a penknife was ripped asunder by carthorses in the centre of Paris, to the uninhibited delight of spectators, including women, from the highest rank of society. Most people, if sentenced to be pulled apart, would prefer for reasons of speed to have the operation performed by elephants. In addition, the French execution was preceded by a long series of the most hellish tortures, which the victim at Hue was spared. In fact if Bishop Pigneau had lived a couple of years longer it is most improbable that he would have found the ceremony in any way blameworthy. The commonest punishment for highwaymen and burglars in the France in which he had been brought up was breaking on the wheel—a hideous ritual which had been carried out on several occasions during his last short stay in Paris, almost within hearing of the fashionable salons in which he had shown off Prince Canh, and the knowledge had not perturbed his equanimity. As for the church, its thunders were directed not against the legalized beastliness but at the Revolution which put an end to it.

The truth is that as far as Western Europe as a whole is concerned, it is essentially the French Revolution which marks the point from which Christendom may fairly be said to show greater humanity in its penal laws than China or Vietnam. The judicial torture, for instance, which shocked foreigners in China during the nineteenth century was no worse than the procedures employed a generation or two earlier on the Continent of Europe. The normal Chinese methods of capital punishment, namely beheading and strangulation, compared very favourably with those in use, say, in France before 1789.

We have left Father Marchand in prison at Hue, and in his case, because his offence was regarded as a particularly heinous attempt against the security of the state, the severest penalty seemed called for. This was of Chinese origin and the name given to it by foreigners has passed into the languages of the world as a term of reproach against the country which invented it, for it was the infamous 'Death of a Thousand Cuts'.

On the last day of November, 1835, the priest was taken from a tiny cage in which he had been confined and carried on a stretcher —for he was unable to walk on his cramped legs—into the presence of Minh Mang and his Court. He was dragged to the King's feet and compelled to kowtow five times. From there he was conveyed to the Tribunal of Punishments, where in the course of an interrogation his thighs were ripped with five pairs of red-hot pincers, which were left adhering to the flesh until they had cooled. This infliction was repeated three times. After the interrogation a stone was put in his mouth and kept in place by a sort of bit made out of bamboo. Thus gagged, Father Marchand was conveyed into the suburbs to the outskirts of a Christian village, where he was handed over to four executioners. One of these had the task of dragging with a pair of pincers at the flesh to be severed, another, armed with a knife, did the actual cutting, while the last two respectively called out the number of the wounds and entered the details in a book. The business started with the amputation of the priest's eyebrows. Then, as the blood poured down over his eyes and face and blinded him, his breasts were detached from his body. The buttocks were next to be cut off, following which the knife began to slice away the fleshy part of the legs. At this stage Father Marchand breathed his last. His corpse was quartered and thrown into the sea; his head, after a preliminary parade through the provinces, was ground into powder and fired from a cannon.

Father Marchand was fully prepared for death: it was a prospect that he had faced for years. Nevertheless even his enormous faith and courage must have been tried to the very limits of endurance and there were surely moments when, alone among implacable enemies and surrounded by everything that was most alien and abominable, the despairing thought entered his mind that he had been deserted not merely by man but by God Himself. It would be odious and disloyal to say a word to disparage his martyrdom. Yet he had undoubtedly taken part in a rebellion which, assisted by a foreign army, had put the dynasty in serious peril, and even by European standards Minh Mang was justified in treating his conduct as an unpardonable crime. At the risk of appearing perverse it ought to be mentioned that until the nineteenth century a man convicted of treason in England was still sentenced to be hanged, drawn and quartered, or in other words to be suspended from a gallows, cut down while alive, his sexual organs amputated, his belly opened with a butcher's knife, and his heart and entrails torn out and burned before his eyes, after which his head and limbs would be severed from his trunk and exposed to public view at appropriate vantage points. Alabaster, a leading western authority on the old Chinese criminal law declares without hesitation that even the so-called 'Death of a Thousand Cuts' was far less atrocious than its English equivalent.[8]

Marchand was not the only foreign priest to shed his blood. There were seven other French and Spanish victims of Minh Mang's severity, but none of the others—perhaps because they were guilty merely of illegally entering the country to propagate Christianity—was called upon to endure the sufferings of Marchand, and in general beheading or garrotting was considered sufficient. The case of one of these men, a French priest named Jaccard, is especially interesting, since it illustrates how unpredictable the king's humour could be. Despite his infraction of the law by landing in Vietnam at all, Father Jaccard was summoned to Hue in 1827 and put in charge of the translation of western books on such topics as the campaigns of Napoleon and the wars of the British in India. For three years he was entertained as a distinguished guest and was even offered the rank of mandarin. Perhaps his polite refusal of this honour angered Minh Mang: at all events, in 1830 he was suddenly arrested and sentenced to death, a penalty which at the last moment was commuted to service in the army. But there was obviously no intention of allowing his talents to go to waste, and far from being turned into a soldier he was set at liberty and for another three years continued with his translations, while at the same time, as discreetly as he could, he exercised his ecclesiastical functions. In 1833 he was brusquely required to surrender all the religious objects in his possession, and on his protesting, he was sent into the country Here for nearly five years he devoted himself to translations of geographical and historical works, with particular reference to America and Japan, and taught French to a class of young men chosen for the purpose by Minh Mang himself from the members of his Court. Then in 1838—three years after Marchand's execution—he was again thrown into prison, and sentenced to be strangled for having persisted, after his former reprieve, in disseminating Christianity. This time the judgement was put into effect.

The news of these deaths aroused strong emotions in Paris. At the mother house of the French Foreign Missions, whenever word came of the martyrdom of any of their alumni, a feast day was declared: the gardens were hung with coloured lanterns; and hymns of triumph were chanted. At a later date the famous Gounod himself was to compose a special piece for these celebrations. But if the slaughtered priests were the envy of their brethren, the persecutors were regarded as the Devil's children. Minh Mang soon won the reputation of a modern Herod, and was pictured as the very type of heathen tyrant. It was inevitable that other vices besides his hatred of Christians should be attributed to him, and before long the story was being circulated among the French that the king had seduced his sister-in-law, Prince Canh's widow, and that when the incest had resulted in her pregnancy he had forced her and two of his nephews to commit suicide.

Meanwhile Minh Mang was well aware of the tension that was building up beyond his northern frontier, as the Chinese authorities at Canton started to enforce their government's ban on the importation of opium. War between China and Britain lay unmistakeably on the horizon, and such a conflict would be bound to have incalculable consequences for Vietnam. Even now foreign men-of-war were becoming uncomfortably familiar visitors to Vietnamese waters. Perhaps after all, it would be wise to try a direct approach in Europe itself to see if aggression could be warded off before it was too late by the granting of some commercial privileges. In 1840 an embassy consisting of two mandarins and two interpreters, the latter no doubt pupils of poor Father Jaccard, set off for the West, and reached France at the end of the year.

Their arrival was almost as much of a sensation in Paris as that of the boy prince half a century earlier. Like him they were lionized by society hostesses, and their presence at the Opera completely diverted the attention of the audience from the artists on the stage. They were invited to assist as spectators at a session of the House of Peers, and were received by Marshal Soult, whose name twenty years before had proved so intractable to Minh Mang's scribes. The cordiality of their reception alarmed good churchmen, the Catholic press raised its voice in protest, and letters from the hierarchy warned Louis-Philippe and the government not to forget the blood of the martyrs. Privately, neither the king nor his ministers were much concerned for the advancement of religion. The Vietnamese envoys caused an uproar by revealing that a certain 'highly-placed mandarin'— generally taken to be Soult himself, though he denied the imputation—had gone so far as to assure them that the decapitation of missionaries was 'a good riddance'. Still, the Church carried the day and Louis-Philippe refused to grant the ambassadors an audience. They paid a short visit to London with no greater success, and by the time they returned to Vietnam their sovereign was dead, and the events in China which had been the prime cause of the unlucky embassy were taking a course which was to determine the fate of Vietnam also.

54

✻ CHAPTER THREE

'With opium in one hand ...'

THE Chinese call their country Chung Kuo, or 'the Middle Kingdom', and the name is a just one, for throughout most of her history China has been the centre of an East Asian world separated from the other great civilizations of mankind by vast distances and daunting physical obstacles. Yet in spite of the barriers set up by nature, there was from very early times intercourse between China and Europe; intercourse, however, which was largely a one-way traffic. The West bought from China luxuries unobtainable elsewhere. In the days of the Roman Empire, silk was the great item of a commerce transacted by successive relays of middlemen. When in the thirteenth century the Mongols for a short while imposed unity on most of the Eurasian continent, some western travellers such as Marco Polo were able to see with their own eyes that the vague reports of Chinese wealth and industry picked up from the gossip of caravanserais were no more than the truth, and the vision was so alluring that after the disintegration of Mongol power and the consequent interruption of the land route it inspired the Spanish and Portuguese navigators to find a way eastwards by sea. In 1516 Portuguese sailors reached Canton, and from then on the traffic was continual. From the start it assumed the form it was to retain for over three hundred years. European merchants were not admitted within the country, but bought what they required at harbours along the coast: by the latter half of the eighteenth century this maritime trade was confined to the single port of Canton. Something has already been said in the first chapter of the activities of the Catholic missionaries who, in this respect luckier than the merchants, were able to win the toleration and to some extent even the favour of the Court of Peking by their attainments in such diverse branches of knowledge as gunnery and astronomy (the latter science enabling them—a task of vital importance in that agricultural society—to devise a more exact calendar). They profited from this advantage to preach the gospel among every class of Chinese: by 1700 they could claim at least three hundred thousand converts and the future of Christianity looked bright indeed. A few years later, however, the Pope's condemnation of the Confucian rites of ancester-veneration angered the Chinese government into a persecution, mild by European standards, but which reduced the number of Christians by the end of the eighteenth century to about two hundred thousand.

The first military threat by Europeans to Chinese territory came not from the sea, but from the Russian settlements in Siberia. Already in the 1640s Cossack adventurers had made their way southwards to the River Amur; and they were so persistent in their attempts at colonization that had there not been at that precise moment a dynasty originating in Manchuria, and so with a special interest in that region, establishing itself on the Dragon Throne, the northern bank of the Amur would have been lost to the Chinese Empire in the seventeenth century instead of in the nineteenth. As it was, Moscow was in no condition to challenge Peking to a full-scale war on the issue, and the dispute was resolved in 1689 by a treaty which acknowledged the country north of the Amur as far as the Stanovoi mountains to be Chinese territory. Furthermore, Russia was put in a different category from the other European powers by being allowed to send periodic trading caravans to Peking, and later, to maintain a religious mission in the capital to provide for the spiritual comfort of a group of Cossacks taken prisoner in the frontier clashes who had elected to serve in the Chinese army. (As a matter of interest, a descendant of these Cossacks, though after more than two centuries of inter-marriage indistinguishable to the eye from a Chinese, died in 1966 as the Orthodox Bishop Simeon of Shanghai.) It should be emphasized that the conclusion of a treaty in no way implied, at any rate in the Chinese view, that China was dealing with Russia on equal terms. The Tsar if he addressed the Son of Heaven at all must, by the law of nature, do so as a subordinate. The Russians, to Peking, were simply another Central Asian people beyond the periphery of the Empire whose geographical position made it reasonable for them to approach the seat of civilization by travelling overland.

As the eighteenth century drew to its close, Britain, then at the peak of the Industrial Revolution, chafed more and more at the restrictions which prevented her from finding in China a market for her manufactures. In 1793 and again 1816, British envoys were dispatched to Peking to ask that China should be opened to commercial and diplomatic intercourse. Each time the request was refused. China, said the Son of Heaven, had no need of foreign trade, since she produced within her own borders everything essential to her sustenance. After all, what had the British to complain of? They were free to come to Canton, as they had been doing for so long, and to supply themselves with all the silk and tea and porcelain that they could afford, not to mention the rhubarb which kept their bowels working regularly.

The snub was infuriating, but in the mid-eighteenth century the resourceful foreigners had discovered one commodity for which there was a ready market in China. Opium, cultivated with special intensity in British-ruled Bengal, could find customers anywhere, and by the beginning of the nineteenth century the effect of the importation of narcotics was visible not only in the growing addiction to opium—chiefly among rich merchants and officials, though extending gradually to humbler sections of the population—but in the fact that for the first time in history China had an adverse balance of trade, since she was paying out more for the drug than her own exports were earning. For all these reasons, the Chinese government made the traffic illegal, but it continued to flourish so openly under the nose of officials bribed to look the other way that it seemed almost a misuse of words to call opium contraband. At last Peking decided that radical measures were necessary and appointed as supervisor of foreign trade at Canton the celebrated Commissioner Lin, who in 1839, by blockading the British 'factories' extorted the surrender of their stocks of opium which he triumphantly destroyed. It was a heavy loss to the merchants, who called upon their government in London to seize the opportunity to go to war and open China not merely to opium but to British commerce in general. There were those in England, however, who felt the proposal was iniquitous and it was only after a heated debate that Parliament in April 1840 passed the legislation necessary for the war.

The course of the hostilities does not concern us here. The British had undisputed command of the sea and were able to capture various cities on the coast and some distance up the Yangtze: it was on board a British battleship three hundred miles upstream from the mouth of the great river, that was signed in August 1842 the Treaty of Nanking which put an end to the war, and began for China a century of humiliation. Curiously enough, opium, which had occasioned the conflict, was not mentioned among the peace terms. Five coastal ports from Shanghai to Canton were opened to British trade and residence. The island of Hong Kong was ceded in perpetuity to the British crown and a swingeing indemnity of twenty-one million silver dollars imposed upon China, who at the same time without realizing that she was surrendering her tariff autonomy, accepted that henceforward her customs rates would be fixed only by mutual agreement with the foreigners. A supplementary treaty at Canton the year following dotted the i's and crossed the t's by providing that British residents would not be subject to Chinese laws but would be under the jurisdiction of their own consular authorities: in addition, foreseeing that other countries would soon be following in Britain's wake, it introduced the doctrine of 'the most favoured nation' by stipulating that any extra privileges granted to a third power would be enjoyed by Britain also.

Few Europeans will believe that from the start there could have been no doubt as to the final outcome of the war. On the other hand, Communist Chinese historians point to the heavy losses from sickness among a relatively small British army which never numbered more than fifteen thousand men. Communication with Britain in the days before the Suez Canal were slow and difficult. True, the British were masters of the sea, and could in consequence strike at points on the coast or up the Yangtze. But they could not venture any distance inland. In these circumstances was it not clearly in China's interest to continue resistance? If the struggle dragged on and British casualties mounted, the opposition to the campaign already voiced in London could hardly have failed to increase to the point where the government would have had to bow to the storm. Even granting that in the circumstances of the time nobody in Peking could have known anything of the British political background, yet it ought to have been obvious that China was far from being in a position where she was obliged to sue for peace. The reason for the surrender, say the Communists, was that the ruling dynasty, conscious as Manchus of being more distinctly a privileged and minority caste than would have been the case with a native Chinese regime, were afraid to mobilize their subjects lest the latter should turn against them as well as against the British. It is true that when Commissioner Lin formed a local defence militia at Canton, the force was promptly disbanded by a Manchu official who succeeded Lin in his post, and generally speaking there is a good deal in the Communist argument. Yet even so it would be an anachronism to attribute to the Chinese of 1840 a nationalism which it took a century of foreign aggression to develop. In any case, it is far from certain that the Emperor or the country at large considered the peace of 1842 as being a defeat. In official statements it was declared that the outer barbarians had at length yielded to the imperial will and ceased their piratical invasion: the withdrawal of the British ships from Nanking after the signing of the treaty confirmed this impression. It was to be a good twenty years before the true meaning of what had happened was appreciated by Chinese minds, and even then, as we shall see, only a handful of people had the capacity to understand the lesson.

Among the officials who witnessed the ceremony at Nanking there figured one neutral spectator, a French naval captain named Cécille who had forced his way to the scene by commandeering a junk for the voyage up-river. His attempts to initiate negotiations on behalf of France were snubbed by the mandarins, but their respite was a brief one. Washington was hastening to have its own treaty; and it may be imagined that Paris was in no mood to see such a vast market become an Anglo-Saxon preserve. But the Sino-French agreement of 1844 contained a provision which the two Protestant powers, in their exclusive pursuit of commercial gain, had not thought it worth-while demanding. It stipulated that all Chinese restrictions on the practise of Christianity should be removed: nothing was said about the entry of missionaries which continued to be illegal.

The forty years from 1800 to the Opium War constitute in some ways the most glorious period of the Catholic church in China. With court patronage altogether removed, a stream of devoted priests, most of them French, entered the country in disguise, trusting their lives entirely to the loyalty of the scattered Christian communities. For the most part, these men would never see their own country again, and might go for years without a word from home. The difference between their situation and that of the few Protestant missionaries to reach the Far East, living with their wives and children in the comparative security of Macao or Malacca, struck even the dullest observer, and is something the Roman church may justly be proud of. Yet Chinese Catholics point out that even in those days, before the gospel became associated with the idea of foreign aggression, too many of the missionaries were already betraying signs of arrogance not merely towards their lay congregations but more surprisingly towards their colleagues, the clergy of Chinese race, who by then existed in considerable numbers. To take a single example, the last priest-mandarin of the glorious old mission of Peking, a Portuguese bishop who survived until 1838, on his death-bed handed the title-deeds of his church and its property not to one of his native priests, but to an Archimandrite of the Russian Orthodox establishment, showing unmistakeably that in a matter of such importance he would rather trust a European schismatic than an oriental fellow-Catholic.

Mao Tse-tung is fond of reminding his countrymen that the West came to China 'with opium in one hand and the Bible in the other', and it must be confessed that the gibe is no more than the truth. The first Protestant clergyman to sail the length of the China coast, the Rev. Mr. Gutzlaff of the London Missionary Society, accomplished the voyage as a salaried member of an opium-running expedition, and distributed religious tracts together with consignments of the drug at the various ports of call. During the war itself, he accompanied the British forces as advisor. It was noted that when he died in Hong Kong in 1850 he left behind him a sizeable fortune, which he could scarcely have acquired as a colporteur of New Testaments. The Catholic missionaries, to be sure, were not personally involved in the campaign, but for the most part they hailed it as a new Crusade and applauded the British victory as the work of God, who was mysteriously employing Protestant hands to chastise His enemies. Here and there in the midst of the jubilation a few discordant notes were heard. One Chinese peasant, a naively earnest convert to Christianity, excused himself for not making his Easter communion on the grounds that his heart was full of uncharity towards the opium smugglers.

It would have been unreasonable to expect the missionaries to be deterred from entering the country by the fact that the agreement with France did not permit them to travel outside the five designated 'treaty ports', and understandably enough they contrived to find their way into the interior in greater numbers than they had previously. Now, a certain hankering after power and status, which even before the war was discernible to sharp eyes, was reinforced by the latest turn of events until it became a standing reproach to the Christian name, a reproach for which the Chinese church in our own time has been called upon to pay the penalty. Antipathy towards the stiff-necked pagan mandarins who set themselves in opposition to the gospel was replaced by contempt for their military inadequacy. This new attitude was manifested particularly in the shape of demands for the restitution of land or buildings owned at one time by the church and since confiscated. Many of these claims were made in Shanghai, where the missionaries were now admitted openly, and were pressed with such scant regard for the rights of current occupiers, that more than a hundred years afterwards stories about them lived on in the memory of the people and were seized upon by Communist historians as ready-made propaganda. In a word, already in the 1840s the missionary question was casting an ominous shadow over the future.

The France of Louis-Philippe, its hands full with the establishment of a dominion in Algeria, and anxious not to alarm British susceptibilities, had no stomach for large schemes of colonization elsewhere. Yet faced with the British acquisition of Hong Kong, Paris too began to hanker after a naval station in Far Eastern waters, and a subsidiary task of the mission which signed the Sino-French treaty of 1844 was to try and hit upon a suitable locality for the purpose. Pigneau's agreement of 1787 was called to mind, for it granted to France not one but two such stations, the island of Poulo-Condore, off the Mekong delta, and the harbour of Danang, admirably situated half-way up the Vietnamese coast. But Poulo Condore was notoriously unhealthy, while Danang had the disadvantage of being on the mainland and was likely therefore to draw a foreign occupant into precisely the kind of large-scale continental adventure which at the moment France was determined at all costs to avoid. Besides, Paris admitted candidly, France could not claim any rights since none of the promises made by Louis XVI had ever been performed. A more attractive location was the Sulu archipelago, between Mindanao and Borneo, and early in 1845 the reigning sultan agreed to sell one of his islands, named Basilan, to the French government. Unfortunately Spain was up in arms in a moment, protesting that Basilan formed part of her Philippine possessions. Paris coveted a Spanish alliance, which it was endeavouring to cement by a dynastic marriage, and for the sake of European politics abandoned Basilan without a murmur. In retrospect we can see this was a momentous decision. If France had had the opportunity of creating an island rival to Hong Kong and Singapore in the midst of the eastern seas, it is just conceivable that she might have been content to leave the mainland in peace. As it was, the renunciation of Basilan spelt doom to Vietnam, though the disaster took its time in arriving.

At Hue, Minh Mang the persecutor had been succeeded in 1841 by his son Thieu Tri, a man a good deal less stern than his father, for while continuing to arrest missionaries he made little difficulty about handing them over for deportation to visiting French naval vessels. By 1847, thanks to this milder policy, there was a perceptible change in the atmosphere, but in that year an incident occurred which ruined all hopes of amelioration. Two French ships arrived at Danang for the double purpose of obtaining the release of a priest who had been imprisoned for re-entering the country after an earlier expulsion, and of drawing the attention of Thieu Tri to the fact that his overlord the Chinese Emperor had promised to tolerate the exercise of the Christian religion. As regards the missionary it was soon discovered that he had in fact been already set at liberty, so that in this respect the expedition was otiose. The letter to the king encountered difficulties of protocol which so exasperated the French commander that he seized the sails of five Vietnamese ships, declaring that he would not hand them back until he had received an answer from the Court. We can understand that tempers must have been on edge, and at last the French, in the belief—whether justified or not is now uncertain—that the other side was meditating an attack, opened a merciless bombardment, and many Vietnamese were killed. The visitors then sailed away, leaving behind them a country seething with rage. The King, his mildness forgotten, ran wildly about the palace smashing whatever objects of western origin he could lay his hands on and expressing his opinion of Christians in such uninhibited terms that on his sudden death in November of the same year, 1847, the pious missionaries announcing the news to Paris discerned the hand of God in the event. Meanwhile it could not be concealed from the French public that the commander of the expedition had grossly exceeded his authority, but protected as he was by the church he escaped with a simple reprimand.

Just over the Chinese border, in the province of Kwangsi, Christianity was in process of making an even more spectacular intervention in Far Eastern affairs, though the Christianity in question was not Roman Catholic but Protestant—an augury that in the century which the Opium War had just opened, and which was to last till the Communist victory of 1949, the Anglo-Saxon presence was to ensure that the reformed churches would enjoy greater intellectual influence in China than their older rival. A country schoolmaster named Hung Hsiu-ch'uan, having come across a pamphlet of evangelical doctrine, persuaded himself that he had been granted visions of God the Father and of Jesus Christ, who had assigned to him the task of instituting the Kingdom of Heaven on earth.

From what has been said earlier, it will have become clear that the dominance of Confucian agnosticism posed a difficulty in the way of Chinese acceptance of Christianity. Yet Confucianism was essentially a creed for a sophisticated elite, and the mass of the people while to a certain extent shamed by its sceptical example from indulging in the grossest form of superstitition did nevertheless turn constantly to magic and the supernatural. Furthermore, even in those educated classes where Confucianism was paramount, it was felt, especially in times of personal crisis, to be a somewhat dry and comfortless doctrine. There is indeed throughout Chinese thought and literature a lack of dramatic tension, and it was this lack that the Christian message, alien though it was, supplied with a terrible urgency. In our own day, it may be argued that it is the Judaeo-Christian zeal in Marxism which has inspired the fervour of the Maoist revolution. Similarly, although agrarian rebellion encouraged by popular superstitions was endemic throughout Chinese history, and much of Hung Hsiu-ch'uan's economic programme—'land, food, clothing and money must be held and used in common, so that there is no inequality anywhere, and nobody wants for food or warmth'— may be traced to speculation of ancient Chinese philosophers, yet the notion that all men are the children of a Heavenly Father, much more strongly personified than any of the dieties in the native pantheon, soon showed it had a unique power to gather followers. Compelled to give up his school teaching because he threw away the ritual image of Confucius as a heathen idol, Hung buried himself deep in the countryside where in a year or two he assembled round him a group of disciples, consisting for the most part of poor charcoal-burners and the like, but including a few men in relatively comfortable circumstances. The times were ripe for unrest. Although the Chinese market was not coming up to the glowing expectations that the West had entertained of it, there was a sufficient influx of foreign manufactured goods, especially of Lancashire cottons, to disrupt native industry. The war indemnity had necessitated a heavy increase in taxation. Also there was a problem of purely domestic origin. From the middle of the seventeenth century there occurred in China an increase of population equivalent to that which was happening in the same period in Europe. The number of inhabitants from about one hundred million in 1650 had by 1850 risen to over three hundred million. This in turn resulted in a perceptible pressure on land. Added to all these causes of dissatisfaction there was, especially in the southernmost provinces, a lingering racial antipathy towards the Manchus, which made it easy for Hung to identify the Tartars and their dynasty with the forces of darkness he had been enjoined to overthrow. In 1851 the banner of rebellion was raised, and a new regime proclaimed under the title of the Heavenly Kingdom of Taiping, the last word conveying the sense of a utopian peace and equality. Hung, the founder, received the style of Heavenly Prince, while his chief lieutenants became princes too, though of subordinate quality.

It was a highly regimented body of about ten thousand men and women that set out from Kwangsi on the conquest of China. Discipline was maintained by the strict separation of the sexes, and by the prohibition of looting for personal gain: all booty was put in a common stock. It was decided not to waste time en route by conducting lengthy sieges: walled cities which held out were left behind without more ado. However the so-called Wuhan conurbation on the Yangtze in the very centre of China was a prize worth any trouble which its capture would require. Hankow on the northern bank fell quickly enough, but the fortifications of Wuchang, on the opposite shore, proved a tough nut to crack. Rising to the challenge, the rebels, who had recruited into their ranks a large number of boatmen, erected two great pontoon bridges across the river for the passage of troops, so that Wuchang was completely surrounded on all sides. Extensive tunnelling operations were then carried on, one of the walls was mined, and the Taiping army entered through the breach.

At this stage, in January 1853, we can see that one of two decisions ought to have been taken. Either the rebels ought to have consolidated their grip on Central China, or they should have profited by the enormous élan their triumph so far had generated— not to mention their vastly increased forces, now more than eighty thousand strong—and staked everything they had on a drive against Peking itself. However, close at hand were the rich and prestigious provinces of the Lower Yangtze Valley, with the great metropolis of Nanking where the house of Ming had first established its rule after the overthrow of the Mongols. The temptation proved too much. Wuchang was abandoned and the Taipings moved downstream. Nanking passed into their hands in March 1853, and was renamed the 'Heavenly Capital'. Certainly Peking was not forgotten: a column marched northwards in May, but the Heavenly Prince did not accompany it, preferring to stay behind and watch the building of a magnificent palace. Even so his men reached the outskirts of Tientsin by October, but then, like good Southerners, finding the onset of winter and the northern diet of millet too much for them, and lacking the inspiring presence of their prophet, they fell back in retreat.

Meanwhile far away in the rear, in Hunan (one of the provinces through which the Taipings had hurried so light-heartedly on their dash to the Yangtze), there had begun a process which was to end in their ruin. The landlords and gentry, finding that the government was incapable of defending their estates from the peasant rebels, had decided to take matters into their own hands. Tseng Kuo-fan, a high mandarin back in his native province for his mother's funeral, was asked by his friends to organize a corps of volunteers to be raised among the tenantry for local defence. Until recently there was a belief, owlishly repeated among westerners, that the Chinese were a people totally lacking in all military qualities, and despising soldiers as the vilest of mankind. It was not explained how, if this were true, the Chinese had already managed, a century before Christ, to stretch their dominion half-way across Asia. Actually, the Chinese attitude to soldiers was exactly the same as that of Europeans before the days of conscription. The only men who would enlist as private soldiers were those who were incapable by their defects of character of earning a regular living: wastrels, drunkards—'the scum of the earth' as the Duke of Wellington called his troops. But military virtues, bravery, resourcefulness, bodily agility and strength, were admired in the old China, service in the army earned certain legal privileges, and officers—as opposed to the men under them— were regarded with due social respect. Not only that, we shall see

66

in the period with which we are dealing more than one example of the case with which a mandarin, who had gained his rank by way of the literary examinations, assumed the rôle of field commander.

Tseng Kuo-fan's first outstanding achievement was his rapid success in introducing an *esprit de corps* into what was in origin a miscellaneous rabble of peasants. He did this by means of constant indoctrination in the principles of Confucianism, and by persuading his followers into seeing themselves as the champions of traditional China in all its aspects—including even bound feet and Buddhism—against the crude iconoclasm of the rebels. To be sure, the morality thus inculcated had its limitations. It did not, for instance, restrain Tseng's soldiers from demanding, as of right, the pillage of a reoccupied town: after all, plunder and rape were universally recognized as the proper rewards of valour. Nor, again, did their loyalty usually extend beyond their own commander. But they were incomparably more serious opponents than any the rebels had encountered so far, and the latter had, by yielding to the lure of Nanking, played into their hands, for Tseng resolved to deny them re-entry into the Wuhan area and Central China generally. In a year or two, the Taipings found themselves more or less confined to the Lower Yangtze Valey. with all access barred to the upper reaches of the river.

At the same time, too, a marked deterioration was visible in the rebel morale. Even during the march across China, the Heavenly Prince had made no secret of the fact that the austerity imposed on his followers did not apply to one as exalted as himself and now in Nanking he and the other princes indulged themselves without stint in all the pleasures of the flesh. Power brought not only enjoyment, but jealousy and distrust. In 1856 the Taiping Court was convulsed by the feuds of rival grandees: one group butchered another, only to be suppressed in its turn with merciless slaughter, until the freight of corpses, borne downstream, led the Manchus to hope that soon there would be none of their enemies left. In fact, the rebellion had still eight years before it, but from now on the Heavenly Prince kept himself more aloof from his subjects than ever and rarely ventured beyond his seraglio, leaving one or two younger leaders to maintain the Taiping cause in the field.

As was natural, the Protestant missionaries were at first much excited by the news that a Christian sympathizer had set out to win the throne of China, and their emotion was shared to some degree by their governments. Closer inspection, however, was less encouraging. The Taipings showed themselves well disposed towards the foreigners, whom they accepted as fellow-worshippers of the One True God, but so far from acknowledging the missionaries as their teachers they made it clear that their own version of the faith—odd though it looked to western eyes—had been established once and for all by their own prophet. Furthermore, although they were perfectly willing to open their country to trade, they would have no truck whatever with opium, which was still a principal source of foreign profit. The western powers before long came round to the belief that on the whole it would be better if the Manchu dynasty were kept on the throne, especially if the privileges already granted by treaty were extended still further, and North China and the Yangtze Valley brought within the sphere of international commerce.

To achieve such a result, the use of force was again unavoidable, and as it happened an occasion was ready to hand. Canton, which had been delared one of the five open ports by the Treaty of Nanking, stubbornly refused to admit the aliens within its walls. An incident concerning a British-registered ship in 1856 provoked the Royal Navy into shelling the city, upon which a mob sacked the foreign business ghetto in the suburbs. London decided upon a full expedition, and as France, too, had cause for complaint in the death in prison of a French missionary, she signified her readiness to join in the venture. After some delay because of the Indian Mutiny, the campaign known to the Chinese as the Second Opium War, began at the end of 1857.

It started with the seizure of Canton, but the real goal of the Allies lay elsewhere. The war was carried to the North, where an agreement was reached at Tientsin in 1858. The following year, however, an attempt to ratify this led to yet another clash, and at last nothing would serve but a full scale invasion. The Anglo-French forces entered Peking in September 1860 and compelled the signing of the treaties they required. Foreign diplomatic missions were to be stationed in the capital. Ports in the North

China and the Yangtze Valley were to be opened, notably Tientsin and Hankow, and foreign naval vessels could sail up the great river to the latter city. The whole country was made available to the missionaries. Kowloon, on the mainland opposite Hong Kong, was ceded to Britain. There was of course a huge indemnity to be paid by the Chinese into the bargain. Meanwhile Russia, by a mixture of threats and cajolery got what she had been coveting for two centuries—Manchuria north of the Amur, and the Maritime Province with the harbour of Haishenwei, now baptized as Vladivostok.

After that, it was plain that the Manchus had earned the right to retain the throne. The area in which foreign help could be most effective against the Taipings was without doubt the country lying between Shanghai and Nanking; but it was considered desirable that the brunt of the fighting should be borne by the Chinese themselves, with a stiffening of European advisers and soldiers of fortune. Tseng Kuo-fan was doing wonders, but he was fully committed further up river to the west of the rebel capital and could not divert any of his attention to another theatre. Instead he selected one of his lieutenants to form a new army to collaborate with the foreigners in Shanghai. This man was Li Hung-chang, a name which was to dominate the Chinese political scene for the better part of the next forty years. To assist Li, the British Army seconded the future General Gordon of Khartoum, then a colonel, who thus entered the history books as 'Chinese Gordon'. Assailed from every side, Nanking fell in 1864, the Heavenly Prince having anticipated the event by suicide, and the great Taiping Rebellion, during which twenty million people are reckoned to have lost their lives, and the consequences of which are visible to this day, at last came to an end.

But before that, in the middle of the Second Opium War, the French had profited from a lull on the Chinese front to embark at long last upon the conquest of Vietnam.

CHAPTER FOUR

The First French Offensive

THE advent of the Second Empire in 1852 marked a decisive stage in the development of French policy towards Vietnam. To the great pleaders for armed intervention the missionaries and their friends at home, the essentially anti-clerical governments of Louis-Philippe and of the Second Republic had found no difficulty in turning a deaf ear. But Napoleon III was heavily indebted to the support of the Church in his rise to power, and the turn of events in the East made it unlikely that he would be allowed to forget his obligations.

It was usual, both in China and Vietnam, for a sovereign to designate as his successor whichever of his sons seemed most suitable for the post, and Thieu Tri had had no difficulty in making a choice, for his younger boy had all the qualities looked for in a Confucian monarch, being highly intelligent, well-versed in Chinese literature, and, in contrast to his rather volatile parent, of an even-tempered disposition. Still, whether in Vietnam or in China, the passing-over of seniority in favour of merit often provoked resentment, and we hear without surprise that the first act of Tu Duc, on coming to the throne in 1847, was to anticipate trouble by imprisoning an elder brother who obligingly hanged himself while in custody.

Sweet-natured as the new king of Vietnam normally was, his reign commenced only a few months after what he could be forgiven for regarding as a most atrocious crime on the part of a Christian power, and filial duty, if nothing else, was enough to thrust him along the path indicated by his father and grandfather.

'The religion of Christ [ran one of his first proclamations] is obviously contrary to nature, for it does not honour dead ancestors. Its European teachers, who are most to blame, will be thrown into the sea, with a stone around their neck, and a rewards of thirty bars of silver will be given to whoever takes one of them. The Vietnamese teachers are less guilty, and will first be tortured to see if they will abandon their errors. If they refuse, they will be branded on the face and exiled to the most unhealthy regions of the kingdom.'

Three years later, in 1851, this indulgence offered to native priests was abruptly rescinded. Henceforward: 'whether they trample on the cross or not, they will be cut in two at the waist.' In that year and the next, four French missionaries were beheaded and their bodies flung into rivers or into the sea. The Catholic press in France cried out in horror, and the agitation found a sympathizer in the Empress Eugenie, particularly when among later victims there figured the name of a Spanish bishop whom as a girl she had known in Andalusia. But probably the most persuasive enemy of Tu Duc was the great oriental traveller Father Huc, who oddly enough had never set foot in Vietnam in his life, but more than made up for the omission by his experiences in China.

The inefficiency of the old Chinese surveillance of foreigners is amply demonstrated by the fact that this priest by simply wearing Chinese dress and a false pigtail was able to enter the country unchallenged through Canton in 1840, at the very height of the Opium War, and for years wandered at liberty as far afield as Mongolia and Tibet, in which latter region his identity as an illegal immigrant was finally detected, and he was arrested and sent under guard to the coast for deportation. He and his companion, a fellow countryman named Gabet, seem to have been treated with marked consideration by the Chinese authorities. Perhaps Huc's naturally domineering temperament was made worse by having become used to the extreme deference habitually shown by converts to their foreign pastors, which far surpassed that exacted by the most highly-placed mandarins from their subordinates. At all events, his rage at what he considered an indignity knew no bounds, and even when some well meaning official tried to behave amiably, the attempt was repulsed as an impudent familiarity. Expelled from the interior, he spent some years in Shanghai and Hong Kong, embarrassing French consulates by his demands for strong measures towards the Chinese, until in 1851 he returned to Paris, where his published account of his travels made him famous overnight. As a writer he contributed materially to the creation of the black legend, which represented China as a hell-on-earth of pagan vice and cruelty, and vast prestige accrued to him as an authority on all matters concerning the Far East.

In his written memorials, and later in personal conversations with Napoleon III, Huc insisted that France had an 'incontestable right' to the territory ceded to her by the treaty of 1787, and that the naval and military expedition sent to participate in the Second Opium War against China was more than adequate for any enterprise in Vietnam, particularly since the population of that country, groaning under the tyranny of Tu Duc, would rise as one man to welcome the French as liberators. In April 1857, Huc's advice led to the appointment of a commission to examine the feasibility of occupying a point on the Vietnam coast. While not entirely concurring with Huc's opinions on the treaty of 1787, the commissioners agreed that the help given to Gia Long by individual Frenchmen could be reckoned as a move towards putting the treaty into execution, and this, coupled with the persecution of missionaries, was sufficient to justify a military intervention by France. Of more importance than any legal hairsplitting was the fact that for the time being London and Paris were fast friends—as shown both in the Crimea and in China—and it seemed improbable that there would be any hostile British reaction to a French adventure in Vietnam, a region where no British interests were involved. The Navy had consistently supported the interventionists, and now was all eagerness to get its hands on Danang. Indeed in September 1856, six months before the Commission had come into existence, a French sloop, after trying in vain to get an official letter transmitted to Huc, had excelled the example set in 1847 by not only bombarding Danang, but in addition putting a company ashore to spike the Vietnamese guns. Accordingly in November 1857, instructions were sent to

72

Admiral Rigault de Genouilly, who commanded the French fleet in the Far East, that he should carry out forthwith a 'demonstration' in Vietnam. It was specified that the exercise must include the occupation of Danang, but everything else was left to the Admiral's discretion. The vagueness reflected the lack of precise aims on the part of the government, some members of which confessed they had only the faintest notion where to locate Vietnam on the map. The clear purpose was to put a stop to the religious persecutions, and it was thought that Danang, situated so close to the capital, was an ideal spot from which to bring pressure to bear on the Court.

In the event it was not until September 1858 that the Chinese campaign allowed Rigault de Genouilly to turn his attention southwards, and his expedition, when it took place, was in conjunction with an ally, for Spain also felt it her duty to avenge the sufferings of her missionaries, and dispatched a corps of Filipino troops to share in the exploit. The Admiral was at home in these waters for he had been present at the bombardment in 1847, and now he found little difficulty in establishing a bridgehead, consisting chiefly of a neck of land which served as a breakwater for the really magnificent harbour. Apart from this initial success, his expectations were sadly deceived. In spite of all the assurances by the missionaries, not a single native Christian rallied to the invaders. As for an attack against Hue itself, tantalizingly so close at hand, the missionaries had again proved too sanguine. Even stationed at Danang, the foreign soldiers were succumbing in alarming numbers to cholera, dysentery and other tropical ailments, and an advance inland on foot was simply not to be thought of. The River of Perfumes flowed from Hue to the sea, but was navigable only to vessels of shallow draught, and as ill luck would have it a number of small gunboats specially constructed in France for the Vietnam campaign had had to be diverted to Lake Garda for use against the Austrians in the war which had broken out in Northern Italy.

It soon became obvious that no purpose whatsoever was to be served by loitering at Danang. But where else could they go? Missionary opinion, supported by the Spaniards, was for striking a blow to the north, in Tongking, where it was alleged Christian converts were especially strong, and where a claimant of the old Le dynasty was eager to put himself under French protection. By this time, however, the Admiral had had enough, and more than enough, of ecclesiastical counsel. There was one place about which there could be no doubt: the southern part of the country was the great rice-producing area, whose loss would be a severe blow to Hue, and the metropolis of the South was Saigon, a city which could be reached directly by river, without the necessity of marching across an abominable countryside. There were some stormy scenes, but the Admiral was intractable. On February 2, 1859, leaving only a few hundred men behind at Danang, he sailed southwards with nine French and one Spanish naval vessel, accompanied by four leased cargo ships with supplies. On February 12th, having silenced the Vietnamese guns at Cap St Jacques, the expedition entered the river leading to Saigon and for three days slowly made its way past fortified positions screened by the dense jungle on the banks. Then Saigon came into view, looking for all the world like a scattering of hamlets across an arcadian landscape, for the great citadel was hidden by a grove of trees.

Defence works on the waterfront had to be put out of action by cannonade before the first troops could be landed, and then on the second morning, February 17th, the assault on the citadel began. It lasted for about five hours, during which it was noticed that the Vietnamese marksmanship was inferior to that of the attackers. By noon the garrison was in flight and Saigon was in foreign hands. The victors were delighted with their quarters in the fortress, especially when they discovered large quantities of ammunition, food—it was estimated that there was enough rice to feed eight thousand men for a year—and strings of the copper coins which were the local currency. These last were distributed among the troops, who used them according to their own national idiosyncracies. Poultry was on sale everywhere, but while the French were interested in eating it—and only breast of chicken at that—the Filipinos, with a livelier imagination, organized a gala of cock-fights. For a time it was quite a fiesta, but in the Admiral's mind there was always the nagging doubt that Paris might not approve of what he was doing. Therefore, in March, he retired northwards again to Danang, contenting himself with leaving eight hundred men to hold Saigon. Judging that the citadel would be unmanageable for such a modest garrison he blew it up and established the defenders in a redoubt with access to the river. As it turned out, Danang did not repay the trouble that had been given to it and when after nineteen months of occupation the allies at last withdrew in March 1860 the only thing to show for their pains was a cemetery of one thousand graves—and this without reckoning the men who died elsewhere of illness contracted in that pestilential harbour.

On the whole the Vietnamese could congratulate themselves on their good fortune at Danang. The officer who commanded them there provides yet another example of what had been remarked upon in the last chapter, namely the apparent readiness with which a bookish Confucian scholar took up the profession of arms. While in China men such as Tseng Kuo-fan and Li Hung-chang were giving the lie to the general European belief in the essentially unwarlike qualities of the mandarin, the same lesson was being demonstrated even more convincingly in Vietnam, for Nguyen Tri Phuong, who led the resistance at Danang with the title of Marshal, had been a literary tutor of the king, and was over sixty years old besides. With this reputation behind him, he attempted to enhance his laurels by driving the aliens from Saigon. There, however, he was not so lucky. It was true that, just as at Danang, the European invaders had discovered that all the stories they had heard about the welcome awaiting them not only from Christian converts but from the population at large were entire nonsense, and that it was quite as much as they could do to cling to their restricted foothold on the waterfront: even so, Marshal Nguyen, although now and then coming pretty near to it, never actually succeeded in pushing them out; and when at the end of 1860 peace was signed with China, it meant that the whole of French military and naval power in the Far East could be concentrated against the Saigon area, whose commercial and political importance was by this time sufficiently appreciated in Paris.

The change in the situation was obvious immediately. First of all, in February 1861 a counter-offensive was launched against the trenches from which until then the besiegers had operated against the garrison. For two days there was a furious struggle over a terrain every yard of which was bristling with fearsome spiked bamboos, whether planted in almost impenetrable hedges or set into skilfully concealed booby-traps. The venerable Marshal Nguyen, in spite of his white hair, took part personally in the engagement and was wounded in the arm. At last the superiority of European weapons began to tell, and the Vietnamese withdrew. Heartened by the victory, the French pressed forward through the Mekong delta and captured a number of places such as Bien-Hoa and Mytho, which were readily accessible by river navigation. The countryside in between, however, for the most part eluded their control and remained in the hands of men who acknowledged only the authority of Hue. Yet in Hue itself resolution was less firm. The Christian claimant to the heritage of the Le dynasty—though knowledgeable people insisted that he had no relationship at all to the old imperial family, being nothing more than a commonplace protégé of the missionaries—was proving himself such a nuisance in Tongking that a full-scale expedition would have to be sent to suppress him, and a war on two fronts was not to be recommended. In the last week of May, 1862, a French cruiser steamed into Saigon, towing behind her a battered old sloop flying Vietnamese colours and having on board two ambassadors from the King, who were empowered to discuss terms of peace. On June 5th, there was signed on board the French admiral's flagship the so-called Treaty of Saigon, by which Tu Duc, in addition to granting free exercise of the Catholic religion throughout his dominions, and agreeing to pay an indemnity of four million dollars, ceded to France the island of Poulo Condore, and the three provinces of Bien-Hoa, Gia-Dinh and Dinh-Tuong which formed that half of Southern Vietnam lying east of the Mekong.

These were hard conditions by any standards. For a good Confucian like Tu Duc they were specially grievous since his mother, and her mother before her had been born in the land now lost to him, and the graves of his maternal ancestors were to be in consequence taken out of his possession. This sentimental consideration weighed in his mind even more heavily than the economic disadvantage of parting with a region on which his capital city depended for its rice. But the revolt nearer home demanded prior attention and Marshal Nguyen, recovered from his wound, conducted an army against the Le pretender who a year or two later, deserted by his followers, was seized and carried to Hue, where the King's rage at the cost of the uprising led to the infliction of a punishment no longer applied in Britain, for the wretched captive was disembowelled and quartered.

Meanwhile in France itself public opinion was becoming alarmed at the cost of the operations in Vietnam, particularly since the parallel campaign in Mexico was going so badly, and certain elements in the government were unhappy at the degree to which Paris was being confronted with a situation created on the spot by its naval representatives in South-East Asia. In these circumstances, Tu Duc had the idea of making an appeal to Napoleon III for the restitution, or rather the redemption, of the lost provinces, for the King proposed to pay a ransom either of forty million dollars outright, or in the form of a perpetual tribute of two or three million dollars a year. To persuade the French Emperor, an embassy of sixty-six members was sent to Paris in the summer of 1863, headed by Phan Than Giang, one of the most dignified ministers of the throne, who had represented Tu Duc in negotiating the Treaty of Saigon, and whose age seemed to claim a respected hearing, for he had been born in 1796. No better spokesman could have been chosen to plead what was essentially the cause of filial piety. In Phan's boyhood, his father, a small official in local government had committed some offence for which he had been condemned to a penal settlement. Young Phan insisted on accompanying his parent in his disgrace, and thus attracted the attention of the mandarins, who encouraged him in his study of the Confucian classics and set him by way of the examination halls on the road to success. With this experience he found it hard to credit that Tu Duc's anxiety to retrieve the graves of his mother's ancestors would not melt the heart of the French Emperor. And indeed during his stay in Paris it seemed that he had achieved what he came for. The French Minister of Finance was particularly enthusiastic at the prospect of a solid accession to his annual revenue, and it was arranged that a new draft treaty would be sent to Hue providing suitable terms for the redemption of the three occupied provinces. But no sooner was this negotiation set on foot than the partisans of colonial expansion began to recover their predominance, and when in July 1864 a French officer signed an agreement in Hue, Paris was induced to deny ratification on the grounds that certain changes had been introduced into the text.

So far from contemplating the surrender of territory, the colonialists had from the start assumed that in due course they would go on to seize the three southern provinces still in Viet-namese hands to the west of the Mekong, now cut off from the rest of the country by the occupied zone. An excuse was soon found, for it was undeniable that the free areas were a breeding ground for the guerrillas who continued to harass the French administrators. Preparations went ahead in complete secrecy and then in June 1867, without warning of any kind, the blow was struck. Among the first victims was the septuagenarian Phan Than Giang, who after his return from Europe held the dangerous post of viceroy of the threatened provinces. He addressed a note to the invaders:

'I was living at peace with you, and relying upon your good faith, but you now march against me with forces so large that it would be madness to resist. If we fight it will bring misery to innocent people, and will only end in defeat. I therefore yield to you what you demand, and protest against your violence.'

As a good Confucian there was only one way for him to preserve his family honour. He fasted for some days in order to weaken him-self, and then swallowed a lethal dose of opium in a solution of vinegar, having in his last words enjoined on his sons never to serve under foreigners. We read that the French were greatly distressed at the occurrence, though on the credit side they could inscribe the last triumph abroad of the Second Empire. It was seven years, however, before Hue could be induced to acknowledge the *fait accompli*.

From the earliest days of the colony it had been the hope of its governors—who were in fact a series of admirals, successors to Rigault de Genouilly—that the administration might be carried on by means of a native mandarinate. So marked was their anxiety to see this come about that they outraged missionary susceptibilities by proclaiming their admiration of Confucianism and by patronizing the study of Chinese literature. Yet their efforts were in vain: the educated class of Vietnamese stayed aloof, and showed plainly that they recognized no government but that of Hue. The Christian community supplied a certain number of volunteers, but in too many cases there was nothing for it but to depend on the services of the least reliable section of the population. In such circumstances it was essential that there should come into existence a highly-trained corps of French experts on Vietnamese questions.

In the year 1864, the so-called 'Chinatown' of Cholon, at present forming one city with Saigon, but in these days separated from it by a stretch of open country was put under the authority of a naval lieutenant of twenty-five, acting as inspector of native affairs. This was Francis Garnier, who is to play an important, and tragic, part in our story. He came from a stock remarkable by its enthusiasm for the cause of Bourbon legitimacy. As a serving officer, his father had literally broken his sword across his knee rather than swear loyalty to Louis-Philippe, and shortly afterwards, in 1832, was among the fanatics who took up arms on behalf of the Duchesse de Berry. It is said that the family fortune was badly impaired by this foolhardiness, and it called for considerable cheeseparing to send Francis through naval college. His lack of inches had during his childhood earned him the nickname of 'Tom Thumb', but his fellow cadets called him 'Mademoiselle Bonaparte', and indeed, apart from the indispensable sidewhiskers of the epoch, his gaunt face and smouldering eyes, as shown by photographs, do put one in mind of the First Consul. In 1860 he had an experience which was to determine the course of his life. He took part in the Anglo-French expedition against North China, and ever afterwards the memory of that wonderful country enchanted his imagination: although his duties soon called him to Saigon, his eyes were constantly fixed on China, and to him Vietnam was chiefly important as a gateway to the southern and western provinces of its vast neighbour. It was an idea which had been in circulation for some time, and as was to be expected the British had no intention of being forestalled: they had been in Lower Burma for forty years, and were manifesting so much curiosity concerning trade routes across the frontier between China and what was still independent Upper Burma, that no rational observer would give much for the latter monarchy's chances of survival. But communications between Burma and China would for the most part be on land. What a triumph for France, now established on the Mekong delta, if that mighty waterway should prove to be navigable from Yunnan to the sea! Saigon would at one stroke become the great commercial entrepôt to which would flow the wealth of Yunnan and Szechwan, and the French Far Eastern Empire, now coming into being, would surpass in riches even India itself.

It appears that Garnier had, as early as 1863, conceived the notion of exploring the upper reaches of the Mekong. In 1864 he and some of his friends submitted a formal plan to the Governor, and when the matter was referred to Paris it happened, as good luck would have it, that the Navy Minister, the Marquis de Chasseloup-Laubat, was president of the Geographical Society, and therefore particularly disposed in favour of such a venture. Although Garnier was without doubt the heart and brain of the enterprise, his youth and subordinate rank ensured that the command must go to an older man, Captain Doudart de Lagrée.

The party set out from Saigon on two gunboats on June 5, 1866, but made a halt of some weeks in Cambodia to procure necessary documents and it was not until July 7th that the journey proper began. One of the gunboats was left behind at Pnompenh and the other was able to continue the voyage for only six days before being obliged to turn back owing to the shallowness of the stream. The expedition, which comprised eight Frenchmen, and nineteen Asian servants of various nationalities, had to transfer to canoes, hewn from tree-trunks with a straw roof to keep off the rays of the sun.

It soon became clear that Garnier's dream of a Mekong navigable to China was condemned to disappointment, for almost at once they encountered rapids which forced them to take to the banks, along which they carried their equipment until the channel again became free. This procedure had to be repeated so constantly that their boots became worn out and they had to walk in their bare feet, often over rocks which the sun had rendered blisteringly hot.

5   Francis Garnier

6 Liu Yung-fu

The Black Flags, a French representatic

Mosquitoes and leeches made their lives a misery. Garnier nearly died of typhus and one of his companions of dysentery. Finally they had to abandon the river altogether and direct their march entirely overland. It was not until October 1867 that, more dead than alive, the explorers crossed the frontier into the province of Yunnan.

CHAPTER FIVE

The French Explore

I N spite of the painful journey, Laos had had its charms.
'I should like to live in Laos, [wrote Garnier to a friend]. It is
a marvellous place, full of calm majestic forests, reflected in the
water of the river, with monkeys swinging from creepers like
clusters of grapes. [But in Laos and Cambodia, with their pre-
dominantly Indian culture, the westerner had to pay for the
picturesqueness of his surroundings.] Picnics on the grass are all
very well [Garnier noted in his diary], but when for month after
month you have been struggling to discover a comfortable way of
eating while squatting on the ground, it is wonderful once again
to be among people who not only use chairs and tables but know
how to make a table appetizing into the bargain.'

Three centuries earlier, the Jesuits had remarked that the
Chinese, alone of the peoples of Asia, sat in a posture befitting
human dignity.[9]
There was an added reason, besides the luxury of being able to
sit properly why Garnier and his friends were glad to have
reached the goal of their journey. Of all the regions of China,
Yunnan has beyond doubt the most agreeable climate, for the
greater part of the province consists of a plateau which lies at an
average height of six thousand feet above sea-level. Thanks to this
elevation, even in summer there is no unpleasant heat, and in the
winter, which was the season our explorers stayed there, the
climate is especially brisk and invigorating, with light frosts at

night—occasionally even snow—and bright sunshine by day.

But it was not the bracing air, however delightful after the sweltering tropics, which had brought the Frenchman all those weary miles. Yunnan for centuries had been the great supplier of tin and copper to the Chinese Empire. It was from the latter metal that were manufactured the coins which were the medium of ordinary trade. Silver, zinc, lead, and precious stones were also found in considerable quantity, and marble in Chinese is called 'the stone of Tali', from the name of a Yunnanese city. All these treasures were still being exploited by primitive methods, and Garnier went into raptures at the thought of what could be done by European technicians equipped with the latest machinery. It would be child's play, provided a convenient means of communication could be established. At the moment everything had to be carried across country to the Yangtze or the West River on which it then went by boat to Shanghai or Canton. If only the Mekong route had been feasible, all this lucrative business would have been naturally diverted to Saigon. That was now, of course, out of the question. Was there another way? In the first days on Chinese soil, Garnier's attention was directed to a river called the Hoti which flowed south-eastwards through a deep ravine. At this point, and indeed for many miles downstream it was not navigable, but if followed patiently it led, he was told, to a market town called Manghao, the resort of merchants from Kwangtung and Kwangsi, from which place boats could make the journey without difficulty across the Vietnamese border to Hanoi and the sea: and no wonder, for the Hoti, it seemed, was nothing less than the upper course of the Red River, the great artery of Tongking. Garnier was unable to confirm these reports by doing the trip himself, but he carried his investigations far enough to give general credence to what he heard, though the disappointment over the Mekong was a warning against building castles in the air.

Three years had passed since the suppression of the Taiping Rebellion, but although the central government of China was once again solidly in the grip of the Manchu dynasty, the country was still far from being at peace, for the Taiping had been merely the most formidable of a whole catalogue of uprisings which, encouraged by mutual example, agitated the country for more than twenty years. In particular, the Muslims were up in arms, not only in Sinkiang where they were Turki by race and fought for the independence of their land against an authority at once pagan and foreign, but also in the north-western and south-western provinces of China proper. Here, although very numerous, and indeed in some areas forming a majority of the inhabitants, the followers of the Prophet, whatever admixture of alien blood may have occurred centuries back when Islam arrived from Central Asia, were now indistinguishable in racial type and language from the mass of their neighbours. Their religion they cultivated privately. No muezzin was heard to summon the faithful to prayer. Their mosques were not distinguished by the minarets of other Muslim lands. Few of them knew Arabic. The one obvious peculiarity which marked them off from their fellow-citizens was their aversion to pork, a remarkable scruple in China, where the common word for 'meat' signifies first and foremost the flesh of the pig. But this was their only dietary prohibition. Go to a Muslim restaurant, which to this day in many a Chinese city is the great purveyor of mutton and beef, and you may enjoy alcohol by the jarful. On the other hand, they nearly always chose wives from among their coreligionists, though apart from this they seem to have regulated their family affairs according to the teachings of Confucius. In fact, one of the leaders in the revolts just mentioned, used to insist that he was not only a good Muslim but a good Confucian too, a saying which in the circumstances shows as well as anything can the extent to which, in China, even Islam, the most jealously exclusive of faiths, had been softened by the general absence of fanaticism.

But although throughout history the Chinese have been in matters of religion the most easy-going people in the world, their very freedom from anything in the nature of doctrinal intolerance, until Marxism in our own day brought with it from Judaeo-Christian Europe the theological hatred of heresy, has made it difficult for them to sympathize with the feelings of others who happen not to be so broadminded. A suspicion that Christian converts, and even the native clergy, were not to be trusted to maintain the nicer points of dogma was one of the chief reasons why western missionaries were so noticeably reluctant to resign posts of authority in the Church into Chinese hands, and given their point of view their hesitation was justified. In 1948, in an editorial article lamenting Gandhi's murder, the principal Catholic newspaper in the Chinese language quoted with approval Romain Rolland's description of the Mahatma as 'Jesus without a cross', a phrase which for combined blasphemy and heresy would have caused hair to stand on end in the most ecumenical western seminary. Even so, this was only the amiable side of an indifference to dogma which at times wore a less charming aspect. For instance, towards the end of 1945 there was an unpleasant incident provoked by some army officers in Sian who out of curiosity decided to pay a visit to an ancient mosque which is one of the sights of the city. As they entered the sacred building they were accosted by a caretaker who implored them to take off their boots. They ignored the request, which seemed to them completely ridiculous, and when the man persisted and became, as they thought, obstreperous they lost their temper and kicked him out of the way, after which they stamped through the place to their heart's content. Meanwhile the caretaker had run off to give the alarm, and in no time at all a sizeable crowd of very angry Muslims burst in to put a stop to the sacrilege and manhandled the culprits so vigorously that one of them died, drawing his final breath, we may be sure, in the blankest ignorance of having done anything objectionable. Actually, the very fact that a place of worship should seek to protect its sanctity from intrusion by unbelievers was in itself sufficient to arouse suspicion that it had something to hide. In the year 1873, a Japanese pilgrim was told by the abbot of a Buddhist monastery in Peking that if you could penetrate into the holy of holies in a mosque you would discover the idol which the Muslims adored, namely the statue of a donkey in copulation with a woman.[10]

The absence of theological enthusiasm, then, did not always guarantee that there would be no friction between a religious minority, such as the Muslims, and the rest of the population. In Yunnan economic causes sparked off the outbreak, which began in 1855 as a dispute between miners. Silver workings in a certain area were being exploited both by ordinary Chinese and by Muslims. The latter, who clannishly kept to themselves, were lucky enough to find the more productive seam, so much so that their pagan neighbours proposed to join forces with them. The offer was not accepted and the refusal led to bad blood and rioting between the two communities. The Muslims in general had the advantage, but they were soon prevailed upon by the Viceroy to return peaceably to work in exchange for his promise of official protection. Behind their backs however, certain mandarins in the provincial government who distrusted them sent reports to Peking in which it was alleged that the followers of the alien religion would not be satisfied until Yunnan had been altogether detached from the Chinese Empire. At the provincial capital of Kunming the same calumny was being relentlessly dinned into the ears of the Viceroy, with the suggestion that it was his duty to strike first and frustrate the treason. The Viceroy, a weak but well-intentioned man, resisted his counsellors as long as he could, but in the end his will-power was undermined and he and his wife escaped from their misery by hanging themselves. Pending the appointment of a successor by Peking, which distance and the chaotic state of the country—the Taiping rebellion was then at its height—would delay for months, the administration now passed into the hands of the enemies of Islam, and secret orders were sent to the mandarins of the province to assemble as many men as they could spare for the extirpation of the Muslims.

This oriental St Bartholomew was fixed for May 19, 1856. In many places it succeeded according to plan, and the streets ran with Muslim blood, while the murderers rewarded themselves for their efforts by appropriating their victims' belongings. Elsewhere, however, the assassins encountered a resistance none of them had bargained for. In Tali, already mentioned for its marble, the entire city and its environs with an enormous stock of booty fell into Muslim hands. In other parts of the province, too, the intended victims held firm and civil war flared across the land.

One man stood out on the Muslim side, for his claim to be considered as leader of the movement was undeniable. In a country where white hair alone gained great respect, Ma Te-hsing was sixty-three. Among his coreligionists even his age and patriarchal appearance were less impressive than his attainments in theology. Not only had he studied Arabic for years in his youth; in 1839, when he was forty-six, he had made his way across country to

Burma, and had embarked at Rangoon in a sailing ship with other pilgrims for Mecca. From there he had travelled through Egypt, and so in due course reached Constantinople, where for two years he steeped himself in Islamic learning and picked up the rudiments of astronomy. Something of his quality may be discerned from the fact that having casually heard from one of his Turkish instructors that at Singapore the days were of equal length throughout the year he called at that city on his way home and remained there a full twelve months to satisfy himself that the report was true. Returning by way of Canton in 1846 he was received with awe by his old friends, as the only Hadji in Yunnan.

This qualification by itself would have established Ma Te-hsing's title to be the spiritual leader of any Muslim revolt, but his age made it necessary for him to have a deputy in the field. A much younger man was fortunately ready to hand, who had in his boyhood taken Arabic lessons from Ma Te-hsing, but whose more practical temperament had sent him into mining affairs where he became an expert in the exploitation of silver diggings. He was named Ma Ju-lung (the surname Ma is exceedingly common among Chinese Muslims), and it seemed his destiny to be a soldier, for his excellent physique and taste for gymnastic exercises had from his youth given him the notion of advancing his career in the service of the State, not in the civil mandarinate, for he had no aptitude for Confucian book-learning, but in the military establishment, entry to which was procurable by examination in such subjects as archery. Having for years entirely given up his spare time to these pursuits, he had in due course been rewarded with a baccalaureate in military science; but now his brother had been killed by the pagans, and dreams of an officer's commission had to be abandoned to the duty of revenge. This last was accomplished beyond all reasonable expectations. In a few months' time, the forces of the imperial government were everywhere on the defensive against the people they had imagined would by now no longer be in existence to trouble them.

The revolt of the Yunnanese Muslims was to be an event of decisive significance both to Vietnam and to France, but this is not the place to trace its story in detail. Passing over its first few years, we find that by November 1860 the rebels were in effective control of the greater part of the province, which they administered by their own system of officials. The city of Tali, in the west, which had been in Muslim hands from the start was governed by a regional leader named Tu Wen-hsiu. The main rebel force, led by Ma Ju-lung in person, was besieging the provincial capital of Kunming, which was expected to fall at any moment and to bring down with it the last remnants of Peking's authority in Yunnan. The position of the garrison was so desperate that it is said an average of one hundred persons a day were dying of starvation. With the end in sight, the mandarins inside the walls decided to treat with the besiegers, hoping at the most that a speedy surrender might perhaps save their lives. To their bewilderment, once their envoys had made contact with Ma Ju-lung and the old patriarch Ma Te-hsing, they discovered that the rebel chieftains were disposed to go far beyond what would already, in view of the injury they had received, be the extreme of generosity. Not only would the mandarins be spared: if they, and Peking, agreed to make the change worth while, the two Mas and all their troops would return to obedience and the Muslim revolt would be over. Throughout history Chinese governments have been readier than western ones to offer generous terms to rebels who manifest a change of heart and what to foreign observers seemed a humiliating concession on the part of Peking was in Chinese eyes an eminently reasonable compromise. Both the Mas were offered high office in exchange for their transfer of loyalty, but in the event the patriarch preferred to receive a substantial pension while the lifelong ambition of his younger colleague was gratified with a general's commission.

Today, a century later, the motive of this spectacular trasformation remains a conundrum. Did the two leaders foresee that their triumph was ephemeral and that ultimately the power of the central government would prevail ? While negotiations were in progress at Kunming, Peking was in the hands of an Anglo-French army and the Emperor a fugitive across the Great Wall: it would have taken a bold man to prophesy that the dynasty would survive at all, or that it would ever be able to reassert itself at the remotest limit of the Empire, for the Taipings were solidly entrenched in the Lower Yangtze Valley and paid scant attention to the affairs of Yunnan.

The temptation to create an independent Muslim State must have been very strong. To the third chieftain, Tu Wen-hsiu of Tali, it proved irresistible, and very likely it was the knowledge of Tu's personal ambitions that convinced the Mas that the rebellion, if continued, would inevitably be rent asunder by jealousy and that for themselves the established order offered greater security. As it was, they faithfully carried out their part of the bargain. Kunming passed quietly into their possession without any molestation of the imperial mandarins or of the inhabitants of the city and it appeared at first that the revolt was at an end. But such a gentle climax was too much to be hoped for. In spite of all pleas from his former comrades, Tu Wen-hsiu remained obdurate. Now that the Mas had abandoned the cause, it was he alone who emerged as the champion of Islam, and he adopted a title worthy of his position: henceforward he would be Sultan of Tali.

Although the men under Ma Ju-lung's command acquiesced in their leader's decision, and by so doing shared in the imperial bounty, yet at heart many of them hankered after the old frank days of Muslim brotherhood, and had no enthusiasm for the new duty which awaited them, for of course it was an inescapable consequence of their transfer of allegiance that if Tu and his followers refused to lay down their arms peacefully they would have to be subdued by force. Indeed Ma's followers showed so little stomach for fighting their fellow believers that some of the mandarins began to wonder how far Ma himself was to be trusted. Their suspicions were unfounded: the new general, as if to demonstrate that he deserved his commission, had more than twenty malcontents among his soldiers put to death under the eyes of their companions, and was clearly all eagerness to drag the Sultan from his throne, yet disppointingly, although his men continued to obey his orders, much of their virtue had gone out of them, and the war dragged on.

In the winter of 1867, when the French explorers arrived on the scene, the rebellion still showed no sign of coming to an end, and the situation was anything but advantageous to the government side. Sultan Tu, in his stronghold in the western part of the province, had taken advantage of his geographical proximity to Burma, to establish regular caravans which brought him, among other supplies, British muskets from Rangoon, thirty years old but far in advance of the antiquated matchlocks which provided the fire-power of the imperial army. It was known that Tu was expecting even more substantial help from abroad, and that in India and in London the British were deliberating the advantage of becoming the patrons of a Muslim Yunnan. Such an idea had occurred to Frenchmen too: one of the original purposes of the Mekong expedition was to investigate the nature of Tu's Sultanate which in its early days some of the French missionaries, who were the only Europeans in Yunnan, had imagined might be more favourably disposed to Catholicism than the regime of Imperial China. But the travellers on crossing the frontier found themselves in territory held by Ma Ju-lung's troops, and naturally proceeded to visit the commander himself at Kunming. He was observing the fast of Ramadan, and oddly enough, instead of entertaining his visitors after sunset, when he might have eaten and drunk in their company with a clear conscience, he treated them to an elaborate Chinese feast during which he sat at the table without allowing a morsel to pass his lips, though his guests were not convinced by his abstinence, and on the contrary drew one another's attention to their host's red-rimmed eyes as testifying to the orgies he indulged in during the night. What did impress them, on the other hand, was his obvious love of fire-arms. On the way into the banquet, the Frenchmen almost tripped over the sacks of ammunition that littered the corridor, and even the chairs they were given to sit on were riddled with bullet-holes, for Ma was in the habit of blazing away at household objects whenever the fit came upon him. With such a hobby, it may be imagined that he was an avid collector of guns, and it was no surprise to discover that he had an excellent little armoury which he had stocked at great expense from Shang-hai and Canton. The tragedy was that difficulty of transport made it impracticable for him to equip his army from the same sources: as it was, his hard-pressed troops were glad to use cannon a couple of centuries old, on which the IHS monogram testified to Jesuit manufacture.

Everything they saw in Kunming confirmed the explorers in the opinion they had formed long before they had ever set foot in Yunnan, namely that in southwestern China a vast market was lying unexploited. The likelihood that Britain would back the rebels must have suggested to them that France might have a chance of stealing a march on her rival if she supported the imperial cause, but they took the precaution nevertheless, of trying to establish contact with the Sultan for themselves. The venerable Ma Te-hsing was helpful enough to give them a letter in Arabic which he assured them would serve as a safe-conduct, and a small party set off for Tali, but their reception there was so menacing that they were glad to escape without the favour of an audience. After that there was no doubt in their minds that their best hope lay in supporting the authority of the Chinese government, and this feeling must have been confirmed by Ma Ju-lung's readiness to oblige them with a loan of money.

It only remained now for the expedition to return to the outside world and describe their exploits and discoveries. The first part of their homeward journey took them overland to the upper reaches of the Yangtze, from where they embarked in a junk and were carried in relative comfort to Hankow and the Shanghai steamer. The leader, utterly broken-down by the hardships suffered on the long trek through Laos, died two days short of the Great River and it was Garnier who emerged into the limelight. The Geographical Societies of Paris and London each awarded him a gold medal. The first international geographical congress, meeting at Antwerp, voted two special medals of honour, one to David Livingstone, the other to Francis Garnier. To a man hungry for glory, all this was gratifying indeed, but not so important to his future career as a chance conversation he had had on his journey down the Yangtze. During the brief delay at Hankow he had been introduced to a fellow countryman: it was a meeting which altered the world for both of them.

The writings of Father Huc had made Europe aware of the existence of the great conurbation in the very heart of China formed by the three cities of Hankow, Wuchang and Hanyang, and one of the results of the Anglo-French intervention of 1856–60 had been to make the area accessible by the opening of the Yangtze to foreign shipping, and the designation of Hankow as a treaty-port. The first British naval squadron to put the agreement into effect reached Hankow in March 1861, with a Frenchman, Jean Dupuis, among other civilian passengers. He was then thirty-three years old, an adventurer who had come to China to make his fortune in trade, and with a useful knack of wheedling favours out of those in power which had won him, a few months before, inclusion as an observer with the Anglo-French expedition to Peking, and was now giving him a start over potential rivals.

Huc, remembering Hankow before the devastation of the Taiping, had pictured it as a thriving commercial metropolis. The specacle of wretchedness which greeted Dupuis on his arrival would have dispirited most other men, but the newcomer, who for a long time thought it safer to take up quarters on a junk in the river rather than sleep ashore, had interests of a special kind to which the war raging around him were propitious. He had come to sell arms precisely at the moment when the Chinese authorities were beginning wholeheartedly to recognise that modern weapons were indispensable for the restoration of public order, and when, as we saw in an earlier chapter, the local anti-Taiping armies on the Yangtze were establishing direct contact with foreign sources of supply.

The suppression of the Taiping in 1864 did nothing to lessen the demand for new guns, and the arms dealer from abroad was a familiar figure in the Chinese landscape down to the Communist victory of 1949. Jean Dupuis, one of the first of the breed, was not the least attractive. He had of course an insatiable appetite for money, but money was clearly not the only motive of his activities. Excitement was to him the spice of life, and there could be no more alluring kingdom of adventure than the China of those days. Without a hundredth part of Garnier's intelligence, he nevertheless reached an appreciation of the Chinese spirit far deeper than Garnier's. The latter's dreams of French greatness were inextricably bound up with a romantic Catholicism which detested the eighteenth century Enlightenment as the enemy of Pope and King and in the last resort felt obliged to condemn Confucian China if only because Voltaire had admired it. The less complicated Dupuis savoured to the full the life around him without any philosophical misgivings. He learned to speak Chinese fluently, and a knack of sociability ensured that even highly-placed mandarins enjoyed his company without detecting the latent uncouthness of his temperament, while with the less pretentious army officers he was from the start a perfect hail-fellow-well-met. In sum, by his fortieth birthday, which he celebrated the year he met Garnier, 1868, the French adventurer had to a large extent donned a Chinese personality, a fact which he emphasized by wearing Chinese clothes in his travels about the land. As he sported an enormous Gallic moustache, downward drooping in a comically woebegone curve, the effect was of Vercingetorix dressed up as Chu Chin Chow.

This was the man who met Garnier on the latter's transit through Hankow and who among other items of information seems to have heard then about the Hoti River and its presumed identity with the Red River of Tongking. At least that is the account given by Garnier. Dupuis acrimoniously insists that he had no need to be told what he knew already: if we believe him, he had been aware for six or seven years that Yunnan was joined by river to Vietnam. Perhaps this was so, but it is significant that it took the conversation with Garnier to send him to kill two birds with one stone, first to make personal acquaintance with Ma Ju-lung, who was until then merely a name to him, and secondly to prove by inspection that the Hoti flowed into the Red River and that the latter was navigable throughout its entire course in Vietnam.

Dupuis and Garnier met in June 1868, and the former set out on his travels the following September. First of all his affairs summoned him to the imperial army fighting the most important Muslim rising of all, that raging in the far northwestern province of Kansu. He travelled in state as a Chinese functionary, for as purveyor to the Emperor's armies he had been accorded the temporary rank and privileges of a mandarin. The journey of two months, through country harassed by brigands, was rewarded by a series of lucrative orders, and it was in the best of spirits that in December 1868, he turned his face to the south on the enormous safari across the map of China which lay between him and Yunnan. From Kansu, the way was through Szechwan. On January 21, 1869 he reached Chungking where a representative of the provincial government of Yunnan had been sent to meet him, and to convey him for the next fortnight in a sumptuously appointed junk along the upper course of the Yangtze, before he committed himself on horseback to the last and most dangerous stage of his adventure. When he arrived at Kunming on March 11th, he had

had more than one narrow escape from the rebels, who, in fact, a few days later succeeded for a while in cutting the road by which he had just travelled.

The provincial authorities were in the circumstances all the more eager to clutch at the prospect of European aid. Dupuis was completely reassuring. Foreign arms, and French instructors to demonstrate how to use them, would pacify Yunnan within three years. He talked also of broader schemes, in particular of the Red River, but he had to admit that the present moment was not propitious for so uncertain an enterprise. The immediate necessity was to bring in weapons by the known and tried way, cumbersome though it was. At the beginning of April 1869 he was en route once more, this time via Hankow, Shanghai and Hong Kong, for Canton, bearing a letter of credit which would enable him to draw on the Kwangtung provincial treasury for the cost of the arms required and the hire of the European instructors.

Back again at Hankow with the mission accomplished Dupuis heard with pleasure the encouraging reports that followed the receipt of the new weapons on the Yunnan front. The months passed, and with them came the news of the Franco-Prussian war, but Dupuis saw no reason on that account to make any change in his plans. In January 1871 he returned to Kunming and finding his Chinese friends in a more cheerful mood—especially General Ma who during Dupuis's last visit had been under a cloud because of his reverses in the field—he told them that he must now absolutely insist on uncovering the mystery of the Red River.

Even in the middle of China, a region that lay on the frontier between one province and another tended in times of unrest to become a kind of no man's land, with each provincial authority passing the responsibility of enforcing law and order to its neighbour. Forty years ago Mao Tse-tung profited from such a condition of affairs to build up a Communist force in the mountains between Hunan and Kiangsi. In the 1860s, with a great rebellion raging in its own territory, one can scarcely blame the Yunnan administration for keeping the affairs of the Vietnamese frontier at arm's length, especially since it was notorious that on the other side of the border the Vietnamese government exercised no effective control. General Ma explained that he could not guarantee his friend's safety, and even the majority of the Chinese attendants, who had not shrunk from danger before, showed that they would not follow their master in this leap into the unknown. Nor was it simply the fear of brigands that made them recoil. The journey would plunge them from the healthy altitude of Kunming into a dank fever-ridden valley, along which they would have to make their way laboriously until they could take to a boat. After that their progress would be less fatiguing, but just as unhealthy, with dense malarial jungle on either bank, and the likelihood of a violent death at the hands of river-pirates from one hour to the next. Nevertheless, nothing could make Dupuis change his mind. A solitary mandarin was found with enough courage to act as the representative of General Ma, while a local headman was bribed to recruit an escort of eighty men with two guides. Thus provided, Dupuis set off.

The expedition was to open a new chapter in the history of France, of Vietnam and of China, and the world is feeling some of its consequences to this day; but at the time, particularly after the ominous prophecies made at Kunming before it began, what actually happened was an anti-climax. The travellers found Manghao to be a market town largely in the hands of Cantonese merchants who had been driven some years previously from the trading post of Laokay, just across the Vietnamese border, by an invasion of brigands, and their stories of atrocities made a number of Dupuis's escort decide to go no further. However, it was true that the river was now usable, and the Frenchman, with what remained of his followers, boldly put to the water. For one thing, he was aware that the bandits or river-pirates whom he would encounter were Chinese, and he obviously believed there was a reasonable chance that, having been outlawed in their native provinces of Kwangsi and Kwangtung, they might be touched by a message of good will uttered in the name of another provincial government.

As it turned out, his optimism was on the whole justified. Laokay (the name means 'the old market') proved to be a wretched assembly of huts which even in its palmy days could never have been prepossessing and now bore a look of the most abject desolation not simply to be explained by the presence of the freebooters, for after all it was in the interest of these latter to encourage commerce from which they could levy protection-money. What had happened, as Dupuis soon discovered, was that the Chinese brigands had broken up into two warring bands. One of these, calling itself 'the Black Flags' from the colour it had chosen for its banners and its costumes, had its headquarters at Laokay, while its enemies, known as 'the Yellow Flags', by seizing a strategic position down stream were able to throttle its source of revenue and prohibit the transit of boats from Hanoi and the coast.

The Black Flags received Dupuis without hostility, and though he got the impression that they were not precisely enchanted with the prospect of leading a more regular life, at any rate they promised not to oppose the plans of the Yunnanese authorities. The Yellow Flags, however, when Dupuis continued his voyage as far as their stronghold, were unreservedly enthusiastic at the chance of winning an amnesty which would at least ensure that when their time came to die their bones could be carried back to lie in their ancestral soil, and offered to do all in their power to promote the grand design.

Dupuis had now sailed nearly half the length of the Red River from the Chinese border to the sea. So far, the country on either bank, inasmuch as it was controlled at all (for it consisted of jungle-clad hills), lay in the hands of Chinese buccaneers. Further on, he would come to the outposts of the Vietnamese administration, and a fresh problem would arrive with which at the moment he was not ready to deal. At any rate, there was no longer any doubt that the river was navigable. So going back the way he had come, he re-entered Yunnan in triumph and announced to General Ma and his other friends that a bright future lay before them. He would guarantee that steamers of moderate draught could sail upstream as far as Manghao, from where cargoes would go easily by mule train up the valley in a matter of days. In fact it was time for a formal agreement to be entered into. Dupuis would see to the hiring of suitable vessels and to the ordering of armaments. On its side the provincial government of Yunnan would issue papers requiring the Vietnamese officials encountered en route to grant passage to the expedition as being in the service

7   The battle at Sontay, 1884, as drawn by a contemporary Chinese artist

8 Rivière pushing the cannon forward during the battle at Sontay

of their overlord, the Emperor of China. For remuneration, Dupuis would be given a share in the exploitation of certain tin and copper deposits in Yunnan, and French experts of his choosing would be put in charge of the mining operations. A consignment of minerals would be got ready to be exchanged against the first lot of arms.

With this treaty burning a hole in his pocket, Dupuis could hardly wait to reach the outside world. Ships were to be chartered without difficulty at Hong Kong, but in an affair of such magnitude he felt he deserved the support of his country. Late in 1871, he set off once more from Yunnan to Hankow and Shanghai, where he embarked for France. Let us leave him now for a while, and turn instead to the Chinese freebooters he had just confronted on the Red River, in particular to the Black Flags and their extraordinary chieftain.

⚜ CHAPTER SIX

The Black Flags

T
HE Chinese provinces of Kwangtung and Kwangsi have
already been mentioned more than once in this story, as,
with Yunnan, bordering Vietnam to the North, and
throughout the first few centuries of the Christian era forming
with Vietnam a single administrative unit within the Chinese
Empire. We have also noticed that their inhabitants, in the eyes
of Northern Chinese, formed almost a race apart, not simply as
southerners—the term 'South' to an ordinary citizen of Peking
still refers to the Yangtze Valley—but as people halfway in culture
to the Vietnamese across the frontier. This attitude was maintained
even to those in the border provinces who were of indisputably
Chinese race, but a large part of the population, especially in
Kwangsi, consisted of aboriginal tribes, akin to the so-called
'montagnards' of Vietnam, and like them driven from the fertile
lands to the hills before the implacable advance of Chinese cultural
colonization from the North.   Today, under the People's Government, a sizeable portion of Kwangsi has been designated as a
special area in which tribesmen, dignified as a 'minority nationality'
enjoy a certain measure of autonomy, but until 1949, the aborigi-
nals were as a rule on the worst possible terms with their Chinese
supplanters, and often enough at open war with them.

Even so, the very name of Kwangsi aroused in the minds of
educated Chinese the idea of a place like no other, where the fairy
landscapes—pine-clad mountains of fantastic shape rising abruptly
from a lake-studded plain, and breaking through wreaths of mist
to show glimpses of ravine's and waterfalls—which for centuries

had haunted the imagination of poets and artists really existed. It was above all others the province of magic, the region in China the most antipathetic to Confucian scepticism. Wizards and alchemists abounded in those improbable mountains, searching to unravel the secrets of nature and to distill the elixir of life. Confucius would have abominated everything about it, not least the condition of chronic anarchy in which by the early nineteenth century much of its southern part was submerged. For this state of affairs a variety of causes was to blame. Attention has been drawn in an earlier chapter to the rapid increase in population from the seventeenth century onwards which was resulting in a pressure on land. Add to this the secular antipathy between the Chinese proper and the aboriginal tribesmen, and it is clear the government of such a region called for outstanding ability in administration, a form of talent more often than not totally lacking in the men sent by Peking as its representatives. As the situation deteriorated, the old hostility to the Manchus, always glowing beneath the surface in these southernmost districts, burst openly into flame. It was not by accident that Kwangsi was the birthplace of the Taiping Rebellion; nor did circumstances exist elsewhere of a kind to produce a phenomenon quite like the Black Flags.

Their leader, Liu Yung-fu, was born in 1837 in the extreme southwest of Kwangtung province, close to the Vietnamese frontier and within a few miles of the sea. Like the founder of the Taiping movement, he came of Hakka stock. The Hakkas (the word means 'strangers'), were originally settlers from North or Central China driven to the far South by the Mongol and Tartar invasions during the Sung Dynasty, a fact which may be deduced from their speech, for they talk a dialect much closer to standard Chinese than the Fukienese or Cantonese they hear around them. In consequence, they have a great sense of clannishness, and one of them travelling anywhere throughout Southern China or South East Asia will be made to feel at home in the Hakka communities he will meet. This, however, was the only point of resemblance between the Taiping prophet and Liu Yung-fu. The former was a man of some education, a schoolmaster who had competed, though unsuccessfully, in the state examinations, and he came from a modestly comfortable family. Liu's parents, on the other hand, were the poorest of the poor, without settled home or occupation, and he remained all his life totally illiterate.

At the time of his birth, his father was trying to eke out a living by peddling rice-spirit of his own manufacture, while an uncle staying with them worked as a pig-butcher. Liu's mother—another sign of the family poverty—was a widow who married his father when the latter was nearly forty years of age, and she soon became a mainstay of the household by her practise as a midwife, and sometimes as a sort of wise woman who prayed and recited charms on behalf of her clients. At first they had lived in a cottage built of mud bricks—a pathetic attempt at respectability which by the boy's seventh year had to be abandoned as beyond their means. The family, including the uncle, whose addiction to gambling had precipitated the disaster, migrated a short distance into Kwangsi, to stay with some cousins whose prospects seemed brighter; but at the very moment of the removal one of their intended hosts was arrested on suspicion of banditry, the household was ruined by the expense of bribing the local magistrate to release him, and the Lius once more were thrown on their own devises. The father struggled to win a pittance from a strip of soil, the mother carried on her old profession, and the boy, who was already taking a pride in trying to enrich their poor diet with an occasional fish caught in a neighbouring river, soon was so well acquainted with the shallows and sandbanks along its course that he was able to earn an odd copper by acting as a look-out on the boats which used the waterway.

The bond between mother and son was especially close, and sixty years later Liu would recall the nights when as a boy he would sit on a rock outside their cabin waiting for her return from some call upon her services, and his excitement when far off through the trees he would catch the first glimmer of her lantern. She had to go out in all weathers, more often than not for a great distance. One night in the autumn of 1853 she came back drenched with rain and with a feverish cough. Within a day or two she was dead.

The Chinese, even those who rejected the notion of the immortality of the soul, attached enormous importance to the proper treatment of dead bodies. It was a crime to dispose of a corpse otherwise than by burial, and there was a whole science of geomancy to help in the selection of a felicitous site for a tomb. During the centuries, the plains of Northern and Central China became studded with these grave mounds, the existence of which proved in our own day to be a most awkward impediment in the collectivization and mechanization of agriculture, for it is out of the question to manoeuvre a tractor where every hundred yards you have to swerve to avoid desecrating the last resting-place of somebody's ancestors. Communist notabilities when they die are invariably cremated: pending the general adoption of this custom, the country people have been persuaded to agree to the reinterment of their forebears' remains in comparatively unfertile ground dedicated as public cemeteries. In South China the problem was not so urgent, since graves were already as a rule situated in rocky and unproductive tracts of hillside.

Not only was the choice of a burial place an important matter, there was the preliminary question of the coffin itself. Wealthy families often prepared by ordering these receptacles in advance, made out of the finest timber. There was so little of the macabre in all this that one of the commonest sights in any Chinese town was the coffin-maker's shop, open to the street and showing its rows of lacquered caskets to passers-by. Indeed, in 1950, a modern undertaker's show-window, in Avenue Joffre, Shanghai, exhibited a tailor's dummy—of foreign manufacture to judge by its European features and blond head—clad in a Chinese shroud, a cheerful crimson cloak with a hood which gave the figure the appearance of Santa Claus.

The poverty-stricken Lius were naturally unable to provide their dead with such comforts. But the poor midwife had been well-liked by her clients, and although some of these must have been almost as impoverished as the bereaved family they collected between them enough to pay for a simple deal coffin in which she was put into the ground. Her husband, a broken white-haired man at fifty-six, survived a bare two months and the destitution of the orphaned Liu Yung-fu may be gauged by the fact that, finding even the crudest coffin utterly beyond his means, he dismantled the primitive bed on which his father had died and fastened the body between the planks to protect it from contact with the bare earth.

A few weeks later, just before the Chinese New Year of 1854, the uncle followed his brother and sister-in-law, and this time the most that could be done was to bury the corpse wrapped in a straw mat.

Left to his own resources, the youth was active enough to scrape a living here and there in the surrounding country, sometimes on the river-boats, sometimes as a charcoal burner. It was while he was engaged in this latter occupation that he had an experience he was never to forget. One day, deep in the mountains, overcome by fatigue he fell asleep. In a dream there appeared before him a venerable man with a flowing white beard, who addressed him with the words: 'General of the Black Tiger, why are you hiding yourself here? Go out from this mountain into the world!' He awoke with a start to find the sun had set and a chill wind was moaning across the hillside.

To one like himself, imbued with peasant superstition, there was no doubt that the vision was of divine origin, and announced some grandiose future. He became more enterprising: it is reported, though not too reliably, that it was at this time that he made his first visit to Vietnam. Even if the story is true, it is not suggested that he ventured any great distance beyond the frontier, and working, as he is said to have done, among fellow Chinese, he cannot have been consciously an exile, He certainly did not stay away very long, but whether in Vietnam or elsewhere he seems to have come into possession of a useful sum of money. According to his own account, he stumbled upon a packet of opium which smugglers from Yunnan, where the poppy was being cultivated, had abandoned in fleeing from a posse of Kwangsi customs officials. However acquired, the money enabled him to rid himself of a nagging remorse that had been plaguing him ever since his parents died. Through lack of means, he had been forced to bury his father and mother on the bit of land they had tilled, although he was well aware of its unsuitability, for a few inches down one struck water, and in wet weather it was often flooded. His imagination was enslaved by nightmarish fantasies concerning worms and putrefaction. Now he remembered how years ago, when as a boy he had been minding the water-buffalo of a wealthier neighbour, he had overheard a geomancer, who was surveying the district for good grave-sites, praise the shape of a certain ridge as resembling the spine of a tiger. How odd that the old man in the vision had referred to the same animal! The money in hand was just sufficient for him to act on the hint. He did everything in style, hiring a geomancer to make the final choice of place and an astrologer to calculate the most auspicious moment for the ceremony. We read occasionally in the Chinese books of filial sons who carry their parents' bones on their back when transferring them to a new home, and as Liu made two trips—for the bodies were placed in separate graves—it is conceivable that he also employed the same classical method, though as only three years had elapsed since the first burial it is probable that the corpses had not yet been reduced to fleshless skeletons and that they were put into elaborate coffins requiring a number of bearers immediately on exhumation. This last operation must have been appalling in the extreme for although the chronicler who compiled Liu's memoirs in his old age spares us the horrible details, he lets us catch a glimpse of one revealing incident. The astrologer had fixed the hour of the father's reburial for the middle of the night, and a violent storm broke out as the funeral procession was proceeding towards the new grave. Liu cried out that the rain must have flooded the hole, and would not be satisfied until by touching the earth at the sides and bottom with his hand he discovered that it was only very slightly damp. And so, his duty to his parents fulfilled, he was free to go out into the world, as the old man had urged, and seek his fortune.

In the dream he had been hailed as a 'General', so as a first step he became a bandit. To be fair, he never thought of the matter in that light. Then and afterwards in his own eyes he was always a soldier—sometimes, to be sure, a soldier of fortune, but not less honourable on that account. Indeed, now at the very outset of his career, fate gave to his actions a stamp of respectability, almost certainly undeserved, but which to his countrymen serves to palliate his freebooting exploits. As we have seen, the great Taiping Rebellion had broken out in Kwangsi in 1851, and from 1853 onwards had established itself at Nanking as a regular dynasty, which to many observers seemed likely to reduce the whole land into obedience. We have described, too, how in their haste to reach the richest part of China, the Lower Yangtze

Valley, the Taipings had marched through large areas of the country without bothering to establish bases in their rear. In consequence of this neglect, they had to all intents and purposes abandoned the very birthplace of their movement, so that by 1857—the year when Liu-fu, at the age of twenty set out on his new profession—there seem to have been no Taiping forces, properly so called, in Kwangsi province. On the other hand, the glamour of the Taiping name, and prestige of serving a dynasty fighting a patriotic war against the alien Manchus, encouraged some of the freebooters spawned by the anarchy of the region—for the absence of the Taiping did not mean that the central government had resumed effective control— boast of their allegiance to the national cause. One of these, a man named Wu Yuan-ch'ing, the leader of a band which infested the vicinity of Nanning adjacent to the Vietnamese frontier, actually claimed to have been created a Prince by the Taiping ruler in Nanking and held a solemn ceremony of inauguration, which so impressed young Liu that he enthusiastically attached himself to Wu's fortunes.

During the next few years the life of Liu Yung-fu is, to a western reader at any rate, a dreary record of forays and skirmishes at places for the most part too insignificant to be traceable on the map, fought between men whose names, without the accident of Liu's presence on the scene, would have long since disappeared in a merciful oblivion. Yet it was precisely to these transactions that, in his old age, his mind kept returning. One might have expected that to him the great event of his career would have been the confrontation with the European enemy, which made him into a national hero, but not a bit of it. As we shall see, his exploits against the French, which caused his name to resound not only in Vietnam and China, but in Europe and America, are mentioned by him only when absolutely necessary, and even then he turns away from them as quickly as possible, with obvious relief, to follow the purely Chinese vendettas with which he felt at home. In a way, this is a salutary reminder that we foreigners habitually exaggerate the role we played in Chinese history. When one considers the great number of westerners who lived in China throughout the century which preceded the Communist victory in 1949, it is astonishing how few of them are remembered by the Chinese at large. Probably only two are ensured of immortality, the Prussian Field-Marshal Waldersee who commanded the allied army against the Boxers in 1900—and characteristically he owes his celebrity not to his military exploits, but to his love affair with a Chinese prostitute which has become the theme of innumerable works of literature—and Dr Bethune, the Canadian physician who gave his life in the service of the Red Army and whose panegyric by Mao Tse-tung is included in the canon of Communist scripture. Be that as it may, Liu Yung-fu's incuriosity makes his memoirs, dictated in his old age to an admirer, one of the most boring works ever composed.

The soldiers of the self-styled Prince Wu led a most wretched existence, being lucky when they were issued with the minute dole of rice which they were promised. We are told that once when they were able to eat a meal of pork an entire company was prostrated with diarrhoea. After a year or two Liu seems to have grown discouraged and to have drifted off in search of a more enterprising leader. His material fortunes hardly improved but the toughness and determination he displayed in many tight corners attracted attention; in two or three years he was the acknowledged chief of nearly two hundred men whom he caused to swear mutual fraternity and loyalty before a black flag which, always remembering his dream, he appointed to be the ensign and totem of the band. With this regiment at his back he decided to return to his first allegiance, where in the meanwhile Wu Ah-chung had suceeded to his father in the make-believe princedom. Now, of course, Liu was able to cut much more of a figure, so much so in fact that Wu thought it wise to cement their relationship by offering him his sister's hand. Apparently the young lady was not very appetizing, for though Liu consented to a betrothal he alleged various excuses for postponing the marriage and the year 1865 found him at twenty-eight still a bachelor.

The Taiping Rebellion had been stamped out at Nanking the year before, and in spite of having its hands full with uprisings elsewhere Peking was gradually reasserting its authority in Kwangsi. The prospects for the outlaws were gloomy, and as supplies grew scarcer, Liu asked permission to take his followers on a foraging expedition away from the main body. The request was granted with a very bad grace, and on condition that he returned without fail at the end of one month; but when the period had expired, the Black Flags, instead of keeping their word, unanimously voted to embark on an adventure which must have been in Liu's mind for some time, and which we are told he proposed at this moment partly in order to avoid the unwelcome marriage which he saw he could not stave off indefinitely. His plan, briefly, was to carve out a territory over the border in Vietnam, but to do so with the blessing of the Vietnamese government by presenting himself as an ally of the latter against the 'montagnard' tribes who had for long been the masters of the hill country between the Chinese border and the upper course of the Red River.

On the face of it, nothing could have been rasher than this scheme. Not the slightest attempt had been made in advance to establish contact with the Vietnamese authorities. The march was slow and deliberate, loitering here and there to collect recruits from other Chinese freebooters. At length, when Vietnamese patrols were encountered, a clash was very narrowly averted. The ears of Liu and his men were not yet accustomed to the local speech, but one or two of them seem to have had more schooling than their captain and were able to convey to the Vietnamese in writing that they were peaceable merchants on their way to Yunnan. Probably something in Liu's manner gave an impression that he was not the kind of man it would be safe to provoke. Certainly neither then nor later, to judge by what he said in his old age, was he inclined to rate the Vietnamese very highly as soldiers. At all events, whether his story was believed or not, he was permitted to continue his journey until the Red River was reached opposite Sontay, and he set up a stockaded encampment.

His passage through the country had been observed by the montagnards, though (perhaps because they imagined he might indeed be simply in transit), they did not attempt to bar the way. Now, however, it was clear that an interloper was staking out a claim in what they looked upon as peculiarly their own domain, and they had no intention of putting up with the impertinence. Their leaders regarded their own status as so dignified that they felt a touch of protocol would not be out of place, and dispatched to Liu a bamboo tablet inscribed in Chinese characters as follows:

'We the military commanders of the Montagnards will on a day we have decided come to Sontay at the head of a mighty host, numbering thousands and myriads, myriads and thousands. This is our respectful greeting to you.'

In fact the montagnard army comprised several thousand warriors, and as the Black Flags together with their new allies cannot all told have amounted to more than five hundred, the situation did not inspire confidence. But Liu had never doubted that the tribesmen would come against him in strength, and he had taken precautions. The terrain itself indicated that the enemy would come down through one particular pass in the hills, and instead of trying to hold them at this point, he posted a detachment of his men in ambush to open fire on the montagnards when they were already through, with the purpose of driving them over a tract of land thickly planted with bamboo spikes set in pits and concealed from view by the vegetation. The trick was astonishingly successful; the montagnards panicked and in a matter of minutes were in full retreat, those bringing up the rear (we are informed) trampling on the impaled bodies of their companions.

The Vietnamese authorities watched these developments with fascination, especially when Liu followed up his victory by organizing the assassination by a disgruntled tribesmen of a montagnard chieftain on whose head the government had put a price. The Court at Hue, on the recommendation of their local representative, was induced to grant Liu an honorary commission in the Vietnamese army, and he and his men were encouraged to continue their work of pacification. In 1868, however, he determined to leave the montagnards alone for the time being and to concentrate his efforts on one of the most satisfying prizes available, the river port of Laokay on the Yunnan border, which had for some years been in the hands of an armed group of Cantonese merchants.

When these latter had got wind of Liu's intention, they were able by an unlooked for turn of events to call on a powerful champion. For while the Black Flags had been winning favour in

Vietnam, the situation of their old comrades in Kwangsi, 'Prince' Wu and his army, had been going steadily from bad to worse until, hounded every step of the road by the provincial militia, they too had been driven south over the frontier. A nephew of the 'Prince', named Huang Ch'ung-ying, more active than his uncle, had grouped his own close adherents around him to form a band distinguished by a yellow flag, precisely on the model established by Liu Yung-fu but twice or three times as many in number, and had formed a stockade at a place called Hayang on the Clear River. This is a tributary of the Red River, arising like the latter in Yunnan but further north, and flowing in a southeasterly direction until it joins the main stream, about one hundred miles from the sea. The Clear River, however, obviously could not be such a source of profit as the Red, and an invitation from the occupants of Laokay was more than welcome.

Huang caught up with Liu when the latter had advanced within a few miles of Laokay and greeted him as an old friend and companion. There ensured an episode for which the nearest parallel in the West would probably be found in the history of the highland clans of Scotland. Liu entertained his visitor as lavishly as he could and helped him set up camp on the opposite bank of the river to himself. Yet he did not venture his person among the Yellow Flags until word was brought to him that Huang's feelings were hurt by the fact that his own frequent visits to Liu were never returned. Was it possible that distrust could exist between such old comrades ? So at last, on a day chosen for its favourable omens, Liu crossed the water, unarmed and accompanied by only two followers, and was introduced by himself into a hut where Huang lay on a couch enjoying a pipe of opium. As he went inside he noticed several evil-looking ruffians guarding the door, and his heart sank, but it was now too late to retreat, and he struck up as lively a conversation as he could. There was another opium-pipe lying on a table and although Liu was a life long abstainer from the drug, he picked up the instrument and held it in his hand throughout the interview, ready, in his own words, to dash Huang's brains out with it if the latter should as much as make one suspicious move.

The precaution was unnecessary, since apparently all Huang

desired was to discuss the question of Laokay. He had decided to transfer his Yellow Flags there within the next day or two, he said, and he would be delighted to have his friend's company. The only difficulty was one of accommodation: the Cantonese in the place had offered Huang lodgings in the middle of the town, but they had mentioned that there were vacant buildings on the outskirts which would be very suitable for Liu and as many of his men as he wanted to take. All they stipulated was that their warehouses should be left alone.

Safely out of the lion's den, Liu regained confidence and in due course presented himself with a party of Black Flags at the buildings to which he had been directed. He was fully prepared to rough it but at the sight of what was waiting for him he burst into rage. It was a line of ramshackle sheds, from which emanated a most revolting stench, and no wonder, for the floors and walls were thickly smeared with every variety of excrement, human and animal. This was not to be endured: off marched the Black Flags into the town and without more ado commandeered one of the biggest of the Cantonese warehouses. There was a mighty uproar, and after a few minutes Huang appeared, as furious as Liu, demanding to know why the latter had broken his word. A clash seemed inevitable there and then, but, miraculously, on hearing what had happened, Huang's temper evaporated at once into sweetness and apologies for the unpardonable negligence of which someone had been guilty.

Yet although the incident passed over, there was after it no further pretence at friendship. For a few weeks the two bands remained aloof, watching each other. There was an attempt by some well-intentioned subordinates, who shrank from a fratricidal war, to bring the two leaders together, and a time and place were appointed for a conference, which the participants would attend unarmed. In readiness for all eventualities Liu tells us he deliberately sharpened his finger-nails into points, so as to gouge out his interlocutor's eyes if the occasion arose, but the meeting never took place.

The circumstances of the battle of Laokay, when the inevitable outbreak occurred, are veiled in an almost impenetrable fog of conflicting details. The Yellow Flags struck the first blow, relying not only on their superior numbers, but also on the fact that they had dug a mine under what they thought was their enemies's sleeping quarters. In this they were deceived, for Liu was aware of their machinations and had disposed his men out of harm's way, so that when the charge was detonated it made a great deal of noise but injured nobody. Instead the aggressors were soon paid in their own coin: as they swarmed to attack their own ammunition was set on fire and killed many of them in the explosion. The struggle was waged intermittently for several days and ended when the Yellow Flags, hemmed in on three sides, took to flight by way of the river in such confusion that a number of them were drowned.

The victory marked a decisive turning point in Liu Yung-fu's career. Already allied to the Vietnamese, he now found his help solicited by the government of his own country to whom so far he had been known, if at all, merely as an unimportant bandit. We have seen that his old commander 'Prince' Wu had fled south into Vietnam pursued by the Kwangsi authorities. These latter had decided, with the agreement of the Vietnamese, to hunt out their quarry across the border, and a Chinese army under a certain General Feng was now operating on Tongking soil. This soldier, who plays a considerable part in our story, will require a more formal introduction later on: for the moment it is enough to mention that he had learned of Liu's triumph at Laokay and the news had made all the deeper impression on him because Wu, the nominal chieftain of the bandits, had escaped from pursuit by death—whether natural or violent is not clear—leaving his lieutenant Huang Ch'ung-ying to succeed him. In other words Feng, representative of Peking, Liu the freebooter, and the civil and military mandarins who symbolized the Hue government's claim to authority in Tongking, discovered they had a common enemy, for the Yellow Flags, who were still a power to be reckoned with in the densely wooded mountains between the upper reaches of the Red River and the Kwangsi border, were closely associated with the montagnard tribesmen. In recognition of this state of affairs, Feng sent envoys to Laokay offering to Liu an honorary commision in the Chinese army on more or less the same terms he had accepted from the Vietnamese. Any antipathy still felt by Liu towards the Manchu Dynasty—and it is unlikely in the first place to have been founded on serious principles—was immediately thawed by the cordiality of the message. The truth is that the more the Black Flags saw of the Vietnamese, the greater their pride in their own nationality. 'Prince' Wu, in claiming to give allegiance to the Taipings, must have ordered his men to let their hair grow in the ancient Chinese mode, and we may imagine that until now, if only for reasons of convenience, the Black Flags had continued the style. Henceforward, they changed back to the Manchu pigtail, more troublesome because, apart from the complicated ribboning and plaiting, the front of the head needed the constant application of a razor. The bother, however, was more than compensated by the pride of flaunting the badge of the suzerain power in the face of the satellite population.

The campaign which followed included some of Liu's most remarkable examples of military leadership, especially the feat known as 'the storming of the thirteen passes', in which he led a force of Black Flags through the mountains against Huang Ch'ung-ying's headquarters at Hayang. Hopelessly outmanoeuvered, Huang had to take refuge with his montagnard allies, and for a while it looked, with such a massive combination against them, as if he and his Yellow Flags had reached the end of the road. But the Vietnamese climate, as it had done so often in the past, again proved too much for a Chinese regular army, and General Feng, his soldiers ravaged by malaria and other diseases of the tropics, withdrew from the scene. Once more, the Yellow Flags emerged from the wilderness and established a hold on the Red River between Laokay and Sontay.

The chronology of these transactions is confused in the extreme, but they may with some confidence be assigned to the years 1869-1870. When Dupuis first sailed on the river in 1871, Liu was firmly in control of Laokay while Yellow Flags were active further downstream. That much at least is clear, but in some details Dupuis contradicts himself. Thus in one place he would have us believe that he spoke to Liu Yung-fu at Laokay, while elsewhere he is positive that Liu absented himself on purpose to avoid meeting a European. In Liu's own memoirs there is no mention of any interview of the kind. It should be remarked too that Dupuis was correctly informed of the friendship between the Yellow Flags and the montagnards, but had not apparently been told of the fact that Liu, in contradistinction to his rival, was strictly speaking no longer a bandit but an acknowledged servant of the Vietnamese and Chinese governments. [11]

❦ CHAPTER SEVEN

Jean Dupuis

WE took our leave of Dupuis as he was setting off for
Europe, towards the end of 1871, bearing with him the
news that the Red River was navigable up to the Chinese
frontier. He lost no time on the way, and reached Paris in January
1872. It was, to say the least, not a very opportune moment to try
to get government backing for a scheme such as his. The capital
itself had scarcely recovered from the bloody suppression of the
Commune, and German troops were still on French soil. Yet
Dupuis was not a man to be deterred by obstacles. He had
introductions to the proper quarters and one cannot help marvell-
ing at the effective use he made of them. By the spring, with the
blessing of the Minister of War, he had already negotiated the
purchase of arms, the carriage of which to Yunnan was the immediate purpose of his planned expedition. The next item on his
agenda was the obtaining of permission from the Vietnamese
authorities for the transit up the Red River. To be sure, he would be
travelling with Chinese papers, but there was no telling what the
attitude of the officials on the spot would be, and it would clearly
be a wise precaution, if possible, to provide himself with a safe-
conduct from the Vietnamese Court at Hue. Here was where the
French government might be induced to lend its aid. In April
1872, Dupuis interviewed the Minister for the Navy, Vice-
Admiral Pothiau, who was the member of the government
directly concerned, and asked to be conveyed by a French vessel
from Saigon to Hue. His visit to the Vietnamese capital would be
in order to elicit from the Court a formal recognition of his status

as a Chinese, not a French, envoy, but the application would, he considered, carry more weight if backed by Paris. As was to be expected the Minister emphasized the difficulties of giving any overt assistance to Dupuis's plans, admirable though these were. However, he went on, provided the authorities in Saigon had no objection he thought that a ship might be spared for the mission, on the understanding, of course, that Dupuis would defray the cost of fuel and other expenses. A letter to this effect would be sent to Saigon. As his visitor was about to say goodbye, the Minister added a few words of informal advice. 'If you meet with resistance, and if you think you are strong enough, force your way through. Remember, though, if you or your people get killed, we shan't come in to avenge you!'

In May 1872, barely five months after quitting the Far East, Dupuis was in Saigon all braced for his great adventure. It was merely a flying visit: within days he was off again to Shanghai, at which port and in Hong Kong, the expedition was to be organized. At Shanghai he bought—in what circumstances we are not told— two gunboats of British origin, while to complete his little armada he acquired at Hong Kong a steam-launch and a Chinese junk of four hundred tons burden, which it was intended to tow. The personnel of the expedition consisted of twenty-five Europeans, and a hundred and fifty Asiatics of assorted nationalities, chiefly Chinese, but with Japanese, Filipinos, Malays and Indians. A Frenchman named Millot, with long experience of China, was Dupuis's second-in-command. The war material destined for Yunnan, when it arrived at Hong Kong from France, comprised thirty pieces of field artillery, seven thousand rifles, and fifteen barrels of ammunition, all of which were stowed away on the ships.

Hong Kong was to be the starting-point of the venture, but first Dupuis paid another visit to Saigon. It was now September 1872 and the letter from Paris sanctioning the use of a French naval vessel to take Dupuis to Hue had been duly delivered and taken cognizance of. The Govenor of the colony, Admiral Dupré, was away on leave, and his *locum tenens* had no objection to the idea, especially since a ship called the *Bourayne* was on the point of effecting a voyage to survey the Vietnamese coast. However, the officer commanding this vessel, a Captain Senez, who had been eight years in the country and was esteemed an authority on native affairs, advanced the opinion that it would be a fatal error to depend on Saigon's patronage in approaching Hue. Let Dupuis confront the mandarins with a *fait accompli*; in other words, let him go straight to Tongking and demand right of way not as a Frenchman but as a servant of the Chinese government. Since the channels of the Red River delta were numerous and confusing, the *Bourayne* would be pleased to sail ahead to those waters and indicate the correct route. Convinced by this reasoning, Dupuis returned to Hong Kong at the end of September, and put the finishing touches to his preparations.

The expedition set sail on October 26, 1872, and owing to bad weather did not arrive off the Tongking coast till November 8th. A few days were spent in unsucessful attempts to find the right channel, until the *Bourayne* was discovered at anchor off the proper inlet. Captain Senez was ashore and, with some modification of his original advice, paving the way for Dupuis by telling the Vietnamese what a keen interest France took in the opening of a route to Yunnan. He was back on board on November 18th, and the next day he introduced Dupuis to the royal commissioner in charge of the coastal region. This mandarin, whose name was Le Tuan, looked dubiously at the Chinese documents which Dupuis produced for his inspection. In the first place, he pointed out, they had been issued not by Peking, or even by the provincial governor of Yunnan, but by General Ma, who had not the status to make such a request. The matter would have to be referred to Hue, and as far as Le Tuan could judge it would be helpful if there was some official confirmation by the French of their interest in the matter. Accordingly Captain Senez handed Le a letter in which he declared himself authorized by Saigon to state that the French government would be gratified if Hue agreed to Dupuis's application. It would be reasonable to allow eighteen days for a reply to arrive, and meanwhile Dupuis would be permitted to buy provisions at a fair price and to navigate in the delta. Having thus done what he considered to be called for, Senez sailed away on November 20, 1872.

With his departure, there was at once a change of atmosphere. Notwithstanding the promise, supplies were practically unobtainable. It was suggested by Le that it might well take three months for an answer to come: why didn't Dupuis return and wait comfortably in Hong Kong? The Frenchman refused to budge and when the stipulated delay had elapsed without his hearing a word, he commenced the journey up river to Hanoi. The voyage was impeded in every manner possible short of the use of force, but on December 22, 1872 the destination was reached: it was the first time that a steamship had penetrated to the ancient capital of Vietnam.

There was one group of people in Hanoi who welcomed Dupuis with enthusiasm. The large community of Cantonese merchants had everything to gain from the opening of the Red River to international trade; and besides, to them, Dupuis (accompanied as he was by his secretary Mr. Li, an indisputable mandarin from the homeland, and sailing under the personal flag of General Ma— for scrupulous care was taken not to show French colours) could claim fairly enough to be an envoy from China. He and his senior colleagues were entertained at the establishment, half club and half hostel, which was the centre of the merchants' social life and where many of them lived, and he was made to feel that he was among friends. In fact to this day the Cantonese stand in a curious relationship with westerners, and it is no exaggeration to say that their peculiar provincial characteristics have had a perceptible influence on foreign attitudes towards China. Before the Opium War, maritime trade between China and the outside world was restricted to the single port of Canton, and the inhabitants of that city had therefore a unique opportunity of seeing Europeans in the mass. On neither side was the encounter edifying. Even if they had the inclination to do so, the visitors were forbidden to learn Chinese, and by the end of the eighteenth century pidgin English was a flourishing lingua franca. This undignified speech in the mouths of pigtailed men was already clownish enough, but another circumstance made things worse. The Cantonese dialect has retained final consonants lost centuries ago by standard Chinese and the resultant sounds, especially when represented in the roman alphabet, are to Anglo-Saxon feelings often ridiculous and some-times obscene. Businesses conducted under styles such as Hop Fat or Fook On must in the course of years have reinforced the tendency of English-speaking foreigners not to take China seriously.

The citizens of Canton were remarkable, when at home, for their anti-foreign sentiments. Indeed it was their obstinacy, despite the Treaty of Nanking, in keeping westerners in a ghetto outside the city walls that was one of the causes of the clash with Britain in 1856. This has made them the darlings of Communist historians, who omit to mention that the same stiff-necked patriots, once their city was in British hands, included any number of people willing to hire themselves out as coolies not merely to load the contents of the provincial treasury as booty on British ships, but to accompany the invaders in the subsequent attack on North China, where much of the rape and pillage was the handiwork of the Cantonese labour corps.

In contrast to the Cantonese, the Vietnamese manderins were as unencouraging as they had been at the coast. The citadel of Hanoi, another of Gia Long's Vaubanesque fortresses, was put in a state of alert, with its gates shut and its garrison under arms. Conversations proved futile: no right of transit would be granted till permission had come from Hue. In any case, they said, the water in the river was at its shallowest in winter, and sandbanks above Sontay would prevent the steamers from making the journey. Even a lunch party on board did not win them over. They enjoyed the champagne but shared the Chinese distaste for red wine. Finally Dupuis demanded to be taken to see a Frenchman who he knew was living not far off, Mgr Puginier, the Vicar-Apostolie of Western Tongking. The request was refused, but the Vietnamese said they would do even better: they would bring the Bishop to Hanoi.

Paul Puginier, although in 1872 only thirty-seven, had already been in Tongking for ten years, not directly persecuted by the Vietnamese authorities but confronted daily with the depressing spectacle of a country ravaged by banditry, where the little Christian settlements were liable to be sacked from one day to the next and women and girls carried off into prostitution. To him the imposition of law and order was a moral duty, and he saw no prospect of such an achievement except by European intervention. As a Frenchman and a Catholic he was doubly anxious that the noble task should be assumed by his own country. Meanwhile he placed his converts under the protection of the Blessed Virgin, and found leisure in the midst of his harassment to keep a Latin school with forty pupils. For in judging the quality of these priests it is worth remembering that all over the Far East they propagated the Latin tongue, and not their own national languages, as the key to European civilization. Two hundred years earlier, they had taught Latin to K'ang Hsi, greatest of the Manchu Emperors. In the 1860s, when the French seized Saigon, they were delighted to receive a letter in seminary Latin from a Vietnamese job-hunter. To Puginier, a Roman through and through, this teaching was a labour of love. As a boy, he had been reprimanded for reading Virgil during Mass. It may well be thought that a Vietnamese or Chinese who learns the Latin language and the Catholic faith has acquired the two things which even today lie closest to the heart of European culture. This exceedingly civilized man was the type of Catholic whom Protestants find hardest to understand. He was an acknowledged expert on the theory and practice of indulgences, carrying a text-book of the science about with him on his journeys so that he could benefit to the full from this spiritual treasury of the church, and his tariff of mass-offerings was a masterpiece of theological arithmetic. An offering of a thousand francs gave one the right to participate in the benefits of four masses a month for fifteen years. For one hundred francs there was one mass a month. Five francs entitled you to one mass a year, while offerings under five francs did not merit a mass at all, but merely a share in the prayers after mass. Nevertheless, unecumenical or not, Puginier, like Pigneau before him, was undoubtedly the kind of man anyone would be glad to have at his side in an emergency.[12]

The summons to Hanoi was the first intimation to the Bishop of the great events in which he was destined to play a part. For the moment, though, he was unable to exert any influence on one side or the other. The Vietnamese seem to have thought that he might on their behalf persuade Dupuis to leave, but no such idea came into Puginier's mind. On the contrary he scorned to pretend that the venture was anything but French, and told the mandarins that in the march of civilization the river, if they refused to open it themselves, would certainly be opened by some foreign power, if not by France then by another country. What he said to Dupuis we do not know. He was cautious enough to maintain a semblance of neutrality, but in their private conversations he must have given the enterprise his blessing.

Before the end of December a reply had come from Hue, but Dupuis was not informed of its contents beyond a reminder that the request of General Ma had not been ratified by the Viceroy at Canton, the usual channel of communication between the two countries. Resolved to fritter away no more time, he set about his preparations for the trip. A preliminary outing as far as Sontay showed him that the water was indeed too shallow just then to float his steamers, so he hired three river junks from a helpful Chinese and after loading them with a part of his cargo and turning a deaf ear to the warnings of the mandarins on the dangers of bandits set out on January 18, 1873. He took with him ten Europeans and thirty Asiatics, leaving the rest at Hanoi under the command of Millot.

The journey was slow and painful, for the mandarins, deterred from stopping Dupuis by force, endeavoured to frustrate the voyage at least in the territory they controlled by clearing the villages along the river of inhabitants so that there was no means of finding coolies to haul the vessels upstream. At Hung-Hoa, some distance past Sontay, they found on the north bank an encampment of about one hundred Black Flags, posted there as allies of the Hue government. A barrage had been erected across the whole width of the river except for a space in the centre where the gate should have been and through this aperture they sailed unmolested. Beyond that point it was quite literally a no-man's-land—immense virgin forests with no sign of human habitation—until after eight days they reached Dupuis's acquaintances of two years before, the Yellow Flags, who were genuinely delighted to see them, and supplied food and coolies in abundance. Then on February 20, 1873, they reached Laokay and the main body of the Black Flags who, having learned no doubt of their friendly reception by the rival band, treated them with some reserve. They were informed that Liu Yung-fu was absent, but Dupuis was convinced that this was no more than a pretext to avoid a meeting. From now on, it is noticeable that Liu figures in Dupuis's pages more and more as an ogre: we are told that some montagnard tribesmen who came to pay their respects to the visitors, being for a moment out of earshot of the Black Flags, burst into tears in describing their sufferings at the hands of this evil man. Liu in his own recollections shows himself sensitive on this point, insisting over and over again on his frequent interventions to rescue montagnard women from the Yellow Flag slave-raiders, but as he admits the alliance between the tribesmen and his rivals his account is not especially persuasive.

The Chinese frontier having been crossed, Manghao, the limit of navigation, was reached on March 4th. On the morning of March 20th, Dupuis was in Kunming, to the enormous enthusiasm of General Ma and his other old friends, who were able to tell him the good news that the insurrection was to all intents and purposes crushed. Two months earlier, in January 1873, Sultan Tu, hopelessly beleaguered in his city of Tali, had agreed to surrender himself to the imperial forces on condition that his followers should be spared. Realizing that his life was forfeit, immediately before quitting his palace for the last time he had swallowed a mixture of opium and peacock's droppings with the result that when his palanquin, defiantly draped in the Son of Heaven's own colour of yellow, reached the enemy lines he was already on the point of death, and the executioner had to content himself with operating on a corpse. The head, immersed in a jar of honey, was rushed to Peking by the fastest couriers and the citizens of Tali believing themselves redeemed by the sacrifice of their leader, opened their gates to the conquerors. The latter, once properly installed, invited the Muslim chieftains to a grand dinner, but at the very moment the party was entering the banqueting-hall the guard-of-honour drew their swords and the guests' heads rolled on the ground. Then the sound of a cannon thudded six times across the city. At the signal, the victors everywhere, in the streets or in the houses where they had been quartered, fell upon any Muslim in sight: it was 1856 over again, except that now the victims could not resist.

After that, the campaign became a simple affair of mopping-up rebel garrisons throughout the countryside. General Ma was not implicated in the treacherous slaughter at Tali, and neither that

event nor the manner in which his pagan colleagues were conducting themselves elsewhere—they often, for instance, refused to
spare Muslim prisoners unless they would consent to eat pork—
was calculated to give him pleasure, but remorse and gloom were
dispersed by the prospect of wealth to come, now that Dupuis had
so brilliantly fulfilled his promise. A consignment of metals was
carried down to Manghao on muleback and loaded on the junks,
while the Frenchman and his Chinese partners concerted their
plans. First of all, it was clear that more formal demand for
transit would have to be addressed to the government of Vietnam:
a letter requesting that such a document should be forwarded
without delay to Dupuis at Hanoi was sent post-haste by the
Yunnan authorities to the Viceroy at Canton. Then it was time
for the return journey, a far less painful business than the voyage
upstream had been. Setting out from Kunming on March 29,
1873, Dupuis reached Hanoi on April 30th. His party was increased by one hundred and fifty Yunnanese soldiers seconded
into his service. En route, he delivered to the Yellow Flags a
friendly letter from General Ma, assuring them that an amnesty
would soon be granted in their favour. To this he added a word
of his own: by October at the latest, he said, he and General Ma
between them would see to it that the Black Flags were expelled
from Laokay. Long afterwards he remembered that on the final
stretch of the journey, as he passed through the country held by
the Vietnamese forces, he saw intimations that his confidence
might perhaps be excessive. Military encampments were proliferating, and every few miles along the bank had arisen little
forts of earth, surmounted by bamboo palisades, behind which
fluttered banners of various hues. In his own words, 'something
had changed'.

What had happened, as he discovered on his arrival in Hanoi,
was that the Vietnamese authorities had at last been stung into
action. The Chinese from whom he had obtained the river-junks,
and some others accused of supplying him with provisions, had
been arrested and were now under lock and key in the citadel.
Such an indirect method of reprisal, however, only reinforced
Dupuis in the belief that nothing would be dared against himself,
and he proceeded to show his defiance in every way he could.

First of all, he set up his own headquarters on shore. A Chinese officer, from one of the units of the Kwangsi army which had stayed behind in the country north of Hanoi when General Feng had withdrawn the mass of his troops a year or two earlier, had rented a town-house and now ceded the remainder of his lease to Dupuis. As befitted a Chinese residence, it was a large, solidly-built structure of brick, in a thoroughfare running at a right-angle from the water-front. To complete his installation, Dupuis also took the two houses opposite, and as the street at this point was of the unusual width of thirty feet (further down it narrowed into a typical alleyway), he felt reasonably secure, especially with a substantial Chinese guard around him, against any surprise. Indeed he was no sooner in the place than he started to exert an independent authority. With almost incredible effrontery, on May 4th, less than a week after his return, he seized the chief of police and sent him as a hostage on board one of the French steamers, releasing him the next day in return for the imprisoned Chinese. After this triumph he put up a proclamation, translated into Chinese characters by his secretary, to warn the population that he was properly authorized from China to travel in Tongking and that they must pay no heed to their own officials.

One commodity was excessively rare in Yunnan: salt—so much so, in fact, that a cargo would sell there for thirty times its value in Hanoi. The only snag was that the exportation of salt was vigorously prohibited by Vietnamese law, but this again was not a circumstance likely to frighten Dupuis away from so enormous a profit. By prior arrangement with the Cantonese merchants who owned them he went through the pretence of seizing a dozen river-junks loaded with salt and set about preparing a convoy which in the high water of summer could be towed upstream by a steam launch.

Confronted with energy and determination, the Vietnamese authorities seemed paralyzed. Once again Mgr Puginier was appealed to, but he answered curtly that he was competent to pronounce only on matters of faith and morals and that the activities of his fellow-countryman, being commercial in nature, were entirely outside the purview of religion. At a meeting with representatives of the Hue government, Dupuis adopted a lordly attitude, telling the mandarins in so many words that by virtue of his Chinese commission he had every bit as much right to be in Tongking as they themselves.

At the end of May, an impressive figure arrived from Hue, no less than the same Marshal Nguyen Tri Phuong who had put up so fierce a resistance in the fighting at Saigon eleven years before, and who, as father-in-law of the King, was undoubtedly the second man in the realm. His advanced age (he was now seventy-seven) had not diminished his courage or his hatred of the French. Immediately on his arrival, he posted a proclamation forbidding all and sundry under pain of death to give aid and comfort to the foreigners. As for these latter, if they did not leave at once he would 'cut them into little pieces'.

In Vietnam it was the custom, whenever a proclamation from so high a personage was made public, that the text should be ex- hibited under the shadow of an umbrella, surrounded by armed guards. Now, on learning the news, a detachment of Dupuis's mercenaries marched under arms to the spot in so threatening a manner that the Vietnamese soldiers took to their heels at the sight of them. The intruders thereupon seized the proclamation and the umbrella and paraded them in mock triumph through the streets to the sound of bugles and drums before throwing them into a bonfire. During the next few weeks clashes became more frequent, and on June 2, 1873, one of Dupuis's subordinates was sufficiently carried away by enthusiasm to have the tricolour ensign hoisted over the ships. This action, which Dupuis says was unintentional, signified to viewers that a portion of the city of Hanoi had been occupied by invaders flying French colours, and there and then couriers left to carry word to Hue and Saigon.[13]

The government of Cochinchina was now in the hands of Admiral Dupré, who was chafing at the inaction to which he seemed condemned by the pusillanimity of Paris. The recent war with Prussia had had few repercussions in the Far East. It was true that the Empress Eugenie, when her husband had been taken prison at Sedan, had actually proposed to surrender the new colony to the victors on condition that France should be allowed to retain Alsace and Lorraine, but at the very time the proposal was made the imperial government had fallen and the Empress herself was an exile in England: besides, the offer was not to Bismarck's taste. The Third Republic was proclaimed at Saigon in conditions of complete peace and order. Nevertheless, two things irked the Admiral especially. The Vietnamese government at Hue persisted in refusing to recognize the French occupation in 1867 of the provinces south and west of the Mekong. Then, his superiors at home turned a deaf ear to his pleas for an attack on Tongking: new colonial adventures it appeared, were not at this stage to be thought of. So unequivocal was the attitude of Paris on this point, that most of Dupré's hopes were now centred on solving his first problem, namely to elicit from Hue some formal recognition of the conquest of 1867. Thus, when in June 1873 he received the complaint of the Vietnamese of Dupuis's conduct at Hanoi, his immediate reaction was that he had at last an opportunity, by helping Hue in this matter, to get in return the acknowledgment he desired. Accordingly he addressed to Dupuis a letter, open and by Vietnamese courier so that its contents could be noted by the mandarins, in which he pointed out that the alleged mission of furnishing arms to Yunnan had now been accomplished, payment in the form of metals had been received, and that Dupuis ought therefore to defer to the wishes of the Vietnamese government and withdraw from Tongking. If he refused, then the Vietnamese would be justified in expelling him by any means they thought fit, and he would have only himself to blame.

This message, carried, as was usual with such mail, in a metal container, reached Dupuis in the middle of July, and he made it clear by his actions that he had not the faintest intention of obeying. What he was doing, he declared to those around him, was fully authorized by China, Vietnam's suzerain, and was no concern of the Admiral's. In a written answer, he was more polite but just as resolute: he added that he was sure by now the Admiral would have heard the true state of affairs from his partner, Monsieur Millot.

The second-in-command had in fact sailed from Hanoi to Hong Kong to dispose of the cargo of metals brought down river from Yunnan. Then from the British colony he had made his way to Saigon, where towards the end of July he alarmed the Admiral by revealing that Dupuis, in the absence of encouragment from

France, might be obliged to accept German or British investment in his enterprise. In any case, he said, some foreign country, Britain most likely, would soon intervene in Tongking, unless indeed the Chinese took over the place for themselves. The hint was enough to galvanize the Admiral into doing something positive. He hastily agreed to underwrite Dupuis to the amount of thirty thousand piastres, and as if to emphasize the threat from Anglo-Saxondom which cast so menacing a shadow over French visions of empire, even this transaction had to be effected through the agency of the British-owned Hong Kong and Shanghai Bank. Meanwhile, however, the situation at Hanoi continued to develop in the direction of open war. Bloody clashes were becoming more and more frequent, though the efforts so far made by the Vietnamese had done nothing to impair Dupuis's position: he was still solidly in control of a section of the city, routing all attackers and holding a number of mandarins as hostages. Something would have to be done: the Admiral sent for Francis Garnier.

CHAPTER EIGHT

Francis Garnier

THE Franco-Prussian war had broken out just when Garnier was basking in the glory of his Mekong exploration. Recalled to service, he played an active part in the fighting around Paris. To one of his temper the French capitulation was ineffably shameful, and he was incautious enough to express his disgust too vigorously for the liking of his superiors who had their revenge by barring his promotion. In these circumstances he applied for, and was granted, leave of absence, and with enormous relief, for France had become like a prison to him, he set off late in 1872 on what he intended to be a lengthy tour of investigation in western China and Tibet. He was accompanied by his recently-married wife and could rely on a certain amount of financial support from French business circles, though for the most part he depended on his own resources. In some ways the early months of 1873 must have formed the happiest part of his life. A biographer of his, M. Albert de Pouvourville, remarks on the transformation effected in him by his arrival in China: it reminds one, he says, of the stories in Greek mythology about Antaeus who drew all his strength simply from contact with the ground. Certainly his energy was indefatigable, and even Dupuis, it seemed, would have to look to his laurels. In the space of six months he wandered from Peking in the north to Kweichow in the south-west, noting down everything he saw. His immediate purpose was to establish a base for future journeys, and this he did at the Yangtze port of Chungking in Szechwan. It was on his return in August 1873 from Chungking to Shanghai, where he had left his bride, that he found the Admiral's summons awaiting him, Before the end of the month he was in Saigon, and being briefed for his new mission.

Now that it was obvious that Dupuis would not withdraw from Hanoi voluntarily, it seemed probable that one of two things would happen. It was conceivable that the Vietnamese might be strong enough to expel him by force, in which event the Admiral could inform Hue that the account he had received from Dupuis was totally at variance with that given by themselves, and that as the matter involved the interests of a French citizen he felt obliged to send an expedition to Hanoi to determine exactly where the truth lay; or else—and this was far more likely—the Vietnamese would recognize their own impotence and appeal to Saigon for help. In this case they could be told that, Dupuis having refused to obey an earlier order from the Admiral, the latter had no option but to dispatch an armed force to eject him. There would, of course, be no point in revealing that the Admiral was now committed to financial support of the buccaneers.

As luck would have it, a few days after Garnier's arrival, some other visitors came to Saigon. Hue, having given up hope of the Admiral's intervention against Dupuis, had decided to send an embassy to Paris, and the envoys were at hand to embark for Europe. It was an occasion not to be missed. Naturally, the mandarins were entertained with the consideration their status deserved, and over a convivial glass of champagne they made no secret of the fact that their government was unable to bring Dupuis to order. But, insisted the Admiral, it was a waste of time and money for them to proceed further. He himself was both able and willing to rid them of the nuisance. As they well knew, he had been endeavouring for a long time to improve relations with Hue, and here, surely, was a matter in which it was to the benefit of both sides to collaborate. They wanted Dupuis expelled: the Admiral would send someone to do it for them. In return, it would only be reasonable for Vietnam to enter into a fresh treaty recognizing the existing French establishment in the south.

It is known that the Admiral at first contemplated sending an expedition of a thousand men to Tongking, but during September his ideas changed. A message from Hue made it clear that the

Vietnamese government was unlikely to admit the necessity for such a large number: an officer with a token force would suffice, since it was unthinkable that Dupuis would make himself an outlaw by defying his own government in arms. More convincing still, Garnier also was unwilling to lead what would amount to an invasion of Tongking. The best way to advance French interests, he told the Admiral, was to appear in the north to support Vietnamese authority against all intrusion from abroad, whether this came from China or elsewhere. A few dozen good men would be ample for the business. But what precisely was the business? In the first place, we should look at the written instructions given to Garnier by the Admiral, and dated October 10, 1873. According to these, Garnier was to investigate on the spot the true circumstances of the dispute between Dupuis and the Vietnamese authorities, but whatever the inquiry showed, he was to insist on the prompt departure of Dupuis from Hanoi, provided that he could take it upon himself, if he judged it equitable, to see that Dupuis's claim for damages was satisfied. This was a far-reaching condition, for Dupuis was by now demanding from the Hanoi authorities large sums of money to reimburse him for the frustration of his commerce with Yunnan.

The withdrawal of the French adventurer and his followers from Hanoi would not, however, mean the abandonment of their enterprise. On the contrary, Garnier was to make it clear to the Vietnamese that the Red River must forthwith be opened to traffic not only by their own nationals but also by French and Chinese merchants. Customs dues would be levied at Hanoi and near the border with Yunnan, and a portion of the money so received must be paid to France to meet the cost of the expedition. There was to be no equivocation about this, and Garnier was to stay to see the demand carried out. As for the disorders which had convulsed Tongking for years, if the Vietnamese mandarins cooperated loyally with the French, Garnier would assist them to restore the rule of Hue over the territory. On the other hand, if the Vietnamese indulged in their old trickery, Garnier was to stand aside and let events take their course.

Such were the written instructions. There must in addition have been verbal counsel, but of this our only intimation is that Garnier

9 Li Hung-chang visiting Mr Gladstone

10   Sir Halliday Macartney at Nanking

on the eve of setting out wrote exultantly to his brother at home: 'I have carte blanche! Forward for France!' But how in the world could he have hoped to fulfil his mission with the derisory force he proposed to take with him? It is true that Garnier despised the fighting qualities of the Vietnamese, and Dupuis's exploit must have confirmed him in this attitude; but Dupuis had now gathered around him—counting the hundred and fifty soldiers from Yunnan, and scores of deserters from the Kwangsi provincial army who saw more chance of booty under the European buc- caneer than in their own service—a brigade not far short of five hundred men. The whole thing is a mystery which it is unlikely will ever be thoroughly cleared up.

The expedition was divided in two halves. The first, with Garnier, sailed from Saigon on October 11, 1873; including a gunboat's crew and marines, the total was eighty-three men. The second batch, of eighty-eight, left on October 23rd. Having touched at Danang en route to deliver a letter in which the Admiral requested that the government at Hue send commis- sioners to Hanoi to cooperate with the French, Garnier reached the vicinity of Haiphong on October 23rd. He first made it his business to call at a Spanish mission nearby, where he had been assured he would, in his capacity of defender of Christians, be given the warmest of welcomes. The priests received him with constrained civility, and told him, in a manner which failed to carry conviction, that their bishop was absent. It was the first hint of what in the next few weeks was to become common knowledge, namely that the Spanish missionaries denied that they stood in any need of French assistance, and forbade their converts to associate with the intruders.[14] Transferring his men and equipment to a river junk, Garnier then commenced the intricate navigation towards Hanoi, where he arrived on November 5th towed by Dupuis's steam- launch, for the buccaneer had gone to meet him on the way. It has never been revealed what passed between them, but the circum- stances of Garnier's arrival were of a sort to arouse the darkest sus- picions in the minds of the Vietnamese. A guard of honour, consist- ing of Dupuis's Yunnanese solders, presented arms to the French commander at the quayside as he stepped ashore. Old Marshal Nguyen kept aloof in the citadel, but a very subordinate mandarin informed Garnier that he and his men had been allotted quarters in an inn in the middle of the town. Without pausing for reflection, Garnier at once adopted the posture he was to maintain throughout the entire episode. With a mere fifteen men at his back he strode through the streets towards the citadel, entered the place before the gate could be shut against him, and burst upon the astonished Marshal, who retained enough presence of mind to receive the uninvited guest with what the latter described as 'perfect good manners'. The inn, declared Garnier, without beating about the bush, was quite impossible. If a suitable lodging was not forth-coming elsewhere, he and his followers would bed down in the citadel itself. Somebody—it is uncertain exactly who—recalled that there was in the vicinity a large enclosure used in former times to house the candidates for the Civil Service examinations, and finding it to his taste, Garnier consented to make it his head-quarters. Dupuis ostentatiously helped him to move in.

The overbearing manner assumed by Garnier from the start must have warned the Marshal what to expect. For the next few days the Frenchman confined his activities to the publication of proclamations. The first of these, dated November 7th, was the least offensive: it merely informed the citizens of Hanoi that the newcomers had arrived at the request of the Vietnamese authorities with the intention of defending the district against pirates, so that the people could live and trade in peace. The French soldiers and officials were the brothers of their Vietnamese colleagues. How-ever, when a couple of days later the Marshal in his turn put up a notice to reassure the public that the expedition had no other purpose than to expel Dupuis, Garnier exploded with rage and answered with the following declaration.

'TO THE PEOPLE OF TONGKING

The Governor of this city has just issued a proclamation which misrepresents my mission. I have asked him to withdraw it, but I hear that he has not yet done so.

I have been sent here by the Admiral, Governor of French Cochinchina, to examine the dispute which has arisen between Monsieur Dupuis and the Vietnamese authorities, and to try, if possible, to settle it, but not at all in order to expel Monsieur

Dupuis. Nor have I come, as the Governor's proclamation says, at the order or demand of the Court of Hue to drive out the said Dupuis and to leave with him.

My mission has another purpose, being chiefly to safeguard trade by opening the country and its river to all nations, under the protection of France.'

The mere presence on the scene of such an implacable enemy as Marshal Nguyen must have convinced Garnier from the moment he set foot in Hanoi that no amount of argument or persuasion would advance his cause. Even the Cantonese merchants, whose interests coincided with those of himself and Dupuis, confessed that so long as the old man remained in authority they durst not come out openly on the side of the French, for although he seemed either incapable of driving the invaders into the sea or unwilling to commit himself to outright war, his unit was still all-powerful everywhere outside the few square yards occupied by the Frenchmen and their mercenaries. In other words there was no alternative but to put the Marshal out of action allogether—a daunting prospect, it might well appear, as he was ensconced in the citadel with a garrison of seven thousand men. Many years later, looking back on the whole extraordinary episode, Dupuis attributed Garnier's resolution to the example he himself had set, and to his own availability in the role of ally. This is certainly true. Less than a week after Garnier's arrival, he had confided to Dupuis that he proposed to seize the citadel and take the Marshal prisoner. Pending this, he had Dupuis's Chinese secretary write out a proclamation, which he published on November 16th, to inform the citizens of Hanoi that: 'the Great Mandarin Garnier has decided that, as of this date, the Red River is opened from the sea to Yunnan, to the commerce of France, Spain, and China'—i.e. of the countries having treaty relationship with Vietnam. Haiphong and Thaibinh, on separate inlets of the delta, were named as ports, and customs-tariffs established.

This resounding statement, wherever placarded, was soon torn down by order of the Marshal who, as Garnier correctly suspected, had at long last made up his mind that the situation was intolerable and was merely awaiting the approval of Hue before launching a general attack. The Frenchman decided to strike first, particularly since the detachment of eighty-eight soldiers which had left Saigon a fortnight after his departure had now arrived with two gunboats in Hanoi, doubling his personal army. He issued an ultimatum requiring the disarmament of the fortress and the opening of Tongking to trade. Then, as no reply was forthcoming—indeed he never expected one—he entrusted his fortunes to destiny.

The citadel, which as we have seen had been constructed on a French pattern by Gia Long seventy years earlier was a formidable piece of military engineering. In shape it was a square, each side being more than half-a-mile in extent. The walls were of earth, reinforced by brickwork, and there were five gates surmounted by towers, two being in the south wall, and one in each of the other walls. The whole was enclosed by a wide ditch filled with water across which five bridges, one from each gateway, formed the sole means of communication. The approach to these bridges on the outer side of the ditch was in every case screened by defensive earthworks, yet the bridges themselves were not drawbridges but permanently in position, so that once the outer screen was taken, the ditch at that point offered no impediment. Furthermore, the garrison, though numerous, was wretchedly armed, for the most part with lances and swords. Few of those lucky enough to be issued with flintlocks had any training in the management of their weapons. On the battlements there were occasional superannuated pieces of cannon, so precious because of their rarity that they had been placed not so much where their fire could be effective as where they could best be covered from the tropical rains.

Miraculously the secret was well kept, and at first light on the morning of November 20, 1873, the French were able to take the outer defences of the two gates of the southern wall entirely by surprise, and had crossed the bridges before the defenders were able to rake them with shot from the battlements. Simultaneously the guns of the naval vessels in the river shelled the citadel with such effect that the garrison, totally unaccustomed to this kind of projectile, panicked and began to stream out into the open country from the west gate. Meanwhile the gates on the south were breached by gunfire and within a matter of an hour the tricolour was flying from the highest point in the fortress. More than two thousand Vietnamese prisoners were captured. On the attacking side only one man was killed and then the victim was not French but Chinese—one of the Yunnanese soldiers seconded into Dupuis's service and now lent by the buccaneer to Garnier so discreetly that another French officer, unaware of the arrangement, took them for Vietnamese and opened fire with this fatal result.

On the Vietnamese side the most important casualty was Marshal Nguyen, who was badly wounded by a shell-splinter and fell into French hands in a dying condition. It was a situation after Garnier's own heart, for it enabled him to indulge in the sort of chivalrous conduct towards a defeated foe which he felt was the true hallmark of a gentleman. He ordered the Marshal to be given every care, and presented himself at the bedside with many courteous expressions of the honour it had been for him to cross swords with so noble an antagonist, but the old man did not utter a word. Then Bishop Puginier came on the scene, hoping perhaps for some spectacular deathbed conversion. His offer of spiritual consolation at least succeeded in provoking the Marshal into breaking his silence. 'What!' he exclaimed, 'can't you even let me die in peace? You ought to be satisfied, for it is thanks to the advice of your missionaries that the French have robbed us of Cochinchina, and are going to rob us of Tongking! What I want more than anything else is to die as soon as possible!' And indeed, choosing a moment when the attention of his guards was diverted, he tore off his bandages and bled to death.

In a proclamation issued the day after the capture of the citadel, Garnier was at pains to deny any intention of annexing Tongking. All the French desired, he said, was to open the country to trade. The mandarins he had just expelled were even more hostile to their own people than they were to the foreigner. From now on a new type of magistrate would be appointed, men who would co-operate with France and administer their charge for the benefit of the population. The King himself would be urged to treat his subjects as if they were his own children.

Now began one of the most remarkable episodes of French colonial history. Dupuis pointed out that the main Vietnamese army in Tongking was based on the town of Sontay, westwards from Hanoi up the river, and that the real threat came from that direction. Garnier ignored the warning and immediately after the victory set about the task of reducing the whole of the delta between Hanoi and the sea. In about three weeks a region containing two million inhabitants and a number of fortified towns was subdued by a force which never exceeded one hundred and eighty men, commanded by officers none of whom, apart from Garnier himself, was older than twenty-five. Some of their exploits would sound hardly credible if they were not admitted to be historical fact. Thus for instance the citadel of Ninh-Binh, defended by seventeen hundred soldiers, surrendered to a canoe-load of seven Frenchmen. It was as if the Vietnamese were hypnotized by the spell of these terrible invaders. By the middle of December, Garnier was back in Hanoi and immersed in the thousand and one problems which the administration of such an area presented. Urged on by the French missionaries, Christian communities were rallying to the new regime, and a native militia was being organized. Wherever the former mandarins had fled, no difficulty was experienced in finding replacements, though Garnier was careful not to choose too many Catholics, and to observe an outward respect for the sovereignty of the Vietnamese King. One volunteer magistrate, rash enough to announce that he was acting in the name of France, was divested of his authority in very short order.

The first reaction of the government at Hue to the news of the loss of Hanoi was naturally enough one of anger and outrage. A cry for vengeance arose, and the King, reminded no doubt by some of his mandarins, all of a sudden recalled the exploits of Liu Yung-fu. There and then a messenger set out for Sontay, to the headquarters of Prince Hoang, another of the King's relatives who held the post of military commander-in-chief in Tongking and who, now that Marshal Nguyen was no longer available, was undoubtedly the most important official in the province. The Prince was an old patron of Liu Yung-fu, having been responsible for the latter's original Vietnamese commission, and heartily approved of the idea of employing him against the French. As luck would have it, Liu was conveniently posted down river at Hung-Hoa, and answered the summons to Sontay without difficulty, taking with him a force of several hundred Black Flags to whom, realizing the magnitude of the task to which he was called, he had before departure administered a special oath of loyalty. On his arrival, the Prince informed him frankly that in consequence of the demoralization of the Vietnamese troops he looked to the Chinese to lead the march against Hanoi and to bear the brunt of the fighting. As an incentive to enthusiasm, however, he was empowered by the King to offer substantial rewards in gold for every Frenchman killed, graduated in amount according to the rank of the victims.

During Garnier's absence in the Delta, word started to come in to Hanoi of these ominous preparations. Dupuis, who was naturally the first to hear what was happening, attempted to get in touch with Liu Yung-fu, sending him a letter written by his Chinese secretary to ask Liu to come and talk things over in Hanoi. On December 9th, Dupuis was visited by a Chinese claiming to have come from Liu, and gave assurances that the Black Flags had nothing to fear from the French so long as they kept aloof from the quarrel. Time, however, was fast running out. It was learned on December 18th that Liu and his men were encamped only ten or twelve miles away. Then, on the afternoon of December 20th, it began to look as if there might be a respite after all, for ambassadors arrived in Hanoi from Hue, and were welcomed with all the customary courtesies, including a salute from the cannon of the French ships.

The next day, December 21, 1873, was a Sunday, and the French officers assembled to hear mass and to partake afterwards of white wine and local sweetmeats in the company of Bishop Puginier. Even there, business pursued them, in particular the question of the allocation of the opium monopoly, due to be farmed out the following day. Dupuis was so much involved in the matter that he had to take his leave before the others, in order to return to his quarters in the town to confer with his Chinese secretary about the translation of relevant documents. An hour or so later, it was reported by the lookout that the Black Flags were approaching the west gate of the citadel. Garnier, who was just settling down for a talk with the newly arrived Vietnamese envoys, immediately ran to the battlements to direct operations. He saw at a few hundred yards' distance a huge black banner—it had, in fact, been fabricated specially for this enterprise—surmounting a regiment of what seemed five or six hundred Chinese, easily distinguishable by their shaven fronts and pigtails, while nearly half a mile to the rear he could make out a more numerous army of Vietnamese, with war-elephants and the parasols which announced the presence of mandarins.

Garnier ordered a field-piece to be set up over the gate and within ten minutes the cannon had gone into action. Half an hour of shell-fire had its effect: the Black Flags commenced slowly to fall back. But this was not enough. 'Gentlemen', said Garnier to his officers, 'this is the only enemy in Tongking we have to fear. We must go out and face him. We can't let him stay in our neighbourhood.' However as if to emphasize that, in spite of his warning, he did not regard the Black Flags as posing essentially a more serious threat than the Vietnamese, he took out with him through the southeastern gate a mere eighteen Frenchmen with a field-gun, together with a platoon of local recruits. No sooner had they skirted the southwestern corner of the fortress, than the gun got stuck in the mud and had to be left with a crew of three. The remainder, subdivided into small groups, negotiated a stretch of paddy-fields fringing the western wall until Garnier observed that a party of Black Flags were concealed behind an embankment. Giving the order to fix bayonets he rushed forward up the slope so impetuously that the three men immediately following him were left well behind. With his gaze fixed on the summit, he failed to notice a water-course in his way, stumbled and fell. Instantly a bunch of Chinese sprang upon him and ran him through with their spears as he lay on the ground. Of his companions, one was shot down and the other two were forced to take to their heels. Almost at the same moment, another party commanded by a young lieutenant named Balny, which had also ventured out from the citadel and was a short distance to the west, made contact with the enemy in a manner equally rash, and with a similar result, Balny and two of his men being killed.

The above account of the events of December 21, 1873 is based on French testimony. If we believe the Chinese sources, Garnier and Balny met their deaths not while they were seeking out the enemy, but on the contrary, when they and their men, routed by the Black Flags, were beating a disorderly retreat to the safety of the fortress. Yet if this was so, it is hard to explain how the bodies could have been recovered as promptly as they were: as it was, within a couple of hours three of the five corpses had been carried back inside the citadel. The heads, however, were all missing, and this undoubtedly was the reason for the withdrawal of the Black Flags: their old mercenary instinct had reasserted itself and they had hurried back with their trophies to claim the reward that Prince Hoang had offered them. Garnier was not only recognised as the French commander; rumour had elevated his status, and till his own dying day Liu was convinced that his soldiers had killed the son-in-law of the Emperor of France—news of the Third Republic had apparently not permeated to the Black Flags. A silver watch set with jewels was taken from the body and a picture of young Madame Garnier inside it was shown ever afterwards by Liu to his friends as a likeness of the unhappy princess his men had made a widow.

If there is a dispute about the exact manner of Garnier's death, all the witnesses concur on one point. The disaster plunged the French forces, both officers and men, into a state of complete demoralization. The moment he heard what had happened, the wretched young Lieutenant Bain, who had temporarily to step into Garnier's shoes, at once raised a cry that the entire expeditionary corps must abandon the citadel, take refuge aboard the ships in the river and sail away as quickly as possible back to Saigon. In the midst of the general panic, Puginier and Dupuis were towers of strength. The Bishop especially, however much one may deplore his conduct at other times, presented in the face of this emergency a magnificent example of Catholic commonsense. 'My dear friend,' he exclaimed to the distracted Bain, 'we can talk about this when you have had lunch.' He would not listen to another word until the Lieutenant had eaten—observing that it was half-past two and the poor fellow must be starving. This matter having been attended to, the Bishop proceeded to give his own opinion. 'M. Garnier is dead,' he remarked. 'It is a great loss, but after all only five men are missing, so that to all intents and purposes you are every bit as strong as you were this morning. If you leave Hanoi, the expedition will be ruined, and perhaps you won't even get as far as Haiphong. Then again, to run away like that would be a disgrace to the French flag!' 'But the troops are completely demoralized!' interjected Bain. 'Call on M. Dupuis! said the Bishop. 'He will help you out, and with his support you will be as much in control of the situation as before this tragedy happened.'

Just then Dupuis made his appearance and for Bain's benefit put on his most reassuring expression. Of course he and his followers were at the Lieutenant's disposal. That very night he would bring a group of his Chinese—all of them trustworthy fellows from the Yunnan army—to relieve the garrison of the fort. Things were by no means so bad as they might have been. How providential it was, for instance, that the ambassadors from Hue had turned up so opportunely in Hanoi! They would make ideal hostages. Bain saw the force of the suggestion and gave orders that the envoys should be transferred for safe custody on board one of Dupuis's ships.

Dupuis, who had his ear closest to the ground, was aware that the Black Flags were preparing an assault: the most picturesque stories were current among the Chinese in Hanoi of the construction in Liu's camp of an improbably large number of bamboo ladders to be used in scaling the walls of the citadel. There were other reports, too, of transactions nearer at hand, in Hanoi itself. That Liu had agents posted inside the city had for a long time been common knowledge; a man claiming to be one of them had, as we have seen, already made contact with Dupuis. Of course, he might have been no more than a pretender out to get some personal advantage from such a pose, but now there were alarming tales that an undoubted officer of the Black Flags was intimidating the Cantonese merchants so effectively that many of them had decided to abandon the French cause as hopeless, and put themselves instead under the protection of Liu Yung-fu who could not, they thought, be held at bay much longer, It was actually believed that Black Flags were infiltrating under cover of darkness up the creeks which led to the trading quarter, and were ready to set fire to houses and shops whenever the signal should be given. Dupuis decided there was no time to be lost. By dint of cajoling and bullying, he elicited the address where this dangerous plotter was to be found, and with a sufficient party of Yunnanese soldiers at his back, raided the premises and caught the miscreant red-handed in the midst of a chaotic lumber—packets of gunpowder suitable for starting fires, as well as a miniature arsenal of spears and pikes. He was named Lin, and his physique alone showed well enough why the Kwangsi brigands had overawed the tiny Vietnamese, for he was built like a Hercules, with a huge bull-neck and an enormous head. Further search of the house revealed how successful he must have been in his mission: the store-rooms were packed with silk, opium and money deposited with him by frightened Cantonese in the hope that their treasure would escape the arson and pillage they imagined to be inevitable. Even without the thought of their dead to infuriate them, the French would have had no compunction in ridding themselves of such a foeman. As it was, they had just put Garnier and his companions into the ground and the anger was fresh in their minds. Dupuis tells us how he took farewell of the hero, whose corpse had been laid out in the very room previously occupied by Marshal Nguyen.

'There is nothing so horrible [he writes], as these bodies without a head. There they lie, stretched out on straw. M. Garnier's clothes are in ribbons: his body is covered with wounds made by swords and spears. His chest has been cut open and his heart removed. Both hands are clenched. For the last time, I press his poor frozen right hand and swear that he will be avenged.'

In the circumstances Lin could expect short shrift. He was shot by a firing squad on December 24th, in front of the eastern gate of the citadel. On his person they found a letter addressed to Liu Yung-fu, undertaking to set fire to the town within two or three days, and to profit from the confusion to admit the Black Flags.

Meanwhile the latter were reaping the reward of their victory. Prince Hoang kept his word, the blood-money for the slaughtered Frenchmen was sent in full to Liu's camp and the fame of the Chinese warriors was carried everywhere throughout the country-side in the wake of the ceremonial parade of severed heads intended to convince the population at large of the fate of the King's alien enemies. Then, at the height of the celebrations a jarring note was sounded. A numerous body of Vietnamese soldiers visited Liu, bearing an order from Prince Hoang authorizing them to take possession of the scaling-ladders which the Black Flags had constructed for the coming assault on the citadel. Inquiries revealed that the original plan had been countermanded. So long as the King's ambassadors were hostages in French hands, said the Prince, it was too dangerous to provoke reprisals against the unfortunate gentlemen by attacking Hanoi. The prospect of booty going to waste aroused Liu to protest, but the Vietnamese had been generous enough with their money and now, in addition to the other rewards, letters-patent had just arrived from Hue to name him military commander of the three surrounding provinces. Perhaps too, he was not in his heart so confident of success as he was later to pretend. At any rate, he finally acquiesced with the best grace he could in the Prince's decision.

Meanwhile, thanks chiefly to the coolness of Dupuis and Bishop Puginier the French began to pluck up courage and to believe that the day was still far from lost. The timorous Bain was now relieved at Hanoi by the man Garnier had himself chosen as his second-in-command, an officer named Esmez, who was endowed with far greater firmness of character. It was a quality which was shared by his junior colleagues throughout the Delta, where the mandarins, who had behaved with such poltroonery a week or two earlier, became men once more at the news of Garnier's death and started to raise the people against the invaders. It was now that the French had cause to bless the work of their missionary compatriots. Christian villages furnished streams of volunteer militia who were given heart by the ruthless punishments inflicted on the enemy. Villages suspected of harbouring loyalists were razed to the ground, and mandarins faithful to Hue, whenever taken with arms in their hands, were mercilessly put to death. By the end of December 1873, it looked as if the situation had been retrieved.

Word of Garnier's seizure of the citadel at Hanoi reached Saigon at the end of November, and was received by Admiral Dupré with mixed feelings. To one such as himself, an advocate of colonial expansion, it was a marvellous achievement. On the other hand there were the formal orders from Paris, expressed frequently and in the plainest possible terms, that on no account must the French government be committed to intervention in Tongking. Garnier's enthusiasm seemed to be carrying him forward too quickly. Obviously it was high time to exercise a restraining influence, and as luck would have it, an ideal instrument was at hand for effecting such a purpose.

Ten years earlier, in the days when Garnier was administering Cholon, the 'Chinatown' of Saigon, there was among the other young naval officers put in charge of local government a Lieutenant Philastre. Born in 1837, and so two years Garnier's senior, Philastre stood out from the rest by his devotion to Vietnamese studies, a field in which his attainments have never been equalled by any other European. Not content with learning to speak the language almost perfectly, in addition he mastered classical Chinese which was the medium of all written communication between educated Vietnamese. His version of the laws of Gia Long remains to this day unique as a complete western translation not only of a Vietnamese, but of a Chinese, dynastic code, for Gia Long had adopted without change the legal system of contemporary China. Until recently most Europeans in the Far East held it as an axiom that the study of Chinese characters invariably addled the western brain, so that even if he had given no further grounds for mistrust, Philastre would already have been labelled a crackpot. Worse still, he openly expressed his admiration of Vietnamese institutions and his sympathy with the country in her present misfortunes. Some of his sayings have been preserved for us by his scandalized hearers, for example: 'The Vietnamese have a right to be masters of their own land,' and, 'After all, Vietnamese civilization is as good as ours.' Father Louvet, the historian of Vietnamese missions, is as indulgent as he can towards this moral degeneracy, conceding that Philastre is entitled to his own opinions. 'However,' he goes on, 'if a man is unlucky enough to entertain such ideas, it is wrong for him to accept the grave task of representing the honour and interests of France.'[15]

There used to be a time when Admiral Dupré took small pains to hide his contempt for this untypical officer, and it was therefore with some surprise that Philastre all of a sudden found himself the subject of the most flattering protestations of friendship at Government House. Only he, it appeared, could stave off the ruin into which Garnier's impetuosity was leading all of them. He alone among the French was trusted by the Vietnamese. He must go to Hue and convince his friends that what had happened at Hanoi was the result of a terrible misunderstanding. So that his own mind should be at rest, here were telegrams from Paris forbidding categorically any military intervention in Tongking. Having seen this proof, he could with a clear conscience assure Hue that Garnier must have panicked at the hostile attitude of Marshal Nguyen, and that neither Paris nor Saigon had any designs in Vietnam except to hope that the existing situation in the south would be properly ratified by treaty.

All this, of course, reassured Philastre, who, before leaving on his mission, could not refrain from writing to his old colleague Garnier in terms more of sorrow than of anger.

'Have you thought,' (he asked), 'of the disgrace that will come upon you and upon us when it is learned that, having been sent to expel a vulgar adventurer and to arrive at an understanding with the Vietnamese authorities, you instead allied yourself with the adventurer in shooting down without warning people who neither attacked you nor defended themselves ?'

Hearing at Hue of the French conquest of the Delta, Philastre decided on his own initiative to convey the Admiral's instructions to Garnier, who he thought must really be taking leave of his senses, but on arriving off the Red River he heard the news of the latter's death three days earlier. On January 3, 1867 he reached Hanoi where he at once took over from Esmez as the most senior officer in Tongking. Already, on his way from the coast, he had shown what he was made of. Ignoring the rage of his colleagues, he ordered the evacuation of the citadel of Hai-Dzuong, which lay on his route, and left no doubt that all the other towns of the Delta—the prize of war only a matter of days before—would have to be similarly abandoned. Then an astonishing spectacle was witnessed. The Vietnamese magistrates of the district, so lately driven from their posts, came out of hiding. They had been sheltered by the Spanish missionaries, who had forbidden their own converts to rally to the French cause and who now, acclaimed as benefactors by the restored mandarins, and even to their bewilderment congratulated by Philastre on their correct behaviour, were reaping the reward their soundness of judgment deserved.[16] Far different was the case of Bishop Puginier, to whom Philastre's entry on the scene represented the betrayal of all those Christians whom he and his priests had induced to throw in their lot with the invaders. By the middle of January, as the withdrawal of occupying troops from the Delta cities gathered momentum, the night skies were aglow with the flames of Christian settlements sacked and burned in reprisal. When Puginier protested, he was made to listen to words which in his wildest imagination he had never expected to hear from the mouth of a French officer. The unfortunate converts, said Philastre, were learning that treason against their own lawful government had to be paid for: the real criminals were those who had encouraged them in rebellion. It will be readily understood that Dupuis was not shown any greater consideration: his demands were so bare-faced that it would have been a miracle if Philastre had not lost his temper, and in fact their conversation soon turned into a shouting-match. The Vietnamese authorities, insisted the buccaneer, owed him damages for the loss caused by their interference with his commerce. He had a prior claim against Vietnamese state property contained in the Delta towns, which consequently ought not to have been returned to the mandarins until the debt was satisfied. Garnier himself had recognized the claim as just. Garnier, exclaimed Philastre, would have been court-martialled if he had survived. In any event, said Dupuis, changing his argument, no French officer had the right to order him to leave. His transit through Tongking had been properly authorized by the competent Chinese authorities, for Philastre could not fail to be aware that China as suzerain had an overriding jurisdiction throughout the territory. If he, Dupuis, was an intruder, by what title were the French in Saigon? 'There at least you have a point,' said Philastre. 'We came to Saigon as pirates and bandits!'

This was plain speaking with a vengeance, when one remembers that up to then Philastre had no warrant for his actions; but as it turned out, the Admiral, shocked by the news of Garnier's death and terrified at the thought of the damage the ill-fated venture might bring to his own career, was only too happy to learn that the wretched affair was being wound up as speedily as possible, particularly since it became apparent that Philastre was after all extracting from the Vietnamese, as a reward for giving them back the Delta, a brand new treaty going far beyond what Saigon had for years been soliciting. Indeed the terms of the agreement were so generous that one is led to assume that the Court of Hue, in its haste to recover Tongking, was either making promises it had no real intention of fulfilling, or that it was unaware of the significance of its undertakings. It was inevitable, of course, that French Cochinchina should be recognized as now including the three trans-Mekong provinces seized in 1867; and as Hanoi and the other Delta cities reverted to Vietnamese control with the withdrawal of the foreigners, the mere declaration that the Red River was opened to international commerce, even when Hanoi and Haiphong, as well as Quinhon in the south, were designated as trading ports with resident French consuls, remained somewhat theoretical. Henceforth a French representative would be stationed at Hue, but taking into consideration the fact that France not only waived the residue of the war indemnity still owing under the old treaty of 1862, but made a present to Vietnam of five naval vessels with a quantity of cannon and rifles, it was permissible for King Tu Duc to judge the whole transaction as a respectable victory for himself and his people. Seen against this background, those stipulations which in French eyes were to constitute the legal grounds for future policy, looked at the time—in Hue at any rate— relatively innocuous. The provisions in question were that Vietnam was declared sovereign and independent of all foreign powers. If Vietnam should so request, France would give her assistance against attack from any quarter, while in return for such protection Vietnam would conform its foreign policy to that of France. The 'foreign power' referred to was understood by France to mean China in particular, but neither then nor for years after did Vietnam judge that she had denounced the suzerainty of Peking, still less did she interpret a statement of her independence to mean that she had in fact become a vassal of Paris. On the contrary, it is likely that straightforward oriental minds would have thought such a distortion of language beyond the capacity for perversion of even the most inscrutable of westerners.

The treaty so conceived was signed at Saigon in March 1874 (the last French troops had left Tongking the previous month), and the Admiral carried it back with him to France, where he had been recalled at his request. Thanks to Philastre, his career had

1   The Marquis Tseng awaiting officials

been saved from the ruin which had threatened it, and he was grateful enough to see that his subordinate was promoted to the Legion of Honour. But the award was hissed by the young officers upon whom Philastre had imposed the humiliation of hauling down the tricolour from the captured citadels of Tongking. The French missionaries, looking ruefully at the smoking remnants of so many Christian settlements, reported that on a Vietnamese tongue the name of Philastre is identical with that of Pilate. Still worse was to come. In due course, the episode was commented upon by the hereditary enemy in London, and the hypocritical Anglo-Saxons acclaimed the villain as the one member of the French forces in Vietnam who deserved to be called a gentleman.[17] After that, one can imagine what kind of life awaited the unfortunate man in the colonial service; and it is not surprising to learn that he retired in 1879 and returned to France.

The most obvious victim of events was Dupuis himself. Faced with the formal decision of a France authority, which he knew would have the backing of Paris, he was compelled to lead his private army out of Hanoi to Haiphong. His ships and equipment were put under seal and when, twenty months later, he was readmitted into possession of them, most things of value had been pillaged. To pay off his men he had to fall back on his own resources: not a word about any compensation had been mentioned in the treaty. Declared bankrupt at Saigon, he made his way to Paris where he infested ministerial corridors with his complaints until, a few years later, as we shall see, the wheel of fortune revolved in his favour and a day of imperial adventure dawned again. Bishop Puginier, meanwhile, had at first let it be known that he could no longer look his faithful converts in the eye after such an exhibition of cynicism and treachery on the part of his countrymen, but little by little the reprisals died down, the Vietnamese promised in the treaty to tolerate Catholicism, and by this time his roots were too firmly implanted in Tongking soil to be easily pulled up. In 1876, a visitor found him as busy and as sanguine as ever, ruling patriarchally over his flock, whom he was encouraging in the manufacture of cigars. He too was being reserved by destiny for a brighter future.

And Garnier? The sound of his name had become hateful to

official ears. The Admiral had had no compunction whatsoever in branding the dead man as a dangerous megalomaniac. The fact that he himself had in the first instance solicited Garnier's help was carefully screened from view; and Paris was informed that Garnier, entirely on his own initiative, had offered his services, which his experience seemed to render specially valuable, in getting rid of that nuisance Dupuis—only to commit, himself, a supreme act of folly in total disregard of the orders of his superiors and of the interests of his country. Since they considered that his death had been brought about solely by his own foolhardiness, for years the French government would not grant his widow a pension. When in 1875 his body, reunited with its head, which the Vietnamese had been induced to return, was transported to Saigon, there to lie in French colonial earth, the Arsenal declined to issue lead sheeting to wrap it in, and the Governor of the day had the pettiness to forbid serving officers from attending the funeral, except such as had known Garnier personally. The eclipse was, however, only temporary, and in due course Francis Garnier was to be canonized side by side with Pigneau de Béhaine as a patron-saint of French Indo-China.

🜚 CHAPTER NINE

China—Divided Counsels

WHILE these events were taking place beyond her frontier, China was experiencing what her historians call the 'restoration' of the Manchus. The ruling house had had a narrow escape. When in 1860 the Emperor Hsien Feng fled in terror north of the Great Wall, abandoning Peking to the Anglo-French invaders, it must have seemed to many of his subjects that the Dynasty, already shaken to its foundations by the Taiping Rebellion, had at last come to an end. Some such feeling was very likely in the mind of Hsien Feng himself; unwilling to survive the ruin of his fortunes, he determined to retrieve his prestige by joining the select company of those who have committed suicide by fornication. As may be imagined, an Emperor of China had better means at his disposal for such a purpose than the mass of ordinary mankind; twelve months of unremitting endeavour added to many preceding years of debauchery gave him his wish in August 1861.

Hsien Feng left only one son, a child of five, so there was no dispute about the succession. The sole question was who would exercise power during the young sovereign's minority? The boy's mother was a concubine named Yehonala, and the parental authority ought to devolve not on her but on the legitimate widow. Yehonala, however, was no ordinary woman. Twenty-six years of age, she had never been a beauty, but in some way she had gained an ascendancy over Hsien Feng which at his death earned for her a promotion to the title of Empress Dowager on terms of practical equality with the senior consort. Soon after this elevation she showed her mettle by frustrating a palace plot against herself and the other widow; so that when in November 1861, after their return to Peking, the pair of Dowagers were proclaimed co-Regents, everybody felt that Yehonala had well and truly deserved the honour. The ritual Chinese expression to describe such female rule is 'to lower the curtain and listen to matters of government', and that is precisely what the two ladies did whenever they granted their ministers an audience, for their twin thrones were concealed by hangings through which they could hear and be heard while remaining unseen. Because of this Confucian regard for the proprieties it was announced that the day-to-day conduct of important business would be entrusted to Prince Kung, Hsien Feng's younger brother, who had stayed behind to negotiate with the British and French in 1860 and had in consequence won a reputation as a practical man of affairs. The boy Emperor's reign was styled the period of T'ung Chih, or 'Joint Rule,' and it seemed that the Dynasty had been given a fresh lease of life.

The survival had been costly. For two hundred years the Manchus, while indulging their Chinese subjects in the enjoyment of their old laws and institutions and welcoming them into the service of the state had been careful to keep the key positions of authority out of their control. At the time of the peasant rebellion of the Taiping, however, the great landowners of south and central China had rallied unhesitatingly around the throne (see chapter three), and such men as Tseng Kuo-fan and Li Hung-chang, at the head of their privately-enrolled militia, had become pillars of the Manchu regime to a degree unequalled by any Chinese before them. Whatever the grumbling of Tartar die-hards about members of the subject race who had advanced beyond their station, the facts had to be recognized.

Other innovations, too, had been introduced into the established pattern of life. The western barbarians, who twenty years earlier had gained footholds along the southern coast between Hong Kong and Shanghai, had now forced their way into the Yangtze Valley and the North. Peking itself had to endure the presence of permanent diplomatic legations, and although years were to pass before China reciprocated by maintaining representatives abroad, these changes necessitated the creation of a brand new department of government. A Foreign Office, with Prince Kung in charge, came into being in 1861, and soon showed signs of dwarfing all other organs of administration, for its terms of reference extended far beyond diplomacy proper to cover military affairs and international trade. It was understood that such an institution needed staff with special training, and from 1862 a School of Languages was set up in Peking where it was hoped young cadets might equip themselves to cope with foreigners by learning English, French or Russian. More significant still, the experience of the last few years had demonstrated that China, which a couple of centuries earlier had not been ashamed to learn the science of gunnery from European teachers, must once again turn to the same source of knowledge to bring her armaments up to date. First to appreciate this necessity were the men who commanded the private armies against the Taiping. Li Hung-chang, for instance, memorialized Prince Kung as follows:

'It is my submission that to transform China into a strong country we must acquire the use of modern weapons, and for this we must instal machinery for making these weapons. By learning the foreigners' methods for ourselves, we shall no longer depend on their services. In order to get these machines and the experts to use them, we should create a special branch of the mandarinate, entrance to which will be open to candidates qualified in these technical studies, who will thereafter have their career assured.'

With ideas of this kind current within influential circles, it might have been supposed that China was entering into a period of modernization similar to that which during the closing decades of the nineteenth century was to make Japan one of the great powers of the world. Yet anyone who entertained such a notion would have been sadly deceived, for the truth was that Prince Kung, Li Hung-chang and those who shared their views took for granted certain basic assumptions which prohibited any cultural revolution. To all these men the Confucian theory of state and society seemed the perfect embodiment of human wisdom. They acknowledged merely that the West had perfected certain military techniques which it was incumbent upon the Chinese government to acquire for itself, not least for the sake of preserving peace and order within its own frontiers. Arms must be bought for immediate use, and arsenals established to ensure a future supply. The aim must be to attain self-sufficiency as soon as possible, and an ample reserve of Chinese technicians was necessary to ensure this. The training of these men would have to extend to some branches of western science only indirectly concerned with armaments. Also, since the foreigners claimed to base their conduct on the rules of International Law, this subject could be added to the curriculum for practical purposes. Of course a good foundation in a foreign language was indispensable, since for years to come the knowledge required would have to be learned from alien instructors, but it was not contemplated that there might be any humanistic or cultural benefit to be derived from the reading of European literature, still less that China should look abroad for the pattern of her political institutions.

Even this cautious programme proved too radical for many people. Although in theory we can make allowance for the strength of tradition, it is almost impossible for us today to appreciate the enormous bulk of prejudice, found equally among peasants and mandarins, against which Prince Kung and his colleagues had to fight every step of the way. The mandarins' prejudices were reinforced by considerations of self-interest: few men who had spent years of drudgery over classical books in order to enter government service would be enthusiastic at the news that others might be given the chance to outstrip them without enduring the same ordeal. Pedagogues who depended for their livelihood on teaching the old learning were indignant to hear that barbarian schoolmasters would soon be competing for pupils against them. The innovators themselves were not wholly without bias. Indeed the classical Civil Service examinations and the concomitant system of education were to be the great clog on China's progress throughout the remainder of the nineteenth century. In spite of modern learning, and the grudging recognition by the authorities of the need for technicians, ambitious young men with influence behind them still saw the time-honoured Confucian training as the real gateway to wealth and power, and the modern field was in general abandoned to candidates handicapped in seeking more profitable careers by family poverty. Nevertheless, for thirty years the views propounded by Li Hung-chang in the memorial quoted above formed the basis of Chinese policy, to such an extent that the period may be termed 'the era of arsenals'.

From the beginning, however, it was obvious that even among the modernizers (if Li and the rest deserve such a title) there were most serious dissensions, and that private aggrandizement rather than the welfare of the state was the prime motive of endeavour. As we have seen, the credit for having rescued the Dynasty from the Taiping belonged chiefly to Tseng Kuo-fan and the army he had raised from the peasantry of his native Hunan. At the outset, Li Hung-chang had been no more than a subordinate member of Tseng's staff, and his rise to success was due entirely to Tseng's recommendation; yet by the time the Taiping were crushed in 1864, Li was the stronger of the two, for the force he commanded in the hinterland of Shanghai had more direct contact with the foreign powers pledged to support the imperial cause, and Li profited from these circumstances to secure modern arms and western instructors. The disparity between Li and Tseng was emphasized by Tseng's decision after the victory to disband the greater part of his troops, possibly to avert suspicion in court circles of his ultimate intentions. It was a premature step, for although the collapse of the Taiping had removed the greatest threat to the Dynasty, vast areas of the country were convulsed with other rebellions which awaited the imposition of law and order. The North China plain, for example, was being harassed by peasant guerrillas known as Nien, and it seemed natural to Peking that the task of pacification should be entrusted to Tseng, and that once again Li Hung-chang should act as his lieutenant. This latter proviso was especially necessary as the dispersal of the Hunan Army had left only a nucleus of about three thousand soldiers under Tseng's control, while Li was at the head of seventy thousand well-armed veterans. Not anticipating any unwillingness on the part of one whose career he had promoted, Tseng requested Li to transfer the main strength of his troops to fight the Nien. It was a curious piece of simplicity to imagine that Li could hand over a force on whose creation he had lavished such care, so that another—even his old patron—should be able to win credit from their efficiency. To Tseng's pained astonishment he was told that it was out of the question for the coastal area to be denuded of its garrison. Expostulation proving of no avail, he had finally to appeal to Yehonala, and an order came from the Court peremptorily requiring the dispatch of a number of Li's soldiers for employment under Tseng's command. Even this transfer did not help matters, however, as the men proved intractable, ignoring Tseng's orders and looking still towards Li Hung-chang. Things went from bad to worse, until Tseng, realizing that his position was untenable petitioned to be relieved of his charge, which was thereupon removed to the willing shoulders of his rival.

From then on, Li's progress was uninterrupted. In 1868 the Nien followed the Taiping into defeat, and two years later the victor obtained the most splendid prize in the Empire, the Viceroyship of the Metropolitan Province. Going north, he took up headquarters at Tientsin where he organized around himself what was to become known during the next twenty-five years as 'the second goverment of China'. The development of military industries which he had been fostering in the Yangtze Valley since 1862, with arsenals at Soochow, Nanking and Shanghai, was henceforward directed equally to the creation of a navy; for Li held the view that the coming threat to China would be from Japan, now so ominously aroused from torpor, and his own position at the very gateway to the capital indicated that the first obligation of defence would fall on him. The coastline from Manchuria to Shantung was gradually dotted with installations of every kind, looked after by experts from Britain and Germany. Subsidiary enterprises appeared to offer even more remarkable prospects. A telegraph office, opened in 1880, linked Tientsin to Shanghai and the Yangtze. The year afterwards a few miles of railway were laid down to a coal-working, but this piece of vandalism was too outrageous to public sentiment and it was another quarter of a century before the idea was pursued. The Chinese Merchants Shipping Company, founded in Shanghai in 1872, after five or six years possessed a merchant marine of thirty steamers which, although no match for foreign competition, plied with some success along the coast and up the Yangtze.

Tseng Kuo-fan died in 1872, his last days poisoned by the sight of Li's triumph, but the vendetta was maintained tenaciously by his family and their connections and the feud between Li and the

Hunan group formed the background to the political scene throughout the period of our story. It showed itself in a bitter, watchful jealousy on either side towards the other's sphere of influence, and on Li's part especially in a carefully contrived depreciation of his rivals' achievements; for although the Tseng faction were early out-distanced they did not abandon the rat-race, and they could depend when necessary on a helping hand from the Court, which understandably was not displeased to see that Li did not have everything his own way. While the Viceroy was building his edifice of power along the northern seaboard, the Hunan group sought its opportunity deep in the interior.

We have noticed in an earlier chapter that the Muslim populations in those regions of the north-west and south-west where the followers of the Prophet made up the bulk of the inhabitants had taken advantage of the Taiping war to raise the banner of revolt for themselves. So far it had been the south-western rising in Yunnan, because of its link with events in Vietnam, that has claimed our attention; however, of the two rebellions, that in the north-west loomed as the greater threat in the eyes of the government, not only because the battleground was closer to Peking, but also because the conflagration extended from the provinces of Shensi and Kansu westward into the heart of Asia, where the Turki peoples of Sinkiang took up arms against their Chinese rulers in defence not merely of their religion, but also of their nationhood. The activity in Sinkiang, which aroused the special alarm of the Imperial Court, has conditioned the attitude of Communist historians today; for while they are generally sympathetic to popular revolts against former regimes they deplore the separatist tendencies shown by Muslim leaders as calculated to provoke foreign intervention, and for this reason acknowledge that the Manchu Dynasty's suppression of the rising was to the advantage of the country as a whole. This important task was entrusted by the government to the Hunan group, in the belief that an equilibrium would thus be created between the latter and Li Hung-chang. Tso Tsung-t'ang, a protégé of Tseng Kuo-fan, was put in charge of the military operations. These were as extensive as the urgency of the crisis required. Activities continued from 1867 till 1878. In 1871, in the middle of this lengthy campaign, the fears of the Court seemed justified when, Russia, on the pretext of maintaining law and order, sent her troops across the Chinese frontier to occupy the part of Sinkiang known as Ili. The Russians declared that their forces would be withdrawn the moment China was able to reassume control, but such a prospect was still far off, and while Tso Tsung-t'ang doggedly continued the war, Li Hung-chang profited from his viceregal status to disseminate the notion that Sinkiang had already since its acquisition in the eighteenth century cost far more than it was worth, and that Tso and his Hunan friends were simply throwing good money after bad for the sake of 'hundreds of miles of sand', which the Empire could well do without.

These sneers at his rivals would have been bad enough in secret correspondence, but Li added to the injury by his open rudeness and arrogance. Here, perhaps, it is worth-while to correct a false idea: contrary to the general belief, the Chinese in the mass are not a conspicuously polite people. Only in Peking does one commonly hear such courtesies as 'excuse me', used between strangers in the street. Every now and then, abroad, one reads in the newspaper of some ugly incident in a Chinese restaurant when a foreign customer claims to have been insulted by a waiter. Investigation reveals that on coming to take the order the attendant has not thought it necessary to phrase his question more elaborately than by a curt 'What do you want?', which is simply a literal translation of what he would say, without the least thought of giving offense, to one of his countrymen in his own language. Li Hung-chang was naturally brusque of speech, a quality which in the eyes of foreigners was often accentuated by his ignorance of European manners. Towards the end of his life—to mention one famous example—during a visit to England in 1896, he went to pay his respects to the great William Ewart Gladstone, then in retirement at his country home, and was introduced to the statesman's unmarried daughter. A situation so un-Chinese as Miss Gladstone's aroused his curiosity, and on the way back to London he asked the local stationmaster, through an interpreter, exactly why so rich a man had neglected to find a son-in-law. Such social misunderstandings had nothing to do with discourtesy; but Li seemed to take a perverse delight in flouting the conventions of his own nation and class by a deliberate insolence, usually, as might have been expected, towards inferiors, but quite often aimed at his equals as well—in marked contrast to the affability he displayed in dealing with members of the imperial entourage whose favour he felt it useful to gain. Consequently over the years there was built up against him among a wide section of the mandarinate a dislike, even a hatred, which was more than simple jealousy of his wealth and influence, and which in the long run was to prove too much for him.

The transactions in Vietnam prior to Garnier's death were viewed by a Peking naturally more concerned with the suppression of the Muslim rising in Yunnan; and since even the affairs of Yunnan were dwarfed by comparison with the protracted crisis in the north-west and Sinkiang, there was little interest in what was passing in Hanoi. The first warning came from a fresh source, and the aggressors were not French, but British.

Garnier, in pursuing his vision of a French gateway to the wealth of southern China was haunted by the fear of being forestalled by the hereditary enemy. Lower Burma had been occupied by the British since 1825, and the route of communication through Yunnan between China and Upper Burma had formed the object, in the 1860s, of British parties of exploration. It was an open secret that both in India and in London there had been much speculation on the advantage to be derived from becoming the patron and protector of an independent Islamic state in Yunnan, if such a state could be successfully established by the Muslim rebels in that province. However even though Tu Wen-hsiu's Sultanate of Tali seemed to fulfil all the requirements, he was unaccountably abandoned to his fate: and by 1873, thanks partly to the efforts of the Frenchman Dupuis, and his munitions, the cause of an independent Yunnan had foundered in defeat before Britain could make up her mind to come to the rescue. A year later, the British authorities in India were galvanized by the news of the French treaty with Vietnam into organizing a full-scale expedition to ascertain once and for all the feasibility of a commercial route from Burma through Yunnan to the Yangtze. It was to be headed by a Colonel Browne, and considering the nature of the country to be traversed it is hardly surprising that it should have assumed a para-military appearance, for there were to be nearly two hundred men under his command. Prince Kung at the Foreign Office was induced to issue a passport for Browne and his companions, and it was decided that a young man named Margary, on the staff of the British Legation in Peking and fluent in Chinese, should go across country with the document, enter Burma from Yunnan, rendezvous with Browne and his party, and then accompany the latter back into China.

There are persistent stories in the Chinese books of Margary's high-handed, domineering attitude towards both the common people and the mandarins he encountered on his journey: indeed it would have been remarkable if, with his background, he had behaved otherwise. But Yunnan, of all the provinces of China, was the one in which it was the least advisable to indulge in such displays of self-importance. At the time of Margary's arrival, in January 1875, the post of Governor had been held for nine years by one Ts'en Yu-ying, who deserves a few words of introduction as he was thenceforward to play a leading role in the events that form the subject of this book.

He was by birth in Kwangsi a neighbour of Liu Yung-fu, the commander of the Black Flags, whom he resembled also in his social origins, for his parents were desperately poor. The two had other points in common, both being ambitious, but Ts'en had certain advantages. In early boyhood he had been rescued from the poverty of his home, being taken in adoption by a childless couple of sufficient wealth to provide him with an education which enabled him to qualify for the civil service by passing the public examination. Appointed to a magistracy in Yunnan, he threw himself with enthusiasm into the raising of volunteers to combat the Muslim revolt, then just breaking out, and within the space of a year or two showed himself the most efficient of the imperial commanders. Even so, Ts'en knew that fortune in those early days smiled constantly on the rebels, and he was too careful a planner not to take into account the chance of a Muslim victory. Surreptitiously, he entered into communication with the future General Ma while the latter was fighting against the goverment, and let him know that at the right moment he, too, would be glad to serve in the forces of a free Yunnan. However, as we have seen, Ma finished by changing sides, and having emerged as one of the leading partisans of the dynastic cause, he thought it politic to recommend Ts'en for promotion, imagining no doubt that in this way he would have an able lieutenant who was bound to him by personal obligation. He was soon undeceived. Ts'en kept as aloof from his benefactor as he could: he had not the faintest intention of permitting his own achievements to be overshadowed by the presence of a superior. Once his feet were on the ladder he climbed rapidly, benefiting from the sentiment in Peking that it was as well for the future security of Yunnan to advance non-Muslims to posts of authority so as not to have to depend too exclusively on Ma and his co-religionists. From 1867 onwards, Ts'en as Governor of the province took precedence over the General, a fact which explains the peculiar bloodiness of the campaign in its last stages, for Ma would never have wreaked such a vengeance upon the rebel rank-and-file. Cruelty was an addiction with Ts'en, and its indulgence was the sweetest pleasure his rank afforded. Like the leader of the Black Flags he was exceedingly superstitious, always on the look-out for signs and omens and an insatiable consulter of fortune-tellers. After his elevation to Governor, and while the rebellion was still raging, one of these star-gazers informed him that his progress was being impeded by the nearness of a certain sport of nature, a man with a monstrously large head. As it happened, there was a poor creature of just such a kind living in Kunming, who kept himself from starving by exhibiting his deformity in fairs and peepshows. He was not allowed to ruin the amenities of the place much longer, for the Governor had him buried alive, a method of getting rid of undesirables without making a mess which was practised here and there in rural China down to the 1940s. But there was one eyesore that even Ts'en's ruthlessness shrank from removing. After he had left his own family to go into adoption, his father had died and his mother had taken as a second husband, of all men in the world, a barber. To understand the outrage to Ts'en's susceptibilities we must bear in mind that the profession of barber was listed by the Chinese among those occupations so low and undignified that those who exercized them forfeited for themselves and their descendants to the third generation the right to sit for the state examinations. At first Ts'en hoped that the relationship would not come to light, but the shameless woman, now once

157

again a widow and learning that her child had become a Governor, turned up at Kunming expecting that something would be done for her. She was speedily disillusioned. Ts'en already had a mother, the respectable adoptive one, in residence with him, and the newcomer was not even admitted to the house. There was an attempt to make out that she was mentally deranged. She remained in the city however, and it did nothing to improve the Governor's temper to hear rumours that she was lodged and fed on the charity of some of his colleagues, including General Ma.

Such was the agreeable personage that the young diplomat Margary confronted in January 1875. Ts'en was one of those mandarins whose xenophobia could scarcely be contained even at their most amiable moments: it speaks volumes for Dupuis's capacity for working with the Chinese that he was able to conduct his Yunnanese enterprise so smoothly, though, of course, his contacts were chiefly with General Ma. Young Margary was altogether a brasher type of European, and highly conscious of the respect due to his status. This was the prime cause of the trouble, for he demanded that Ts'en should accord him all the ceremony due to one's official equal. As Ts'en happened at the time, in addition to his Governorship, to be acting as Viceroy of the two provinces of Yunnan and Kweichow, this claim from a comparatively junior member of the legation staff did sound sufficiently impudent, and Ts'en rejected it out of hand. Yet Margary persisted; and in the end, weighing his self-importance against the anger of Peking if he should provoke an Anglo-Chinese incident, Ts'en swallowed his pride and let the Englishman have his way. Still, when Margary had left with an escort of Yunnanese soldiers, Ts'en continued to brood over the affront, and the reports that came in of the foreigner's arrogant conduct en route kept his resentment on the boil. The last Chinese garrison commander that Margary encountered before crossing into Burma, a Colonel Li, although outwardly all smiles and joviality, detested his visitor so much that he is believed to have written Ts'en for permission to eliminate the nuisance for good on the return journey, and to have received an approving reply. At any rate, when Margary reappeared, in February 1875, he was ambushed and killed. Browne and his party, who were some distance behind, managed to escape back into Burma. The news reached Peking the following month, and the Chinese government discovered it had on its hands a crisis of unsuspected dimensions.[18]

The disaster occurred, inauspiciously, in the first weeks of a new reign. The boy Emperor, T'ung Chih, the son of Yehonala, had come of age in 1873, thus ending the Regency. By all appearances, the Dowager's days of power were over. T'ung Chih had little cause to love her, and began to act as if she did not exist. Like a true son of his father, he had a craving for smallfooted Chinese femininity, and when this fit was on him all the Manchu and Mongol beauties of the imperial seraglio could not serve his purpose. With a pair of confidants, he took to slipping out of the palace in disguise after nightfall, and if rumour was to be credited these excursions carried him to some very odd adventures, for he was said to pass by the aristocratic houses of pleasure in favour of robustly plebeian company. The year 1874 was not far advanced before people at Court were remarking to one another about the shocking deterioration in the Emperor's appearance, and as the months passed it became difficult to hide the fact that he had contracted some painful disorder. Repenting his folly, the sick wretch tried to reform and turned for comfort to the young wife he had neglected. This desperate attempt at domesticity made the Empress pregnant, but was too late to save the Emperor. It was given out that His Majesty had been granted the happiness of a visitation of Celestial Flowers, or in other words that he had got smallpox. On January 13, 1875, the Dragon Throne again lacked an occupant.

The decree announcing T'ung Chih's illness declared that the two Dowagers had agreed to handle state affairs during the emergency. By the time her son died, therefore, Yehonala's former authority as co-Regent had been to some extent restored. Yet her future position seemed dubious. If the child T'ung Chih's widow was carrying should be a boy, it would have an incontestable right to the Throne, and it would be hard to deny its mother's claim at least to participate in the Regency. Clearly drastic action was called for if such a possibility was to be forestalled. Yehonala boldly proclaimed that it was out of the question for the throne to remain vacant until the sex of the unborn baby was known: an Emperor must be appointed at once. Here the Chinese law required that the ordinary rules of adoption should apply, and these stipulated that T'ung Chih's successor must be a male of the same clan one generation junior to the deceased. Yehonala however was not concerned with technicalities. Her younger sister had shared in her good fortune by marrying one of her husband's brothers, and the couple had an infant son. To Yehonala the prospect was alluring: another long Regency, and even after that, the throne still in the family. Her formidable presence overawed opposition; the yellow palanquin was dispatched to her sister's house, and at dead of night a frightened child of three was hurried into the palace and made to kowtow before the corpse of his predeccessor. The new sovereign was given the style of Kuang Hsü. There remained the problem of what to do if a posthumous son should be born to T'ung Chih. That, to put it mildly, would be an embarrassment. Yehonala did not shrink from doing what was necessary. 'I feel,' she said, 'that as the Empress is so downcast by the loss of her husband she ought to consider following him.' T'ung Chih's widow took the advice and commited suicide on March 27, 1875.

The business, as may be imagined, caused an enormous scandal: at least one prominent mandarin killed himself in protest; but Yehonala knew that she could rely on some very strong supporters, especially on Li Hung-chang whose constantly increasing power was close at hand, and her vigour and self-confidence carried all before her, as she entered upon what was to be the great phase of her career. In theory she again shared the Regency with the other Dowager, but the triumph was hers. One sign of her prestige was a perceptible weakening of the influence of Prince Kung. The cooperation between them, which in 1861 had seemed to offer such promise for the future, had not lasted more than a year or two: a clash of temperament had turned their friendship into barely-disguised hatred. The Prince was still chief minister and adviser, but Li Hung-chang began increasingly to assume this function.

It was the Margary affair more than any other that made this development obvious to the world at large. The news of the murder reached Peking while the Court and the mandarins were engrossed with speculations aroused by Yehonala's return to power. The British Minister was Thomas Wade, an old resident of the country, whose attainments were later to be rewarded with the first chair of Chinese at Cambridge and who gave his name to the system most generally used in the West today for the romanization of Chinese words. These scholarly interests were insufficient to mollify his native temper, which displayed itself, whenever the Chinese would not let him have his own way, in loud bellowing and table-thumping. For once, it must be admitted, he had an adequate reason for anger. Yet his demands, when he formulated them towards the end of March 1875, went far beyond the incident itself, and Prince Kung not surprisingly rejoined that although accepting such proposals as the sending of a mission of inquiry, and the payment of an indemnity, the Chinese government was quite unable to see the connexion between the unfortunate Margary's death and, for example, the exemption of British goods from inland transit duties. At this, Wade flew into one of his rages, threatening to shut down his mission: simultaneously the Chinese were informed that their obstreperousness was compelling the British to come to an understanding with Russia for the concerting of a joint invasion of China through Yunnan and Sinkiang respectively.

Wade addressed his menaces to Prince Kung and the Foreign Office, but in the meantime similar approaches were being made by another channel to Li Hung-chang. Twenty years earlier, while the Taiping war was at its height, and Manchu officials had been temporarily evicted from the Chinese city of Shanghai by a group of insurgents, it was agreed that foreigners should look after the collection of customs dues at the port on behalf of Peking. What was intended as a short-term arrangement had resulted in the creation of a most remarkable institution, the Chinese Maritime Customs, run by foreigners in the employment of the Chinese state, and headed, until the abrogation of the Unequal Treaties in 1942, by a Briton. During the period we are discussing the incumbent was the Ulsterman, Robert Hart. He and his men did feel a responsibility towards the country they served: in fact their general honesty and efficiency made the Chinese readier to accept the situation than they might otherwise have been. However, under this non-Chinese management the first charge on the customs revenue was the payment of money due to the foreign powers, whether in the form of war indemnities or interest on loans: only when these obligations had been met was the residue handed over to Peking. This by itself was unacceptable to national sentiment, but there were even worse features. The Customs Service, as an organ of the Chinese government, inevitably tended in the days when few Chinese were familiar with western languages, to be used by Peking as a handy means of transacting international business. This was done to such an extent that, as we shall see, Hart was ultimately to play a major role not only in the implementation of policy, but even in its initial formulation. In other words, as the Communist historians tell us, the Customs Service was *par excellence* the instrument by which the West administered China as a semi-colony.

With regard to the Margary affair, Hart soon made it his business to pay a call on Li Hung-chang at Tientsin. The gist of his remarks, noted down by Li, was that Britain was after trading privileges: if these were conceded, the Margary incident need cause no further bother; if they were refused, then there was no saying to what lengths London would go. Hart's words, commented Li in his report to Peking, seemed far from an idle threat. Then, in August 1875, Wade came to Tientsin in person: Ts'en Yu-ying and the other criminals in Yunnan must be punished and satisfactory arrangements made for trade between Yunnan and Burma. Surely Li could see the justice of this? A shake-up was long overdue in the Chinese administration, most of all in the Foreign Office. Nothing loath, Li passed on these observations, adding his own opinion that 'the fault clearly lies on our side, and we cannot evade the issue by glossing things over'. The following month, authorization came for him to represent the government in talks with Wade, but his terms of reference fell far short of making him the plenipotentiary with whom alone Wade thought it worthwhile to hold a formal conference. The Englishman withdrew in a huff to the capital, where the Court was soon humming with stories that he had cancelled his previous demands, and that nothing any longer but the throwing open to British merchants of a wide range of market towns in southern and central China would stay the hand of vengeance. The tension dragged on throughout the winter and spring, until in June 1876 Wade at last carried out his menace, and moved out of Peking at the head of all his staff. A break seemed unavoidable, and Li begged Hart to pursue the obstinate man to Shanghai and at the eleventh hour induce him to draw back from the precipice. Hart obeyed, and in July wrote to Li that Wade would be willing to talk with a Chinese minister, provided that the latter's authority was not restricted simply to the Margary incident. He must be a genuine plenipotentiary, and have a character equal to the greatness of his task. There must be no pettifogging haggling over details. To make his meaning intelligible beyond doubt, Hart added: 'Your Excellency would be far more suitable than any other person.' Li forwarded the letter to Yehonala and at the end of July was gratified with an appointment as envoy with full powers to treat with the British Minister. Their conference was held at the port of Chefoo in Shantung, already a favourite summer resort of foreigners. It ended with the signing on September 13, 1876 of a Convention so amply satisfying Wade's demands that Li expressed the hope that it would obviate any further disputes with Britain for twenty years to come. The terms were certainly far-reaching enough. The foreigners' right of extraterritoriality was to be put on a wider basis, and protocol for the reception of foreign diplomats was to be adjusted to international practice. New treaty-ports were to be opened, both inland and on the coast, among them Chung-king. The frontier with Burma was to be definitely established. Finally as regards Margary's death, which had provoked all the bother in the first place, a high official was to go to London on a mission of apology. This last provision was carried out in the following year, 1877, and was more important than had been anticipated, for the mandarin in question stayed on as Minister to Britain and France, thus initiating the residence of Chinese envoys abroad.

Nevertheless, one demand of Wade's was frustrated. The fire-eating Governor of Yunnan, Ts'en Yu-ying, went unchastised. Colonel Li was taken into custody as a matter of form; but when the Imperial Commissioner arrived in Kunming to conduct an inquiry into the murder, he was overawed by Ts'en, who made a point of receiving him at the head of his troops in full military paraphernalia and flaunting a magnificent Burmese sword. Far from daring to bring any charges against his host—it should by the way be added that Ts'en was of strikingly robust physique—he readily discovered that even Colonel Li was free from blame, and that the real culprits were a bunch of tribesmen, scarcely able to speak Chinese, whose heads could be lopped off with impunity.

The references to Burma in the Convention were explicable only on the assumption that China already recognized that its vassal kingdom had become in some sense a British protectorate. The message was spelt out later, in 1879, when Wade in a convivial moment said to Li: 'We British like Burma very much: it's a place worth getting.' The very childishness of the language suggests that Li must have noted down the Englishman's Chinese speech verbatim. Li, according to his own account, rejoined: 'If you should go to war with Burma, let us know first, so that there won't be any ill-feeling between us.' For indeed, it would have been strange if a man prepared to see Sinkiang lost to the Empire made trouble over the shedding of one of the remoter satellites.[19]

CHAPTER TEN

Halliday Macartney and the Marquis Tseng

THE Franco-Vietnamese Treaty of March 1874, declaring Vietnam's independence of all foreign powers was designed, in French eyes at any rate, to put an end to Chinese suzerainty, and the clauses stipulating that in return for French assistance against attack Vietnam would conform its foreign policy to that of France were intended to create a French protectorate. International courtesy required that China should be notified of this disposal of her interests, yet Paris showed marked reluctance to raise the matter. Indeed it seems that the French pressed Hue to break the news to Peking on their behalf, but the suggestion was not taken up and neither then nor for years to come was there any perceptible modification of the relationship between Vietnamese vassal and Chinese overlord. Meanwhile, as far as Tongking was concerned, the agreement remained a dead letter. So far from being opened to French commerce, the Red River was firmly in the hands of the Black Flags, whose prestige, after the killing of Garnier, had grown prodigiously throughout the northern provinces.

The situation was more irksome to Saigon than to Paris, where the French Foreign Ministry seemed content to leave the question of a protectorate in cold storage. Thus in May 1875, when the French Chargé d'Affaires in Peking at last communicated the terms of the Treaty—already fourteen months old—to the Chinese government, he thought it better, in his covering letter, to 'slide over' (the phrase is his own) that particular problem. His note was addressed to Prince Kung:

'Your Imperial Highness [it said] will see that from now on it is the business of France to look after the security and independence of His Majesty Tu Duc, and I have no doubt that the Chinese Government will understand how necessary it is for the maintenance of the good relations that exist between France and China to give the strictest orders to the Yunnan authorities not only to stop fresh bands of Chinese from entering Vietnam, but even to recall those who are at present committing violence of every kind in that kingdom. The French Government is determined to fulfil the engagements it has undertaken towards King Tu Duc and to secure peace and quiet in the dominions of this monarch. Its first task will consequently be to disperse and destroy these bands who are fomenting unrest and civil war.

'There is a second point to which I should equally like to call Your Imperial Highness's attention, I mean the opening to shipping of the Red River from its mouth to the Chinese frontier. In the Treaties of Tientsin and Peking there is no clause dealing with this eventuality, which could not have been foreseen at that time, but now that it has arisen it ought to be settled at once so as to avoid complications. The French Government concluded this Treaty with Vietnam after long consideration of the burdens and of the benefits to itself thereby created and is determined both to honour its obligations and to take advantage of its privileges. I have therefore been instructed to reach an understanding with Your Imperial Highness on these two questions: (1) the suppression of the Chinese bands who are ravaging Vietnam and (2) the opening of a point in Yunnan where our ships could land and carry regular commercial transactions. I have no doubt that Your Imperial Highness will also understand the necessity of a practical solution of these two problems and will prefer the establishment of regular relations to a condition of disorder which, by forcing the King of Vietnam to take energetic measures to protect the security and the commercial prosperity of his dominions, could have the gravest consequences.'

It will be remembered from the last chapter, that in May 1875, when this communication was delivered to Prince Kung, he was wholly engrossed by the labyrinthine development of the Margary affair; and anyhow, he could not have deduced more from the message than that France, her cupidity excited by what she had heard of the demands made by Britain, had decided to try her luck and compete for a similar entry into the Yunnan market. As to this, he answered then that, as France herself admitted, there was no treaty with any country relating to the opening of Yunnan to foreign trade, but that the matter could be discussed in the future, after an inquiry had been held on the spot. This clearly referred to the investigation of the British demands then being undertaken in Yunnan. It was afterwards maintained by the French that by not specifically rejecting their claim to exercise a protectorate in Vietnam, China had tacitly abandoned her own right of suzerainty, but this is quite simply untrue. Prince Kung informed the French Chargé d'Affaires that: 'Vietnam has for a long time been a tributary of China. The Vietnamese Government has on numerous occasions asked for help from China. China was unable to refuse help and protection to a vassal, and therefore sent troops to drive away the brigands (who were infesting Vietnam).' The chief of these brigands, added the Prince (who must have been aware that the man in question was by way of being an ally of the French), was Huang Ch'ung-ying, the leader of the Yellow Flags. As regards the movement of bandits from China into Vietnam, the Chinese troops on the frontier had as one of their duties the prevention of such migrations, but whenever these occurred they were bound to pursue the criminals across the border. The Prince, in other words, was careful not to provoke a quarrel; but then, for that matter, the French diplomat had been quite as circumspect in his language, and had not by any means denounced the Chinese claims. Indeed during that year of 1875, Paris, and more particularly Saigon, were compelled to watch helplessly while their potentially most effective allies in Tongking, namely the Yellow Flags, were being progressively annihilated.

This action was, of course, nothing more than a continuation of the campaign launched in 1869, which it will be remembered had put the seal on Liu Yung-fu's new-found respectability. Not only did he hold the commission of the King of Vietnam: his own China, from which he had fled as an outlaw, had recognized him as an ally, for an army from Kwangsi province had come south against the common enemy, Huang Ch'ung-ying and the Yellow Flags. At that time, in spite of many initial victories, the malaria infesting the tropical jungle had compelled the Kwangsi troops to withdraw to their healthier native air, and Huang and his followers were left in control of a vast tract of country between the Red River and the Chinese border. Now, however, the hour had arrived for a final settlement of accounts. Soldiers came down for the kill not only from Kwangsi but also from Yunnan, while from the other side Liu was supported by Vietnamese units. The fighting was particularly merciless until, as the attackers drew closer, treachery began to appear among the Yellow Flags, and deserters found their way to Liu, carrying with them the heads or, if these were too burdensome, the ears of their officers and comrades in token of their change of heart. At length, it was evident that Huang's principal base, the stockaded encampment at Hayang, must fall to the Kwangsi army, and the garrison scattered for safety into the surrounding forests. Huang, who had hidden a quantity of gold bars upon his person and was accompanied by his family and a strong bodyguard, seems to have hoped to pass as one of Liu's lieutenants for he instructed his party to sport Black Flags. By a strange oversight, however, the banners, instead of being three-cornered to resemble Liu's, were square, and the deception failed completely. As it became plain that the trap was closed, tempers flared among the fugitives, who blamed their predicament on their leader's rashness. The idea must have entered some of their minds that the best way out of their difficulty would be to make Huang a prisoner and hand him over to their pursuers, but whatever the reason they did not yield to the temptation and contented themselves with slipping off quietly. Finally there remained with Huang only his wife and one of his concubines, and less than thirty of the band, and in a couple of days they were all exhausted with aimless wandering and lack of food. The women, while scrambling over the hillsides, had plucked poisonous herbs here and there and during the night succeeded in chewing and swallowing their find, with the result that the sun rose upon two corpses. Huang cursed them for a pair of bitches, and left the bodies where they lay to be fought over by scavengers. This was the last straw. Two or three miles further on, Huang, who as usual was leading the march, turned his head to discover that now only eight men were left.

As the sun was setting they came to a tiny shrine carved in a cliff and dedicated apparently to the tutelary spirit of the mountain. A large incense-burner stood in front of it, to receive the joss-sticks which the peasantry round about would offer at the new and the full moon. The travellers stretched out for the night upon the ground, but Huang forced himself to keep awake; and when his companions were snoring he arose stealthily, drew out from beneath his clothing some of the gold bars he was carrying, and buried them in the mass of ashes which clogged the incense-burner. This done he lay down again. The others were up before dawn and Huang, hearing them whispering together, prepared himself for the worst. Suddenly one of them came at him with a sword, slashing down at his head, but with the excitement and the darkness he struck merely a glancing blow. The wound bled so profusely that the men assumed, especially since Huang had the presence of mind not to utter a sound, that their leader was dead, and groped in his clothes until they had found the rest of the gold. They then set off the way they had come, no doubt hoping to catch up with their friends.

By this time the sun was appearing, and Huang made out at a distance through the trees the roofs of what was obviously a hill-tribe's village. Leaving the gold where he had hidden it, he struggled forward. On the edge of the settlement he saw a field planted with sweet potatoes, and could not refrain from clawing up one of the vegetables which he began to eat voraciously. A tribeswoman came out from a hut and approached him curiously. Huang asked her if she could spare a little rice-gruel, and she signed to him to stay where he was until she returned. When she came back, she was accompanied by a couple of dozen men, armed with spears, who to Huang's astonishment wanted to know whether he was the famous chieftain of the Yellow Flags. Too weak and ill to pretend any longer, Huang admitted his identity. His captors revealed that the commander of the troops from Kwangsi had spread the word far and wide through the jungle that a handsome reward was waiting for whoever laid hands on the outlaw. The simple tribesmen were overjoyed at their good fortune and treated

Huang with positive joviality, killing a chicken and regaling him with the best they had in food and drink. Meanwhile, some of their number were given the task of constructing a large bamboo crate, such as is used in China to convey pigs to market. In this Huang was placed, and carried suspended from a pole to his former headquarter at Hayang, now occupied by the Chinese army. The officer there toyed for a while with the notion of taking him back in triumph to Kwangsi; but on second thoughts he decided that the prisoner, who so far from benefiting from the tribesmen's hospitality was even sicker than before, and indeed was scarcely able to speak, would not make a very impressive spectacle, even if he survived the journey. Besides, once back in Kwangsi and remote from the scene of events, there was bound to be speculation that the whole affair was a put-up job, and that some starving wretch had been persuaded by the offer of money to his family to sell his life and pass as Huang Ch'ung-ying. Care was taken to assemble witnesses who could certify the culprit's identity, and then he was beheaded in front of the troops. Their mission accomplished, the Chinese forces withdrew across the border.

The loss of so useful an ally did not fail to irk the French, but they were in no position to intervene. Three years later, however, they did react to a rather similar situation, but with results that were far from glorious. Among the officers of the Kwangsi army, there was a man named Li Yang-ts'ai, born and brought up on the Chinese side of the frontier (a native of the same district in southern Kwangtung as Liu Hung-fu), but of a family which claimed to trace its descent from one of the dynastic houses of medieval Vietnam. Piqued at the slowness of his promotion, Li decided to carve out a dominion for himself in his ancestral land, and having first sent agents to spy out the terrain and to propagandize on his behalf, in November 1878 he crossed the border at the head of a force of several thousand. (The size testified to the chronic persistence of banditry and peasant unrest in Kwangsi and Kwangtung.) The matter was treated as urgent, not merely by the Kwangsi provincial authorities, but also by the Government in Peking, which held General Feng of the Kwangsi army responsible for the affair, and let drop a broad hint that unless he retrieved the situation his own future would be in jeopardy. In these circumstances General Feng stood in no need of appeals from Hue to hurry to the rescue—though such appeals came thick and fast, for Li was taken seriously as a contender for the Vietnamese throne.

Once again, Saigon, for it was the colony rather than metropolitan France which felt its passions roused by these transactions, was faced with the unwelcome spectacle of a Chinese expedition to Tongking requested by Hue for that very purpose of maintaining order which the French had attempted to assert as their own monopoly. But this time, even if their protégé neglected to call on them for assistance, they would show the world they were not defaulting on their duty. One hundred French troops were dispatched to guard the consulate at Hanoi, a right reserved by the Treaty of 1874. It is quite certain that Li Yang-ts'ai hoped for some measure of cooperation from the French, and both he and his enemies may be forgiven if they assumed that this movement of troops was merely the preliminary to a large-scale intervention. The Vietnamese had not yet called upon the Black Flags, but now they did so, confirming Liu Yung-fu—and for that matter many of his countrymen—in the belief that only he and his band could cow the foreigner. In fact, to what extent the apparition of the killers of Garnier intimidated the French and prevented their further involvement in Tongking is very much of a mystery. The Chinese books insist that a French plan to seize the city of Bac-Ninh and thus effect a juncture with Li Yang-ts'ai, who was in that vicinity, was actively under way when it was frustrated by the arrival of Liu. At any rate, the fact that the French gesture at Hanoi was not followed up was universally interpreted among the Chinese, both in Tongking and north of the border, to mean that once more their compatriot had rescued Vietnam. So enormous had Liu's reputation now become that the Kwangsi commander, General Feng, thought it necessary to send the Black Flags a message to fall back a little to the south, so that he could redeem his honour in the eyes of Peking by destroying Li Yang-ts'ai himself. The task took longer than anticipated, but in October 1879 Li was made prisoner and sent back to Kwangsi, where at the provincial capital of Kweilin he was put to death at the beginning of the following year. His head was carried under escort to Vietnam, and paraded through the land over which he had hoped to reign. The affront provoked Paris into addressing to Hue a protest (the proper time for which, one would think, would have been twelve months earlier) against the injury to French rights constituted by the request for Chinese intervention.

Like the British in the Margary affair, the French in estimating their prospects in Tongking kept one eye cocked on Russia who of all the western powers was at the moment the most seriously embroiled in Chinese politics. We have seen in the last chapter how Moscow in 1871 profited from the Muslim revolt in Sinkiang to occupy a portion of the province called Ili, protesting meanwhile that her sole purpose was to assure law and order in the absence, and on behalf, of the legal Chinese authority. Yet when in 1878, after years of bitter fighting, the Chinese succeeded in quelling the rebellion, the Russians showed no sign of wishing to honour their pledge, and it was decided in Peking that there was nothing for it but to send a diplomatic mission to discuss the matter. The man chosen was a Manchu named Chunghow and he was given plenipotentiary powers to act for his government. Travelling to Europe by sea, he reached Russia at the beginning of 1879 and set to work negotiating. It was not his first trip abroad: in 1870 he had been sent on an even more unpleasant embassy to apologize to France for the murder of some Catholic missionaries by a mob at Tientsin, and he had in consequence the reputation of being something of an expert in foreign affairs. On this occasion, however, his conduct was so extraordinary that it has been surmised he must have been afflicted by some temporary mental alienation, though to give him his due it should be mentioned that the brain-storm, if there was one, did not occur until after nine months of indescribably tedious haggling sufficient to addle the wits of anybody. Whatever the circumstances the wretched man was bamboozled, in October 1879, at Livadia on the Black Sea, into signing a treaty which would hardly have been drafted differently if it had been imposed on a country defeated in war; for a portion of Ili was ceded to Rusia, who also retained the possession of certain passes into Sinkiang of great strategic importance and gained extensive commercial privileges. To add insult to injury, China was to pay an indemnity of five million roubles to defray the cost of the military occupation.

When these terms became known in China there was a great outburst of anger. Chunghow returned to Peking in January 1880 to find himself everywhere denounced as a traitor. Instead of being thanked for his efforts, he was promptly flung into gaol. Amid the roar of vituperation, one voice alone was heard to plead for calm and reflection: Li Hung-chang, who had never concealed his opinion that the whole of Sinkiang put together was not worth the cost and trouble of reconquest, was not now ready to lose sleep over the amputation of a small part of it. Besides, he said, there was a principle of diplomacy at stake. Nobody could deny that Chunghow had been given full powers of negotiation, with authority to sign an agreement for the government. Any repudiation of the treaty would not only put China hopelessly in the wrong, it was quite likely to result in consequences infinitely more disastrous than Chunghow's bargain would entail. But for once the Viceroy was unable to carry the day. The voice of the very commander whose skill and patience had recovered Sinkiang for the Empire, General Tso Tsung-t'ang, was loud for resistance, and the cry was taken up by the other Hunan militarists, who discerned that Li Hung-chang was not willing to run the risk of having his precious military establishment ruined in a war. Even Yehonala and Manchu advisers at Court, though sharing Li's aversion to the prospect of an armed conflict with Russia, went along with the majority opinion: the Treaty of Livadia was denounced.

At this moment, an old friend arrived on the scene. 'Chinese' Gordon, moving between one unsatisfactory job and another in those years before his ultimate summons to Khartoum, had just resigned in disgust from the most unsuitable of all, that of private secretary to the Viceroy of India, when he received a telegram from Robert Hart of the Customs, inviting him to Peking. It seems that Hart took the threat of war seriously, and felt that Gordon would be a good man to have around: the Russian fleet was, after all, manoeuvring in Chinese waters. On his arrival, Gordon proved more eccentric than ever, but there was wisdom in his vagaries. He let it be known that if war came, no power on earth could prevent the Russians from reaching Peking within a couple of months. To imagine otherwise was idiocy: he emphasized the word by pointing it out in an Anglo-Chinese dictionary. If they insisted on fighting, he told the mandarins, they must fully understand that the Court had to leave the capital and migrate deep into the heart of the country from where a national resistance might be organized. Then, as abruptly as he had come, he was off again. Perhaps, as Hart surmised, the man was, whether through vanity or religious mania, 'not all there'. Nevertheless, his words had an effect; Russia, too, began to reconsider the cost of intransigence. It was not long since she had emerged from an exhausting conflict with Turkey. Fresh conversations were started at St. Petersburg, in which China was represented by the very man who was the incarnation of the Hunan party's hatred for Li Hung-chang, for he was no other than the eldest son of the great Tseng Kuo-fan, and therefore duty-bound by all Confucian principles to pursue the vendetta against one who had behaved to his father with such black ingratitude. Yet on the surface the appointment seemed a perfectly natural one: the Marquis Tseng Chi-tse (for, contrary to the general system which aimed at the gradual extinction of hereditary honours in the course of not more than five generations, the nobility conferred on his father was perpetual) was already Minister to London and Paris, and as there was not yet a resident Chinese diplomat accredited to Russia, there appeared to be nothing out of the way in his receiving this extra mission.

It was indeed only three years since the first Chinese legation had been established in the west by Tseng's immediate predecessor who, having gone to London to apologize for the murder of Margary, had stayed on to act as permanent representative of his country both there and in Paris. In those days it was an enormous undertaking for a mandarin, totally unused to foreign ways, to live abroad for any length of time, and they prepared themselves for the ordeal like men going on safari, with cooks, doctors, barbers and even shoemakers and tailors—for though an occasional student might sport a billycock hat or a frock coat, as a dare, thirty years had to pass before an official could show himself without his long gown and his pigtail. In the matter of footwear, the Chinese preferred cloth shoes to leather boots which chafed the feet and were considered to produce an ungentlemanly clatter inside a house. On the whole, this swarm of orientals, hardly one of whom spoke a word of any language but his own, behaved with such discretion that invocation of diplomatic immunity and the like would have been otiose. Now and again, though, with the best will in the world, incidents happened and then unless they were watched carefully they were liable to lead to grotesque results.

Such an incident had occurred during Mr Kuo, the first envoy's, tenure of office. It will be easily understood that the sight of these picturesque strangers was sufficiently remarkable to attract a crowd whenever they appeared in public. One day in Oxford Street, a Cockney youth was bold enough to tug at the pigtail of one of the servants, who turned round and lashed out at the culprit with his umbrella. Trying to dodge the blow, the young man stepped into the road and a passing cab ran over his foot. The hullaballoo brought the constabulary on the scene, and the Chinese was taken to the nearest police station where he was charged with assault. When his identity was discovered, and confirmed by his employer, the accusation was dropped and the man was released. Mr Kuo, overwhelmed with shame and rage, ordered the decapitation of the offender without delay in one of the legation cellars, and for a time it was touch and go whether the atrocity would be carried out, for none of the Minister's Chinese subordinates dared oppose him. Fortunately, however, there was on the staff a British adviser who after interminable arguments and expostulations succeeded in having the sentence commuted to dismissal and reshipment back to China.

The man who saved both the servant's life and the good name of the legation was Samuel Halliday Macartney, a Scot who in his early days, as a member of the Medical Corps, had been through the Crimean War and the Indian Mutiny. He left Calcutta to take part in the Anglo-French invasion of North China in 1860, and when the Manchu Government made peace, decided that the prospects of a career in Chinese service were brighter than in his present occupation. He therefore resigned his British commission to become not a medical but a combatant officer in the Ever Victorous Army, the international body of mercenaries commanded by Gordon, which was engaged in fighting the Taiping. But while Gordon was merely temporarily seconded from the Royal Engineers, Macartney burnt his boats completely, and staked his entire future on the Chinese need for foreign experts. At first the venture

175

paid off splendidly: after the suppression of the Taiping, he was put in charge of the arsenal at Nanking, one of Li Hung-chang's more ambitious projects. To consolidate his new allegiance still further, he took a Chinese wife. She is said to have belonged to the family of one of the Taiping leaders, and to have fallen into Macartney's hands as a prisoner, but as the lady lived in a condition of virtual purdah until her death in 1878, and was never introduced to any of his friends, a curtain of mystery veiled the whole transaction, and this enhanced the wonder felt by ordinary foreign residents towards this compatriot who had gone native. Awe-struck rumour maintained that he had become completely Chinese in thought and habits. Yet the truth was that although he had picked up a familiarity with spoken Chinese he never to the end of his life bothered to learn the written characters. Moreover, those Europeans who reached terms of intimacy with him were as a rule convinced that in his heart he despised the Chinese as heartily as the most respectable member of the Shanghai Club could wish. Certainly, as the years passed, he grew more and more disillusioned with his post. Friction with his Chinese colleagues necessitated frequent appeals to Li Hung-chang, now up in Tientsin as Viceroy, but still retaining control of the Arsenal in Nanking; and all too often Li did not give him the support he expected. Matters came to a head in 1875 when two cannon, which had been cast at Nanking for Li's army in the North, exploded in a fort at Taku at the entrance to the Tientsin river, killing five soldiers and wounding several more. There was a dispute as to the extent of Macartney's responsibility, and Li insisted that, although he was British, he must as an employee of the Chinese government conform to Chinese practice, admit his guilt and 'petition the Throne for punishment'. Macartney flatly refused, and was accordingly relieved of his duties.

While his relations with Li were going sour, he had in compensation formed a warm friendship with Tseng Kuo-fan, who for some time prior to his death in 1872 had held the post of Viceroy at Nanking, and with Tseng's eldest son, who was sufficiently unrepresentative of his class to embark upon the study of the English language. The Tseng family found they had at least one thing in common with the arsenal supervisor, namely a bitter resentment

13   The destruction of the arsenal at Foochow by the French, under Admiral Courbet, 1884

14 Admiral Courbet

Jules Ferry

of Li Hung-chang, and the discovery drew them together as nothing else could. The goodwill of the Tsengs, and through the Tsengs of the Hunan group as a whole, was an asset whose value Macartney was able to appreciate when, at forty-two, he was compelled to seek a new career. For a while he toyed with the notion of setting himself up as a teaplanter, or of emulating Father Huc and going to Lhasa in disguise, but in the end it was the posthumous influence of poor Mr Margary that determined his plans. It was accepted that a mission of apology would have to go to London, and the unthankful task had been delegated to a high mandarin, Mr Kuo, whose complete ignorance of the outside world made it essential for him to have a competent foreign adviser in dealing with so delicate a mission. By this time the Margary case had become chiefly Li's concern and, ruthless though he was, Chinese sentiment made it harder for him than for a western employer of his type to throw a subordinate into the street. A letter in humble terms pleading for generosity towards Macartney had come from young Tseng. Besides, here was an opportunity not only to salve his own conscience and possibly regain the service of a man who had been useful in the past and might well be so in the future: it ensured that Macartney would not be nursing a grievance in China, under Li's very nose. The British Minister, Thomas Wade, whom Li was specially anxious to placate, had in his younger days also come out to China as a soldier, and consequently had a fellow feeling for the dismissed man. All these were good reasons why Li should recommend Macartney's appointment as adviser to the London mission, and with such backing the nomination was never in doubt—though thanks to the complexity of the Anglo-Chinese negotiations the envoy and his suite did not sail from Shanghai until the end of 1876.

They were no sooner on shipboard than Macartney was noting in his diary the sort of problems he was going to be faced with. To be sure, the behaviour of Mr Kuo himself was unexceptionable, but he was accompanied by a colleague of almost equivalent rank, a Mr Liu:

'who committed many grave breaches of good manners. During dinner, he choked and spat, and on one occasion, after an unusually successful attempt at expectoration called his servant and ordered him to bring the spittoon, into which he spued rather than spat. This was exceedingly disagreeable to the gentlemen sitting on the opposite side of the table, who turned away their faces and manifested the most decided signs of disgust. [The next morning] he called for an egg, and proceeded to open it in such an awkward manner that his fingers went into it, his long nails, or rather claws, meeting from opposite sides. With the yolk of the egg dripping from the points of his fingers and streaming over his hands he presented a curious specimen of the corps diplomatique. [Indeed, Anglo-Saxon disapproval pursued poor Liu everywhere.] Having finished his dinner before the rest of us he retired from the table and entered his cabin. We were still at our wine when his servant was seen to snatch up a lamp and go into his state-room. The captain instantly sent one of the stewards to see what he was doing with it, and in a minute he returned stating that His Excellency was enjoying his smoke (i.e. of opium). The captain sent back the steward for the lamp and with instructions to put out the pipe. This being carried out His Excellency, accompanied by his servant, went upstairs apparently in anything but the best of humours.'

We may take leave of Mr Liu by noting that after creating some discomfort for his colleague in London, he was at the end of 1877 transferred to Berlin, where he lasted only a few months before being recalled to China.

Perhaps one reason for the captain's strictness was the fact that the legation was deemed to be in sackcloth and ashes for the murder of Margary, and so Liu's self-indulgence was all the more reprehensible. The same note of austerity was sounded at Hong Kong. The envoys felt that a visit to the colony's gaol would be a properly solemn gesture, and in the course of it, the prison governor, entering into the spirit of the occasion and anxious that the quality of British rule should not be misunderstood, ordered one of his Chinese convicts to exhibit his bare back, 'all raw and crossed and cut with hundreds of welts, showing how effectively the cat-of-nine-tails had done its work.'

Macartney's employment carried no guarantee of permanence, and he was delighted, on Kuo's resignation in the summer of

1878, to learn that his old friend Tseng Chi-tse had been chosen to succeed as Minister. If it had not been for the long intimacy between them, Macartney might have seen one drawback in the appointment. His own usefulness to the legation depended to a large extent on the envoy's ignorance of European speech and habits; whereas Tseng had for years been a student of English, could follow ordinary conversation, and surpassed Macartney's attainments in Chinese by his ability to read English newspapers and to write simple letters, ungrammatically no doubt but quite intelligibly. All this would reduce his dependence on his foreign adviser. Still, the disadvantage was more than off-set by the genuine bond of friendship which united the two men, and it was possible to predict (accurately, as things turned out), that Macartney's influence under the new dispensation would be stronger and more pervasive than ever.

On his arrival in Europe at the beginning of 1879, the Marquis Tseng was in his fortieth year. Behind an apparent *bonhomie* he was ambitious and thrusting; convinced of his own importance, and alert to spot any sign, reflected in matters of protocol, that this conviction might not be shared by others. Thus, on the voyage out, in passing through Hong Kong he paid a formal call on the Governor, who happened to be that most exuberant of Irishmen, Sir John Pope Hennessy (the original, we are told, of Trollope's Phineas Finn). Sir John greeted him like a long-lost brother, threw all ceremony out of the window, and tried, but without success, to persuade him to move into Government House *en famille* during his stay in port. The hospitality was boundless, and on his return to the ship, Sir John insisted on keeping him company all the way down the Peak to the waterfront. Nothing could have been more charming or more spontaneous, and it would have been a douche of cold water if Sir John had known that his guest, while appreciating his kindness, had noted acidly in his diary that the Governor had neglected to return his visit formally on board the ship.

It will be easily understood that to a man of this type, even had there been no legacy of family illwill, it was infuriating to hear from his foreign acquaintances that in western circles Li Hung-chang's ever-growing establishment at Tientsin was commonly referred to as being a secondary government of China, and that recommendations Tseng himself might make to the Foreign Office in Peking could well be stultified if they clashed with the views of the great Viceroy. His temperament made it certain that he would be up in arms against the national dishonour of the Treaty of Livadia, but when he heard that Li had actually had the effrontery to defend the unlucky Chunghow he threw himself into the war of words with all the energy he possessed. Thus when Li's enemies carried the day, Tseng, as a natural leader of the Hunan group, and in particular as a diplomat already in Europe, seemed the ideal choice for the task of reopening the question with Russia. Meanwhile Chunghow had been sentenced to death, a barbarity so shocking to western susceptibilities that its execution would have prevented any further discussion. Fortunately, however, the poor wretch had been reprieved—at the plea, it was said, of Queen Victoria, forwarded to Yehonala through Li Hung-chang—and the Tsar considered that it would not in these circumstances be derogatory to his honour if his representatives should once again sit at a table with the Chinese and talk about the fate of Ili.

Macartney accompanied Tseng to St Petersburg, where they remained from July 1880 to February 1881. The pair of them made a formidable combination, and there is no doubt that the Scotsman gave invaluable help to the Chinese cause, drawing Tseng's attention to scores of details which the Marquis, who had never before in his life been faced with an affair of such magnitude, would inevitably have overlooked. The actual course of the negotiations does not concern us: it is enough to note that they ended in the signing of a new treaty, restoring to China nearly all the territory in dispute, together with the passes, and limiting the trading concessions previously granted to Russia. Although in revenge the indemnity was increased from five to nine million roubles, this result was regarded by international opinion as a triumph of Chinese diplomacy. At home, the Hunan group exulted in the discomfiture of Li Hung-chang, and waited eagerly for their next opportunity, not knowing that their hero, Tseng Chi-tse was already busily creating it. In November 1880, while still wrestling with the Russians at St Petersburg, the intrepid Marquis had served notice on France that she would have to reckon with China in Vietnam.

✣ CHAPTER ELEVEN

China's Suzerainty Challenged

IT cannot be doubted that in taking what was to prove the most
momentous step in his career the Marquis Tseng was decisively influenced by Macartney. Such appears to have been the
universal opinion in France, though in the chorus of Gallic
vituperation against the Scotsman's ambition and love of intrigue,
nobody seems to have hinted that Macartney may have been
affected by other considerations. For instance, although we have no
evidence of such an encounter, it is scarcely credible that during
Jean Dupuis's long residence at Hankow as an arms' dealer he had
not met Macartney, then managing the arsenal down the river at
Nanking. One would give something to know what the two thought
of each other. Macartney was at all times very much a snob, with a
keen nose for anything in speech or manners which branded a man
as common, and Dupuis had little charm or gentility to recommend
him. Then again, the two were in a sense rivals, and Macartney,
who clearly hankered after a more romantic occupation than
the overseeing of a workshop, must have chafed to see the French
adventurer laying the foundations of what might well be a vast
fortune in Yunnan and Tongking. It would be asking too much
of human nature, especially at a time when his own job at the
arsenal was at its most frustrating, for him not to have been consoled by the ruin of Dupuis's enterprise after the death of Garnier.

Macartney, who now fancied himself as a professional diplomat-
ist, had taken great pains to cultivate the French language, which
unlike Chinese he not only spoke but wrote with ease. His British
biographer credits him, as a Celt, with having an instinctive sym-

pathy for France; and indeed in 1884, at a period when he was regarded in government circles in Paris as their inveterate enemy, he married a young French girl in the place of the Chinese wife who had died six years earlier. Yet the fact that the man who as Minister to London relied entirely on his advice was simultaneously playing an identical role in Paris and depending in the same way upon a French counsellor was itself calculated to inspire uneasiness, not to say jealousy. Macartney's opposite number across the Channel was a Monsieur Giquel, whose career had run on parallel lines with his own, for he had gone from the French navy to head an arsenal at Foochow. Inasmuch as this foundation was effectively controlled not by Li Hung-chang but by the Hunan group, it might seem that the cards were stacked in Giquel's favour, but on the other hand there was the long-standing friendship between Macartney and the Tseng family, coupled with Tseng's personal preference for English ways, a preference partly the cause, partly the result, of his having learned the English language. From occasional expressions in his diary, one gathers the impression that Tseng found Giquel a bit of a nuisance. There were other 'old China-hands', too, hanging round the Paris Legation, whose dislike for Macartney probably arose from a sense of thwarted rivalry, especially now that not only the authorities in Saigon, but the metropolitan government itself was beginning to show signs of awakening interest in Eastern Asia.

For at last, towards the end of the 1870s, the tide in France was flowing in favour of colonial adventure. The Conservative governments coming to power after the disaster of 1870 had been deterred from taking any but the most cautious line. Then in 1879, they yielded place to the moderate Republicans whose leader, Gambetta, saw in overseas expansion the key to the national future. Developing industries clamoured for markets and intellectual circles manifested an ever greater concern with the countries of Asia. Thanks largely to the enthusiasm of men like Garnier, France headed the world in the pursuit of geographical science. In 1878, advantage was taken of the Paris Exibition to hold the first international conference of Commercial Geography.

In October 1879, the French Naval Minister Admiral Jauréguiberry, a veteran of the Vietnamese war of 1858–62, addressed to his colleague, the Minister of Foreign Affairs, a memorandum of great historical significance. He drew attention to the fact that the Treaty of 1874 was for all practical purposes a nullity, as had been convincingly demonstrated by the Vietnamese Court's appeal to China, and not to France, to restore order in Tongking. The Red River remained closed to foreign shipping. Diplomatic approaches to Hue would be worse than useless. Military intervention was the only means of changing the situation for the better. A force of six thousand men, half of whom could be native militia from Cochinchina, would in all probability be welcomed by the people of Tongking, who were only too anxious to be rid both of the mandarins and of the Chinese, and it was reasonable to hope that the commercial advantages, added to what could be raised by taxation and customs dues, would go a long way towards meeting the cost of such an expedition.

It will be noticed that old mirage of a Tongking panting for French intervention had lost none of its appeal. Indeed in the late 1870s there was a revival in the French press of news stories, emanating from North Vietnam, describing in detail the pitiful condition of the population of that region, and in particular the slave trade in women and children carried on by Chinese pirates. These reported activities, it was alleged, formed more than sufficient grounds for action by a Christian and civilized power. Here it may be said in parenthesis that Macartney told the British Foreign Office that 'none but the French seem to have found the pirates in Tongking especially troublesome', but he was presumably referring to piracy against shipping on the high seas: there is little question that the domestic situation between the Red River and the Chinese frontier must have been unutterably wretched, and even the Chinese accounts make it clear that Chinese banditti played a main part in the traffic in women. The very eagerness of Liu Yung-fu to throw the blame for such crimes on the shoulders of his rivals, the Yellow Flags, suggests that he and his men were just as bad. So long as France claimed the Treaty of 1874 had given her a protectorate, it could be argued that further abstention would be dishonourable. Early in 1880, rumours of impending action were so persistent that the Marquis Tseng, in an interview with the French Minister of Foreign Affairs, had inquired whether there were any matters likely to provoke a conflict between France and the King in Vietnam: he felt justified in asking, he said, because Vietnam was a vassal of China. The Minister, however, at once denied the existence of any problems which could create such a conflict. and Tseng accepted the assurance. Yet the rumours continued, and became louder than ever, so that Tseng, urged on we may be sure by Macartney, tackled the French again, and this time in writing. On November 10, 1880, from St Petersburg, he addressed to the Minister of Foreign Affairs in Paris (the successor of the man he had spoken to a few months earlier, French cabinet changes being confusingly frequent), a letter in which, after referring to the assurance he had been given he went on:

'According to more recent information, it would appear that France intends to send, or has already sent, troops to Tongking. I therefore have the honour to ask your Excellency to be so kind as to let me know whether this information is correct and whether since my interview with your predecessor the intentions of the French Government have undergone a change.

'I need not tell Your Excellency that the Chinese Government could not look with indifference on operations which would tend to alter the political situation of a country on its frontier, like the Kingdom of Tongking, whose ruler down to the present day has received his investiture from the Emperor of China.'

The French reply, which was not sent till the end of December 1880, states:

'Our relations with Tongking are laid down by the Treaty concluded 15 March 1874 between the French Republic and Vietnam of which as you are aware, Tongking is a dependency.

'In virtue of article 2 of this solemn Treaty, France recognized the entire independence of the ruler of Vietnam as regards any foreign power, promised him aid and assistance, and undertook to give him all the support necessary to maintain peace and order in his dominions, and finally to defend him against any attack. I should add that the same Treaty placed European interests in Vietnam under the protection of France.

'The Treaty of which I have just mentioned the principal

clauses was communicated at the time to the various governments it might concern. The Chinese Court, in particular, was notified through the French Legation in Peking. Since then, the relations between the French Government and Vietnam are defined with sufficient precision, and I have no doubt that my predecessor, in the interview to which you refer, gave you an explanation perfectly in accordance with the text of the Treaty which fixes the rights and the obligations of France. In my turn, I am happy to assure you that the French Government intends to conform with the requirements of the Treaty of 1874 and to fulfill the obligations which may result from it.

'The French Government readily understands the interest which the Court of Peking, like ourselves, has in the maintenance of order in a country on the frontier of the Celestial Empire, and it will direct all its efforts to see that no difficulty or misunderstanding is caused on this point between France and the Imperial Chinese Government.'

There followed a lull in the correspondence: very likely the Marquis was absorbed by the negotiations with Russia. Meanwhile, a fresh source of irritation for Paris was the dispatch by Hue of yet another tribute mission to Peking. This routine event had occurred once already after the conclusion of the Treaty of 1874, and the establishment, as the French claimed, of their protectorate over Vietnam. That had been in 1877: the French representative at Hue had asked the envoys whether they would pay a call on the French Legation in Peking, and they said they would if the Chinese agreed. In fact they never went near the place, and the French did not take the matter further. When in the autumn of 1880 it was announced that preparations for another mission were under way, Paris cabled Saigon to exert pressure to stop its departure, but the message arrived too late, as the envoys had by then crossed the frontier. Carrying their gifts of precious woods, silks, satins rhinoceros horns and elephants' tusks, they went at a leisurely pace, not reaching Peking till July 1881. A humble memorial stated that the King of Vietnam prostrated himself before the Emperor of China, while the mountains and rivers of his country stood still to await the commands of the Celestial Dynasty.

It is a remarkable fact, and very illuminating as to the essentially passive attitude both in Peking and Hue, that neither government thought it worth while to depart from precedent by maintaining permanent diplomatic relations. A suggestion to this effect was made in the winter of 1881 by the Marquis Tseng in a dispatch to his own Foreign Office. He wrote:

'Over and above the regular tribute mission, Vietnam should send one of its senior officials who understands Chinese and is well acquainted with political affairs, to reside permanently in Peking and report back to his own government. [At the same time, to show that he was fully aware that changes in Vietnam's inter-national relations were inevitable, he went on] the French are always arguing that the Red River was opened to commerce by Treaty, and that the agreement has not yet been carried out. Now China can well refuse to recognize this France-Vietnamese Treaty, but such a refusal is not possible to Vietnam. We should urge Vietnam boldly to open the Red River, but without referring to the Treaty. Instead, the western nations ought to be told that the river has been opened to the trade of all countries in conformity with the command of China. This news would convince the various countries of China's power to arbitrate, and they would see the sympathy which exists between ourselves and the Vietnamese.'

Typically, Li Hung-chang poured cold water on both of these proposals. About the same time, in the course of a conversation with Monsieur Bourée, the French Minister in Peking, Li made the following observation which is all the more significant if we bear in mind that he had already dropped a hint of exactly the same kind to Thomas Wade on the subject of Burma:

'Vietnam has been a Chinese dependency for a long while. If France intends to gobble it up, China cannot let the thing pass in silence. It would be only reasonable to let us know in advance. Our government is much concerned about this matter.'[20]

For once, even the resolute Tseng showed some tendency to compromise, when on his way back from Russia he stopped off in Paris to see the Foreign Minister. After stressing that 'China is as determined to protect Vietnam as she is to protect one of her own provinces,' he weakened the effect of his words by adding:

'Of course China cannot recognize the Franco-Vietnamese Treaty of 1874. However, if France's sole intention is to trade with Vietnam and she has no further aims, then China can tolerate that Vietnam has made a private agreement. China has no wish to interfere with established French rights or to make France lose face.'

In his dispatches home he complains of excessive fatigue at this period, and the strain of his recent efforts at St Petersburg may well explain this rather muted warning. Nevertheless, his repeated declarations that China did not recognize the Treaty were taken seriously enough to induce the celebrated Gambetta, who in the game of political musical chairs landed for a couple of months the post of Foreign Minister, to write to him on New Year's Day 1882, reminding him that the text of the Treaty had been communicated to the Chinese Government in 1875, and triumphantly quoting from Prince Kung's reply at the time to the French representative in Peking to demonstrate that China acquiesced in the French claim. The words Gambetta relied on certainly did convey such an idea. Prince Kung had remarked, according to the translation furnished by the French Legation, that 'Vietnam was formerly a Chinese dependency'. This mention of history, said Gambetta, in no way constituted an objection to the Treaty, and France could not now, all these years after the event, take cognizance of any belated protests. Only then did Tseng become aware that in addition to other failures of understanding, the French interpreter had bungled his translation, for the original Chinese words read plainly 'Vietnam has been for a long time a Chinese dependency,' and refer not to a closed chapter of history but to a state of affairs which continues to exist. When confronted with the evidence, even the French had to admit to the blunder, but the situation had deteriorated too far to be retrieved.[21]

In that winter of 1881–2, while the Marquis Tseng was fighting on the diplomatic front to assert China's rights in Tongking, another champion whose very name was by now synonymous with the same cause was making a pilgrimage of filial duty. It was sixteen years since Liu Yung-fu had set foot on Chinese soil. He had fled from Kwangsi an outlaw with a price on his head, scarcely knowing how or where he and his followers would find their next meal. Today, the ex-bandit was an official of the Vietnamese state and, what was even more surprising, held a commission from the Chinese authorities. The Black Flags and their chieftain were a household word throughout Tongking, but now he owed it to the memory of his parents to let them share in his glory. He must go and sweep their graves, as the Chinese phrase expresses it.

Once across the frontier it was a triumphal progress: the Kwangsi peasantry flocked from far and wide to gape at the hero, while the mandarins vied with one another in the lavishness of their entertainment. Away in Saigon, the colonial authorities watched the excitement with foreboding. Strangely enough for a people themselves much given to ritual grave-visiting, they could not credit their formidable enemy with sentiments of family piety, and decided that his purpose must be to attract recruits for his band. In fact Liu's activities were exclusively religious and social. He bought land near his parents' burial-place, and started to plan the building of a house to which he could eventually retire. Meanwhile there was the necessity of communicating the glad tidings to the dead. This was frequently done in China, since official honours were deemed to reflect a lustre on the holder's ancestors, who must therefore be informed of their descendant's achievement. To pass on the news was simplicity itself. All you had to do was to write a letter to the deceased on a special kind of yellow paper, by setting fire to which you dispatched the message from this world to the next. When Liu had done this, he assumed not unreasonably that jollity and high spirits were the order of the day. Troups of actors summoned in advance to this remote spot performed in relays day and night for forty-eight hours. Upwards of one thousand spectators sat down to alfresco banquets on the hillside, and told one another that Kwangsi had never witnessed such princely hospitality. The festivities were at their height when a messenger arrived from the Vietnamese frontier town of Langson. Liu's presence was urgently needed in Tongking, for after more than eight years the French were invading again. It was the month of April 1882.

CHAPTER TWELVE

Henri Rivière— Tragedy Repeated

FOR the past three years, since 1879, the colony of Cochin-china had had its first civilian governor. Charles Marie Le Myre de Vilers, aged forty-six at the time of his appointment, had indeed spent some years of his youth in the navy, but had resigned as long ago as 1861 to enter the administrative service, in which he had gradually mounted the ladder of promotion to reach the position of Director of Civilian and Financial Affairs in Algeria. On going to Saigon, he had been given particular instructions to keep his eye on Tongking and to try to devise a way of remedying the unsatisfactory situation there. He had now made up his mind to intervene, but to do so without coming into armed conflict either with Hue or with Peking. As he saw it, the real enemy thwarting France in her design of opening the Red River was the Black Flags. There was no way to cope with them without using force, but if sufficient prudence were employed, the fighting could be restricted to a simple police action. For instance, at high water, the encampments from which Liu Yung-fu and his men controlled the river could be shelled from gunboats, without landing soldiers to go inviting disaster in the jungle. The only trouble was that it was essential that the expedition should be commanded by an officer chosen with the utmost care. What was needed was someone as unlike the impetuous Garnier as possible, a sensible, solid man quite without romantic visions of becoming the founder of a great empire in the East.

As it happened, just such an officer came to Saigon in the autumn of 1881 to take charge of the naval station. Even the physical presence of Captain Henri Laurent Rivière was re-assuring. A tall, massively-built Norman of phlegmatic manner, at fifty-four his professional advancement had not been specta-cular, and it was an open secret that his great ambition was to be known not as a leader of men but as a writer. His talents as a novelist had unlocked for him the most select literary salons, and he dreamt of the day when he would be admitted to the French Academy.

Meanwhile the shifting course of events in Paris had once more brought Admiral Jauréguiberry, the advocate of conquest in Tongking, back to his former post as Naval Minister, and although he considered Le Myre de Vilers a partisan of half measures, he approved the latter's plan for the time being. On March 26, 1882, Rivière sailed from Saigon with two ships and two hundred and thirty men, ostensibly to strengthen the garrison of the concession at Hanoi. The instructions he carried impressed upon him the importance of abstaining from all use of force except in case of absolute necessity. A war of conquest was totally ruled out. The Black Flags were to be considered as pirates, but even so if any of them should fall into French hands they were on no account to be put to death. On the contrary, to display Rivière's solicitude for human life, they were to be sent to Saigon as a prelude to their internment on the island of Poulo-Condore. If Chinese regular troops were encountered, all care was to be taken to avoid a conflict. On April 2, 1882, having made an uneventful transit up the river, the expedition arrived at Hanoi.

The Treaty of 1874 had restricted the number of the French garrison to one hundred men, and the apparition of this flotilla was inexplicable to the local mandarins except as the spearhead of a fresh invasion, for no matter what the excuse, the newcomers were by their presence plainly violating the agreement. A visit of courtesy which Rivière paid to the Vietnamese governor at the citadel did nothing to ease the tension: throughout the interview the captain was watching out of the corner of his eye a couple of herculean servants who would, he was convinced, have strangled him on the spot at a word from their master. There were war-elephants, too, in the courtyard, which had been trained to trample men to death. Altogether he breathed more freely when he was back within his own lines, but soon he had another cause for complaint. The governor refused to venture out of the citadel to return his call. Still worse, the defences of the place were being reinforced by the summoning of troops from the countryside and the renovation of those parts of the fortification which showed signs of dilapidation.

Le Myre de Vilers would have been astounded if he had seen the effect of Tongking on the phlegmatic Norman. It was remarked that once he set foot on the classic ground of Garnier's triumph and death, the fiery spirit of his predecessor seemed to take possession of him. Not only was the obstinacy of the Vietnamese an insolence to be castigated, he could see that the preparations going forward in the fortress were capable of being used for attack as well as for defence: these things were unendurable. On April 25th, heartened by the arrival the day before of another two hundred and fifty French troops, Rivière served an ultimatum on the governor, requiring the immediate surrender of the citadel. When this remained unanswered, the French ships opened fire under cover of which a storming column moved up for the assault, carrying scaling ladders with them. In two hours the exploit of Garnier had been repeated and the citadel was in French hands. The victors had only four men wounded. The unfortunate governor had avoided captivity by hanging himself. After so brisk a morning's work, Rivière was exhausted: a good stretch on the matting in the governor's quarters and a bucket of cold water emptied over his head refreshed him for a triumphal luncheon at which he ate a whole chicken.

Still, he was well aware that the news of his achievement would be an unpleasant shock to the man who had entrusted him with his mission. He was quite right. Le Myre de Vilers seethed with anger and for a moment toyed with the notion of recalling him. However, the ill feeling at Saigon was somewhat appeased by the information that less than a week after seizing the citadel Rivière had returned most of it to Vietnamese occupation, and had pulled down the tricolour in favour of the flag of Hue. The French kept the heart of the fortress, called the 'Royal Pavilion', in their own hands, and ensured that the Vietnamese should be so lightly armed as not to pose a threat to their security.

Meanwhile, at the first word of Rivière's arrival, the supreme representative of the Vietnamese government in Tongking, the King's relative, Prince Hoang, dispatched from his headquarters in Sontay the message which, as we saw in the last chapter, disturbed Liu Yung-fu's holiday at his old home in Kwangsi. Liu obeyed the summons at once, but when in a matter of days he appeared all travel-stained in the Prince's presence, the interview was less than agreeable. Liu spoke far more freely than he had ever ventured to do before. It was quite true, he said, that as the holder of a commission from King Tu Duc he was under an obligation of loyalty. But he had a duty to his men, too, who were grumbling that the Court of Hue, and for that matter the Prince himself, seemed unconscious of their existence until an emergency made their service necessary. As regards money and supplies they had been more or less abandoned to their own devices. It was really not good enough. The Prince was unaccustomed to being addressed in these terms and had difficulty in containing his resentment. All he could think of answering was that he had a mass of things to attend to, and that in consequence it was inevitable that certain problems should have been overlooked—an excuse so fatuous that Liu, who was probably inflamed by his own eloquence, curtly took his leave, and shortly afterwards set off up river to his stronghold of Laokay from where, in morose silence, he watched the situation develop.

About this time there were rumours in Chinese circles that the French entertained the idea of bribing Liu to change sides, and it is not unlikely that he himself had conquered his instinctive aversion to Europeans sufficiently to contemplate such an eventuality. By now, also, it must have been clear to him that the Vietnamese government was powerless to retrieve the situation. If he had any hopes of being invited to turn his coat, however, he was disappointed, for there is no evidence that any offer of the sort was made and indeed French sources suggest that a feeler from Liu was refused. Still, whatever the cause, there was during the summer and autumn of 1882 an unnatural calm in Tongking. Rivière had contented himself with a brief reconnaissance by gunboat of the Red River for a distance of forty or fifty miles upstream from Hanoi, but after this single outing, which lasted for three days at

15 General de Négrier

General Feng Tzu-ts'ai

16 French soldiers march towards Langson, 1884

The battle at Langson

the beginning of June, he stayed quietly in the citadel, cursing the heat and whiling away the tedium as best he could with his writing, and with nightly roulette parties.

What signs of activity there were came not from Vietnam but from China. At last the warnings of the Marquis Tseng, confirmed as they now were by the present French seizure of Hanoi, were having some effect on official circles and to a varying extent at the Court itself. In June 1882, the Marquis's uncle, Tseng Kuo-ch'uan, was named Viceroy of Kwangtung and Kwangsi, an appointment which meant that a stalwart of the Hunan group was immediately concerned with Sino-Vietnamese relations. The provincial armies of Yunnan and Kwangsi began once more to move over the frontier, alleging that the state of banditry in the border area made police action unavoidable. These events were observed by the world at large, but another occurrence just as fraught with consequences passed unnoticed by foreign eyes in the autumn of that same year.

Among the mandarins in Peking was an assistant-secretary in the Board of Civil Office named T'ang Ching-sung. As a native of Kwangsi he was inquisitive about Vietnamese affairs, and he had contrived to strike up an acquaintance with the members of the tribute-missions from Hue. It was in this way that he heard of the exploits of Liu Yung-fu. When he learned besides that the hero was of Hakka stock like himself, he began to take a kind of proprietary interest in the Black Flags and their achievements. In August 1882, encouraged by some colleagues, he made bold to submit his view in a memorial to the Throne. The document was two thousand characters in length and was composed, in the heroic Chinese mode, after a session of drinking, but the ideas it expressed were anything but confused; on the contrary they could only have come from a particularly sharp intelligence.[22]

South Vietnam, said T'ang, had been in French hands for years: today the foreigners had designs on Tongking, the shield which guarded the way through Yunnan to the provinces of western and central China. Talk of international law was futile. The Vietnamese forces, both officers and men, were useless. So far, the French had been thwarted only by the Black Flags. It might well be said that Liu Yung-fu was once a bandit, but after years among the Vietnamese who had tried to tempt him into their service, he showed his true feelings by his insistence upon wearing Chinese dress. He must be longing for more recognition from his own country. What harm would there be, for example, in sending a mission to him with a message of felicitation from the Throne? At the same time he could be advised that the most effectual way of frustrating French intentions would be not to try and rescue Hanoi directly, but rather to lead his band towards Saigon. Even if he did not succeed in taking that city, he would plunge the southern provinces into such chaos that the French would be obliged to abandon Tongking altogether and concentrate their strength on the defence of their base in Cochinchina. The original two thousand Black Flags had been recently increased by numbers of their old enemies from the now dispersed Yellow Flags. Furthermore, there were still many Chinese banditti in Tongking: would it not be more profitable, instead of organizing periodic expeditions to suppress them, to encourage them into casting in their lot with Liu and marching to the south?

The memorial succeeded in what was obviously its chief purpose. Early in September 1882, T'ang was posted to the staff of Ts'en Yu-ying, Viceroy of Yunnan and Kweichow, with the responsibility of treating with the Black Flags. Instead of going overland, he decided to travel via Hong Kong and Vietnam. Setting out late in September 1882 he did not reach Hong Kong till the end of November. His delay was caused principally by the irresistible pleasures of Shanghai; for by the 1880s that port was already in many respects the cultural capital of China, a role it was to fill until the Communist victory in 1949. As early as the Taiping war, the security of the foreign settlements had attracted numerous men of letters, and now, twenty years later, it was the centre of the publishing world and the favourite rendezvous of mandarins in transit between the Yangtze Valley and Peking. The choicest singing-girls—and the hinterland of Shanghai is cele- brated for its beautiful women—flocked to entertain so generous a clientele. Chefs specializing in the cuisine of particular provinces offered treats for the palate such as none of the wretched chop-suey parlours masquerading today in the west as Chinese restaurants can give the faintest idea—though as often as not the fashionable man-about-town would prefer to treat his mistress to a European dinner washed down with champagne. For a blissful month, T'ang savoured these delights as tradition taught him he should, omitting no opportunity of commemorating a drinking-party in elegant verse, and it is hard to credit him when he tells us that he was all the while consumed with anxiety to continue his voyage and was detained solely by the necessity of adjusting his finances. Curiously, he was paying his own way, and had to negotiate loans from friends and correspondents en route.

From Hong Kong, T'ang went directly the few miles up river to Canton, where he remained for a fortnight, seeing the Viceroy Tseng Kuo-ch'uan nearly every day. Tseng, who completely shared his nephew's opinions on the necessity of resisting the French, charmed his visitor by telling him that his memorial to the Throne, the text of which was already known in the South, was the best thing of its kind for thirty years. Even more to the point, he advanced T'ang a substantial sum of money and made arrangements for him to receive more if necessary from the China Merchants, a shipping company with agents on the Vietnamese coast. Thus provided for, and passing himself off as a trader, T'ang boarded a steamer in Hong Kong and after three days' uneventful journey transferred to a sampan at the mouth of the River of Perfumes, and was rowed upstream to Hue, past gun emplacements on the banks and barriers ready to be thrown across the water at a moment's warning.

He had come prepared to receive an unfavourable impression of the country and his forebodings were confirmed. The first offence to his eye was given by the officials at the customs, with gowns reaching only to the knees, and with bare feet, which they were constantly scratching, thrust into heelless slippers. He noticed that his sampan was rowed by women, a phenomenon which he could have observed equally at Hong Kong, and decided on the spot that the Vietnamese men were lazy good-for-nothings. The next morning, he announced his arrival to the Board of Rites, who were already aware of his coming, disclosing his status of mandarin. His announcement received a gratifying response, for almost immediately he was visited by one of the most important ministers of the realm, Nguyen Van Thuong, a man of sixty-three who in the good Confucian manner had risen from obscurity by way of the examination hall, and whose son had married a niece of the King. The pair communicated by means of what was called 'pen-talk', that is to say they expressed their ideas in written Chinese, the universal language of the traditional Far Eastern world. One might have supposed that T'ang would have been touched by this solicitude, but on the contrary all he was conscious of was his visitor's lack of frankness. When he told of the feeling in Peking that Vietnam ought on no account to be bullied or cajoled into accepting a French protectorate, and that Liu and the Black Flags should be employed to the full, all he got in reply was non-committal hemming and hawing, and he said to himself that a king who chose such a man as his chief minister must himself be a pretty wretched sort of monarch. In fact it soon became clear that Tu Duc, though courteously presenting the newcomer with a whole roast pig, would on no account grant him an audience, alleging, according to T'ang's diary, that it would be too dangerous if the matter reached French ears, though T'ang elsewhere admitted that the reason for the rebuff was that he had not been accredited as envoy. Seeing that there was nothing to be gained by staying in Hue, and feeling that the place had little to recommend it—the largest Vietnamese houses seemed to him no more than bamboo huts without proper beds or furniture—he set off inside a week to make his way along the coast to Haiphong from where he would try his luck at penetrating to Laokay and the Black Flags. After a deplorable journey, partly on a craft laden with buffalo-dung, so that he never knew whether his nausea came from the stench or from the rough sea, he was met at Haiphong by a piece of news that made him decide to abandon his mission altogether.

What had happened was that Monsieur Bourée, the French Minister to China, had become alarmed by the reports of troop movements from Kwangsi and Yunnan on the Tongking border, and decided to withdraw from Peking to Shanghai for the winter. While passing through Tientsin in November 1882, he conferred with Li Hung-chang and together they devised, in a remarkably short space of time, what they considered was a masterly solution of the problem. The memorandum presenting their conclusions declared that the one aim of France in Tongking was the opening of the Red River to commerce as far as the Chinese border. To achieve this, it was proposed that Laokay should be a Chinese customs station, through which traffic in goods should pass to and from Yunnan: in effect this seemed to transfer Laokay from Vietnamese to Chinese jurisdiction. It was recognised that the great obstacle to commerce was the bandit-ridden condition of Tongking, and as a means of remedying this, it was suggested that a line of demarcation should be drawn half-way between the Chinese frontier and the Red River. North of the line China would exercise a protectorate for the purpose of restoring order, while France played an identical role to the south; in the meantime, Chinese troops at present over the border should retire, a stipulation which could only be reconciled with the other provisions if interpreted in the sense of withdrawal from any points nearer to the river than to their own land.

Although these proposals were accompanied by the French Minister's fervent denials that his country harboured even the faintest intention of conquest in Vietnam, the facts spoke for themselves, and it was plain that if this was to be the policy of China, T'ang was simply wasting his time. In the worst possible temper, he caught the first boat sailing to Hong Kong, and from there retraced his steps to Canton.

He had expected to find Tseng Kuo-ch'uan as downcast as himself, but the Viceroy's mood was one of indignation rather than despondency. All was not lost. In spite of Li Hung-chang, the government at Peking had not yet ratified the proposed agreement, and it was the duty of every good Chinese to see that the plot came to nothing. T'ang in particular must draft another memorial to the Throne, which the Viceroy would have telegraphed at once. T'ang needed no encouragement to expound his views. He had now seen with his own eyes the state of Vietnam and could testify that under its present government nothing could save it. Yet if the country was indeed to disappear from the map, then China must refuse to be satisfied with the miserable strip of borderland which had been assigned to her. The whole of Tongking, as far south as Than-Hoa, beyond the Red River delta, must pass under her control: anything less would place her southern provinces in danger. France, however, was certain to reject such a suggestion, nor would the Vietnamese themselves willingly acquiesce. One was forced after all by the logic of circumstances to the conclusion that the only possiblity of avoiding an open war with France, while safe-guarding China's interest, was to give discreet assistance to the Black Flags to enable them not only to stand firm on the Red River but also in due course to make their presence felt in South Vietnam.

When a memorial in these terms had been dispatched to Peking, it was obviously high time for T'ang to resume the mission he had prematurely abandoned. Returning to Haiphong, he made his way north to the town of Langson, adjacent to the border of Kwangsi, where he found Chinese troops who had been withdrawn from further south in order to be in the vicinity of their own frontier. At least part of the Li-Boureé agreement was being put into effect. Laokay, however, stayed firmly in the hands of Liu Yung-fu and T'ang sent a courier there to announce that as an accredited representative of Peking he was anxious to confer with his famous countryman: meanwhile, he said, he would await Liu's answer at Sontay; and the Chinese commander lent him an escort to go there. On his arrival, towards the end of March 1883, he had his first glimpse of the celebrated company whose name had been haunting his imagination for so long, for a detachment of Black Flags, under two of Liu's most trusted lieutenants, maintained their old encampment immediately outside the city. But his first visit was to the senior Vietnamese commander in Tongking, Prince Hoang, who seemed genuinely delighted to see him, admitting frankly that nothing he himself could say or do was having the slightest effect on Liu, who was still sulking as he had been for months. It was all the more vexatious in that Rivière in Hanoi was at long last on the move again.

It would have been a relief to T'ang, as he sat twiddling his thumbs at Sontay, cursing the damp heat which—as he noticed with horror—was causing mould to sprout on his bedding, and kept awake at night by the largest and fiercest mosquitoes he had ever encountered, had he but known that the hateful agreement of Tientsin, which had cast so blighting a shadow over all his hopes, was already stone dead, killed by the French themselves. A month earlier, in February 1883, Jules Ferry the great advocate of imperialism in the British manner, had formed his second government in Paris, and the mere suggestion, to one who was to go down to history as 'the Tongkingese', that France should condescend to bargain with China about a province destined by providence to be ruled by the tricolour, was sufficient to provoke an explosion of rage. Poor cautious Monsieur Bourée was informed by cable that his diplomacy was repudiated by his superiors and that having demonstrated his unfitness to represent his country, he must come home and face the music. He lingered on in Shanghai and Peking until June, complaining to his intimates that policy in Paris was being dictated by unscrupulous profiteers and speculators. He was probably thinking of men like Dupuis, who after years of frustration in the waiting-rooms of government offices, was now coming into his own, with the firm promise of compensation from the future revenues of Tongking. In Saigon, too, the prudent Le Myre de Vilers had been replaced by a Monsieur Thomson, whose Anglo-Saxon name was an appropriate augury for the new dispensation. In February 1883, on the heels of Ferry's accession to power, Rivière, strengthened by reinforcements amounting to seven hundred and fifty soldiers, demonstrated how his masters in Paris were thinking by occupying the port of Hongay, some distance north-eastwards along the coast from Haiphong. This operation put the French in control of a valuable coalfield, for which they alleged that the British, behind the façade of a Chinese company, were planning to acquire the mining rights.

Despite the refusal of the Black Flags to cooperate, Prince Hoang had not been idle during the past few months. One of the chief points towards which his activity had been directed was the fortification of Nam-Dinh, a town near the mouth of the southern channel of the Red River, where the Vietnamese, if they took proper advantage of its situation, could impede the passage of ships. French vessels were restricted by the Treaty of 1874 to the northern branch of the river, so Rivière was not justified in complaining that this was a threat to his communications with the sea. As the French intentions became manifest, the Vietnamese felt that a stiffening of Chinese was necessary among the local garrison, and although thanks to Liu Yung-fu's bad temper the best auxiliaries were not available, there was no lack of miscellaneous adventurers from Kwangsi and Kwangtung willing to fight on the terms offered and a corps of some five hundred mercenaries came into being, who looked warlike enough to make their paymasters hope that perhaps Liu was not after all so indispensable as he imagined.

When at length Rivière did attack, he came with quite an armada, consisting of eight gunboats and other craft, and eight hundred troops. In the style which had by now become customary, he sent to the governor of the town an ultimatum, declaring that French honour and security as well as the cause of peace in general required that Nam-Dinh should be surrendered. When the demand was rejected, the squadron opened fire, and the next day, March 27, 1883, the French troops, who included a detachment of Cochinchinese riflemen, went ashore. The defenders, overwhelmed by the invaders' artillery, clung so tenaciously to their positions that it was evening before the tricolour flew over the citadel. As the attackers moved up behind the bombardment, their losses were astonishingly light; only three of their number were wounded, one mortally. The resistance, however, infuriated Rivière, and finding some fifty of the Chinese mercenaries had fallen into his hands, he ordered them to be strung up at the yard-arm of his ships. Granted that he was convinced that the wretches must belong to the detested Black Flags, even so he had been specially instructed by Le Myre de Vilers to demonstrate French humanity by sparing their lives, and this example, set by a cultivated man-of-letters, gave warning that a new phase of savagery was beginning. Soon such events were to become commonplace. One of the most generous and sensitive of the French officers, Captain Gosselin, who without the least trace of hypocrisy, remembering the fate of the Australian blackfellows, congratulates Vietnam on her good fortune in not finding herself under the odious rule of the British, tells us that, some years later when the war of conquest had entered its final stage, he witnessed without any emotion whatsoever the shooting or beheading of 'a very large number' of Vietnamese prisoners—although in France he would hate to be present at a public execution, and even in Algeria he lay awake for hours the night before he had to superintend the shooting of two Arabs. The same authority reveals that a certain colonel instructed his subordinates to 'make sure that orders to send rebel leaders in custody to headquarters are always received too late'. Another French officer, discovering that one of his prisoners was an ex-Catholic who had strayed so far from grace that he had resisted the soldiers of Christ, sent the man a confessor. The priest performed his duty successfully and when a few hours later the prisoner's head was hacked from his shoulders the officer, 'a convinced believer', spoke of the consolation he felt in having helped 'to open the gates of Heaven to a criminal who would certainly never have found such a chance again.'[13]

The fall of Nam-Dinh was a shattering blow to any hope the Vietnamese had of managing without Liu Yung-fu. There could be little doubt that before long Rivière would turn his attention to Sontay itself, the key of the entire delta, and in fact French sloops were constantly chugging up river from Hanoi to observe the fortress from a distance. Then at the beginning of April, with flourish of trumpets and waving of banners, the hero on whom everything depended turned up in person to greet the mandarin from Peking.

Liu Yung-fu was at this time forty-six years of age. It may be remembered that he had entered Vietnam in order, among other reasons, to avoid an unwelcome marriage, but since then he had taken a wife—one of his own countrywomen—who had given him two sons. He was above the middle height and exceedingly lean, with prominent cheekbones that, to T'ang's eyes, 'made him look like a monkey'. This simian cast of features is distinctly noticeable in all the pictures we have of him. He remained as illiterate as ever, though by now he scarcely felt this as a handicap, since he could afford a secretary who knelt at a low table in front of him and took down his dictation. In spite of his want of schooling, he affected some fastidiousness in composition, and was never satisfied until the appropriate words had been found to express his thoughts.

T'ang commenced the acquaintance on the right footing by entertaining Liu to dinner, during which the two of them talked about everything but what had brought them together. Much wine was consumed, and we can infer from the last dish that in spite of the rough-and-ready circumstances the menu was quite adequate, since, instead of rice, dinner ended with a bowl of congee, a common habit of the Chinese when they have enjoyed an elaborate meal of many courses. The ice thus broken, the real business in hand was discussed tête-à-tête later. If we are to believe Liu, T'ang told him directly that the present dynasty of Vietnam was quite obviously doomed. If the country was not to pass into French hands, Liu must act without delay, killing if necessary any Vietnamese official who opposed him, and declare himself King: Vietnam would thus remain a vassal of China. T'ang could confirm that the Court in Peking was of the same way of thinking. T'ang's account of the conversation is substantially different, and since he committed his impressions to a diary on the spot, he is more trustworthy than Liu, who dictated his recollections many years after the events, when, for reasons we shall see, he had fallen out with T'ang. Yet even T'ang admits having advised Liu that his best plan would be to gather under his banner all the Chinese banditti in the region, as well as any Vietnamese with a taste for adventure, and consolidate his power in Tongking. He could then ask Peking to enfeoff him, and, fortified by imperial recognition, advance on the South. T'ang added: 'If you succeed you will be a king. Even if you fail, you will be a hero who defended the Chinese frontier.' We need not attach too much importance to Liu's description of his pious remonstrances regarding his loyalty towards King Tu Duc. More credible is his objection, as quoted in T'ang's diary, that if he attempted such an exploit, the Vietnamese would at once join hands with the French to oppose him.

It is hard to discover the truth among the obscure and contradictory stories of this transaction, but there is no doubt that Liu must have been considerably impressed by the visit of a genuine civil mandarin from a Peking ministry, a man of incomparably higher social prestige than those military officers, as a rule scarcely more cultivated than himself, who in the past were the representatives of Chinese authority with whom he had most to do. At any rate, he was speedily talked into a reconciliation with Prince Hoang, condescending to wear for the occasion the knee-length gown of a Vietnamese functionary; and when, in the middle of April, T'ang left Sontay to rejoin the Kwangsi provincial troops which were now occupying Bac-Ninh, between Sontay and the Chinese border, the Black Flags saw him off with quasi-regal gifts of ivory and rhinoceros-horn. They themselves then advanced to the town of Phu-Hoai, lying a few miles west of Hanoi, where they established their temporary headquarters.

Rivière meanwhile was preparing for the expedition against Sontay, which he recognized could not be delayed much longer. Eighteen months of the Vietnamese climate had had a disastrous effect on his health. His bulky frame was ravaged with dysentery so that he could no longer mount a horse—an animal which in any case as a naval man he held in small esteem—and the activity of a campaign offered the prospect of almost unendurable hardship. Nevertheless he was anxious to be up and doing, since victory in the field would bring the end of his exile all the nearer. As a final goad, there came on May 10th a challenge from Liu Yung-fu, in the form of a proclamation, placarded during the night on one of the gates of Hanoi fort. It ran:

'The warrior Liu declares to the French: Other nations despise you. You have the character of wild animals. Since you have been in Vietnam, you have seized citadels and massacred mandarins. These crimes deserve death: Heaven will not forgive you.

'Today I have been commanded to wage war. My soldiers are as numerous as the clouds. My flags and my lances darken the sky. My rifles and my swords are as many as the trees of the forest. But I have no wish to turn the city of Hanoi into a battlefield, and to ruin its people. That is why I am making this proclamation to the French who are plundering this country. If you are strong enough, you will send your men to Phu-Hoai to fight with my terrible soldiers, and see who is the better.

'If you are afraid to come, cut off the heads of your Commander-in-Chief and of your officers and send them to me! After that surrender the citadel and return to Europe! I shall then be able to forgive you. But if you delay, I shall come to find you wherever you may be and I shall kill all of you. Life is next door to death. Think carefully!'

As if to emphasize these menaces, the Black Flags dispatched advance parties into the countryside between Phu-Hoai and Hanoi and took special pleasure in sacking a Christian settlement. Under cover of darkness, they even bombarded Hanoi itself with cannon that had been carried on the backs of elephants. Rivière had the sensation of being cooped up behind walls and decided, as one of his followers put it, to treat himself to a little fresh air. The excursion was discussed in so free-and-easy a style that all the servants in the officers' mess were acquainted with the plan of action, and word of it was carried to Liu Yung-fu. At daybreak on May 19, 1883, four hundred and fifty French troops marched off along the road towards Phu-Hoai in the best of spirits, laughing and singing. Rivière accompanied them, but in view of his debility permitted himself the luxury of a carriage. They had gone only a few hundred yards when Chinese were glimpsed behind the bamboos which bordered the road. Rivière apparently assumed that these could only be scouts, and gave orders that the column should advance with all speed so that the main body of the enemy would not have time to escape. One of his officers ventured to remonstrate with him on the risk of such a movement, but he would not listen, and pressed ahead. The consequence of this impetuosity became clear a little further on, when they reached a spot called Paper Bridge, which was now to gain a sinister notoriety. Swarms of Black Flags were observed issuing from neighbouring villages, and moving as if to cut off the French in the rear. Packed close together as they were, Rivière's men made an easy target for the Chinese fire, and they halted and commenced to fall back. The field-pieces they had brought with them had been put, against all accepted practice, at the head of the troop, and one of the guns, its crew killed, seemed likely to fall into Chinese hands. Rivière descended from his carriage and, armed only with a cane, led a group of soldiers to the rescue. While struggling with the cannon, he received several bullets in the body and fell to the ground. Dismayed by the loss of their leader, and the fierceness of the assault, the French retreated to the security of the Hanoi citadel.

We do not know in what circumstances Rivière breathed his last. The French heard a story that he had merely been wounded at the bridge, and was conveyed by the Black Flags to a nearby pagoda, from which Liu Yung-fu was directing operations: just as the prisoner was being carried into his presence, Liu got word that one of his most trusted lieutenants had been killed, and in a fit of rage ordered Rivière's throat to be cut. It is a fact that Liu did lose a close friend in the battle, but what truth there is in the rest we have no means of telling. All that is certain is that the heads of Rivière and the other dead Frenchman were severed, pickled in brine, and exhibited as trophies. Next day, the French sent Chinese merchants from Hanoi to offer to ransom the corpses, and it was only then, says Liu, that he knew for certain that the dead commander was Rivière himself and not one of his staff-officers. What followed, as described by Liu, is so grotesque, that one would find it incredible, if it were not confirmed by factual evidence. It seems the rank-and-file of the Black Flags got it into their heads that an enormous sum was being offered for the body of Rivière alone, and they determined to ensure their individual participation in the reward by each acquiring a fragment of the remains. The first comers helped themselves to the fingers, but within a minute or two the process had turned into a frantic butchery, slices of flesh being carved from all parts of the body, so that when Liu found out what was happening the corpse had to all intents and purposes disintegrated, and any thought of ransom had become impracticable. Yet the French continued their efforts, till in September 1883, our old friend Bishop Puginier discovered through one of his converts the place where the Frenchmen had been buried. The heads, which had been interred separately, were exhumed first: Rivière's had been put by itself in a box, under the middle of a highway, where it would be continually walked over by man and beast. When the bodies were traced, it was learned that the Captain had in that matter also received discriminatory treatment. His companions had been thrown into mass graves, while his remains were in a shallow trench barely covered with earth. Besides the head, the hands had been severed, and the Bishop tells us that all that was left of the rest of the body was a mass of bones wrapped in a bloody shirt, from which almost every shred of flesh had been scraped away. We have heard of French atrocities: it is only fair to bear in mind the circumstances in which they were committed. In due course the bones of Rivière were transported to a family vault in the cemetery of Montmartre.[24]

The engagement of May 19, 1883 cost the French fifty dead and seventy-six wounded. Such a loss at the hands of a band of savages was hard to bear, and efforts were made, in the press and elsewhere, to suggest that the savages were not unaided in their foul work. The Black Flags were obviously well armed. Who was to be blamed for that but those enemies of mankind, the British, who in the way of business would sell weapons and ammunition to the devil himself? But even that would not explain their success. There must be Europeans fighting in their ranks, and—a sort of left-handed consolation—Frenchmen. The reading public of Paris was told that there were in Tongking French officers who could, if they chose, actually name men of their acquaintance who had deserted to the Black Flags.

Still, there it was: Rivière had been killed almost on the same spot as Garnier, and by the same foe. Ten years earlier, Garnier's death had been an embarrassment to be shrugged off as non-chalantly as possible. Things were far different now. From Paris there came a voice of thunder: 'France will revenge her glorious children.' Even so, on calm reflection, there were people, at least ordinarily patriotic, who did some heart-searching. Monsieur Rheinhart, for instance, who represented his country at the Court of Hue, opened his mind to a friend on the subject of Garnier and Rivière:

'I respect those who are dead, and admire those who fell bravely, but they have reaped what they sowed, and for both of them their adventure was bound to end badly, as it began in the English manner, that is to say treacherously. We attacked the Vietnamese in violation of all justice, and when they recovered from their surprise and defended themselves, we cried Murder! That is really too English!'[25]

It is the severest condemnation that a French mouth can utter.

CHAPTER THIRTEEN

Hue Capitulates

EVEN before the death of Rivière, the emergence of the
second Ferry government in Paris, its aggressive intentions
towards Tongking plainly evidenced by its indignant repudiation of the draft agreement reached between Li Hung-chang
and the French Minister, had alerted the Chinese authorities to the
immediacy of the crisis. At the same time, an appeal had reached
Peking from Hue, in terms that were hard to ignore, for it illustrated the plight of Vietnam by reference to another satellite
nearer at hand.

'For more than two hundred years, [wrote King Tu Duc],
my country has been a feoff of the Celestial Dynasty (i.e. the
Manchus). Every foot of its soil, every one of its inhabitants is
subordinate to the Celestial Dynasty—Today my country is
threatened by France, just as Korea is threatened by Japan. But
whereas I hear that Korea, thanks to Your support, is able to
enjoy peace, my country, being situated at a greater distance,
does not have the good fortune, which all of us long for, of being
considered as one of Your close dependencies.'

The example was an apt one. Korea and Vietnam shared in
theory an identical relationship with China, but the fact that the
former was on the very doorstep of Peking meant that it was kept
under far more vigilant surveillance by the suzerain power. Even
before the advent of the Manchus, the point had been demonstrated at the end of the sixteenth century when a Japanese army,
having invaded Korea, pushed across the Yalu River to enter
Chinese territory, and the Ming Dynasty was taught in the most

convincing manner possible that the security of its own dominions necessitated the rescue of its vassal. The lesson was taken to heart and is still remembered, as was proved in 1950 when China intervened to save North Korea from extinction by General MacArthur. In the middle of the nineteenth century it had a particular application. No sooner had Japan been compelled by the West to come to terms with the modern world, than she began to copy her mentors and to covet for herself a leading influence in the Korean peninsula. So eagerly did she pursue this, that by the 1880s, by the skilful manipulation of political factions in the country, she was bidding fair to oust the traditional Chinese hegemony. This was something which even the most harassed of Chinese governments could not acquiesce in, and in 1882 when an explosion of violence in Korea seemed about to bring matters to a head, a Chinese expeditionary force had been dispatched to the scene to retain control of the situation.

Of course, King Tu Duc was right: mere distance ensured that Vietnam could not loom so importantly as Korea in the councils of Peking. Nevertheless, by May 1883 the Chinese were impelled to do something to meet what looked like an intolerable threat to the nation's interests. From Tongking itself, messages of jubilation were coming in from the Kwangsi provincial force at Bac-Ninh praising the marvellous diplomacy of T'ang Ching-sung, who had persuaded the Black Flags to do their duty, and asking that, for the time being, instead of going to his post in Yunnan, he should be seconded as liaison officer between the Kwangsi command and Liu Yung-fu. T'ang himself was busily engaged in drafting a proclamation to be disseminated by the Black Flags, which differed from previous announcements in declaring to the world at large the inflexible determination of Liu and his followers to maintain Chinese suzerainty. The document began with a reminder that for a thousand years Vietnam had formed part of the Chinese Empire. With small regard for local sentiment it even boasted that the Ming Dynasty had brought back Chinese rule: there was no mention of the brevity of this experiment.

'During the Great Pure Dynasty (of the Manchus) [it went on], several families have ruled Vietnam in succession, but every one of them accepted the status of vassal, and regularly paid tribute. This fact is known to any lad five foot tall: are the French the only ones never to have heard of it? To wage war on Vietnam is equivalent to waging war on China. France started the present conflict: if the mighty Emperor of China in his anger demands a reckoning from the French for their crimes, what excuse can they offer? Under the guardianship of the great Emperor, Chinese armies have gone out to rid Vietnam of brigands, whereas the French have not helped with so much as an arrow. On what do they base their talk of protection? Strange protection indeed, to seize cities, to kill mandarins, and to plunder treasuries! I, Liu Yung-fu, am a Kwangsi man, and I am bound to defend the Chinese frontier. I also hold a Vietnamese commission, and consequently it is my duty to suppress the enemies of Vietnam. In May, I boldly led my soldiers against Hanoi, burning Christian churches outside that city. On May 13th I personally commanded my men in a bloody battle with the French, three hours in length, during which the guns roared like thunder and lumps of flesh flew through the air. The odds against us were ten to one, but we killed the French commander-in-chief, and more than twenty officers, as well as inflicting innumerable casualties on their men. Since then the enemy have not dared to venture outside Hanoi. The will of Heaven being manifest, if the French repent and withdraw, I shall refrain from further bloodshed. If they persevere in their crimes, then I swear I shall never rest until I have had my revenge. If they make more trouble for China, a summons from me will collect an army of ten thousand men, at the head of which I shall advance to take Saigon. As for you Christian converts, you should be grateful for the generosity which has been shown to you. Now that we are at war, converts are traitors, and will be slaughtered without compunction. If you change your ways, furnish us with information about the enemy, and act as our fifth column, you will be rewarded abundantly. As for you men from Saigon, formerly Vietnamese subjects, how can you have forgotten your native land? By serving as guides for the enemy, you have sinned against your conscience. Turn your arms against your foreign masters, and you will save your lives! Those of you who accept French service, remember I know your names, although I do not choose to reveal them here. Although you are traitors today, I hope you will return to decency tomorrow!'

Besides all this, the partisans of firmer action by China were encouraged by messages from the Marquis Tseng in Europe, which emphasized the domestic problems facing the French government. By May 1883, these influences prevailed so far at Court that Li Hung-chang, vastly against his inclination as we may well imagine, was instructed that the time had come for the southernmost provinces of Kwangtung, Kwangsi and Yunnan to be put on a war footing, and that as the outstanding military expert in the land he must go down in person and assume charge of operations. To Li the one bright spot in the general gloom was that for the time being at least he could restrict the deployment of forces to those already in the South, without touching his precious Northern Army. Even so, he set off on his mission with a noticeable absence of alacrity, and pounced eagerly upon an excuse for loitering in Shanghai.

It was in that port, in June 1883, that he made the acquaintance of Monsieur Tricou, a diplomat who had been transferred from Tokyo to succeed the unlucky Bourée as French Minister to China. To manifest his country's determination, Tricou thought it became him to wear a stern and frowning look, and his language, too, was more openly menacing than is customary in his profession. When Li ventured to express his surprise that France had repudiated so violently the agreement he had come to with Bourée, Tricou declared in ringing tones that: 'as things are nowadays, we must talk in terms of strength, not in terms of right or justice.' No words could have been more to Li's fancy, who in his reports to Peking, stressed that:

'at first sight, the petty victory of Liu Yung-fu seems like good news. But ever since Europeans have invaded the Orient, eastern nations have always won the first battle, and lost the last one. We should be taught by history. As for our coastal defence, our armies are weak in men and supplies, and our navy is still untrained. We are in no state to go to war with a strong European power.'

Li was able to support this opinion by quoting disinterested

advice he had received from one or other of his foreign acquaintances, some of which had a turn of phrase strikingly reminiscent
of his own diction. Thus, one source insisted that a clash with
France, if it came, would be infinitely more serious than a conflict
with Russia would have been. After all, the latter is separated from
China by vast stretches of desert, while the French fleet would
without difficulty seize or sink all China's navy and mercantile
marine. Meanwhile he told Tricou that it was quite conceivable
that the Black Flags had been masquerading in Chinese uniforms,
thus leading the French to assume mistakenly that they had been in
contact with troops of the imperial government. He was glad to
take this opportunity of assuring the envoy that such Chinese
regular soldiers as were at present on Vietnamese soil had gone
there in accordance with a long-established practise, for the sole
purpose of suppressing banditry. It had never been the intention
of Peking to fight for the Vietnamese against the French. No
wonder on listening to this Tricou was all eagerness for Li to
obtain authority to act as a plenipotentiary, and in Li's words
'flounced out of the room with an expression of great displeasure'
when informed that such an appointment was entirely up to the
Court, and could not be solicited by Li himself. At any rate, the
conversations at Shanghai served one useful purpose. They
provided an admirable pretext for Li to delay his journey to the
South, and in July he contrived to call off the trip altogether and
returned to his old post at Tientsin.[26]

A few days before Rivière's death, the Chamber of Deputies at
Paris had by a large majority approved the first reading of a bill
granting the sum of five and a half million francs, which the
government optimistically imagined would be sufficient for the
operations in Tongking, and when the news of the disaster was
received the credits were voted unanimously. Simultaneously,
reinforcements of three thousand men embarked for the Far East.
It was decided, too, that events had proved the unsuitability of
having the question of Tongking managed by the colonial governor
at Saigon, but unfortunately the first scheme devised as an alternative was every bit as defective. A triumvirate was constituted.
General Bouet, a marine officer, was transferred from Saigon to
command the land forces in the Red River delta, Admiral Courbet,

an ex-governor of New Caledonia, was given charge of naval operations, and a former companion of Garnier, Dr Harmand, a navy surgeon who had passed into administration and had made a name for himself as an explorer, was sent from the consulate at Bangkok as a civil commissar to coordinate military and political action. The plan was, briefly, to establish and consolidate French control of the delta, and to sever political ties, and even direct communication, between Hue and Peking. As to this, Tricou's messages, after his meetings with Li, were confident that China would not go to war, but would acquiesce in a French 'act of virility'.

Harmand and his two colleagues held a conference at Haiphong at the end of July 1883, and it became obvious that the roles of civilian overseer and military commander were being performed in reverse, for while Bouet was the very embodiment of deliberate caution, Harmand was all fire and flame, and urgent for brisk work in the field. The time seemed specially opportune for an adventure: a fortnight earlier, on July 17, 1883, that steady enemy of France, King Tu Duc, had said goodbye to a world he must during the last few years have come to detest. To add to his desolation, he had not been blessed with children of his own, and he had in consequence adopted a nephew whom he had nominated as his successor, and who mounted the throne under the style of Van Lang. Within a mere twenty-four hours the new sovereign was dethroned by a *coup-d'état* organized and carried out entirely within the palace in a manner so discreet that from that day to this the reason for the substitution has remained a matter of speculation. In one respect, the change introduced a resemblance between the Chinese and Vietnamese thrones. We have seen that in both countries Confucian law required that in every case of succession the successor must belong to the same clan and be one generation junior to the deceased, just like a natural son. This rule was broken at Peking in 1875 when Yehonala adopted to follow her son, T'ung Chih, a boy of the same generation, Kuang Hsü. In the same way, a brother of Tu Duc was now set in his place.

That the coup was in fact intended as an anti-French move seems highly probable from the wording of the proclamation which announced it. This ran:

'The bird of the fifth happiness has flown through the air and has alighted on the palace of the Nguyen. King Tu Duc, our master, has entered into a consoling rest. The grief of seeing foreigners invade and lay waste his kingdom has killed him: he died cursing the invaders. Preserve his memory and avenge him! The Council and the Court have not thought it proper to keep the crown for the prince whom the dead monarch had chosen. They have accordingly selected another prince who has ascended the throne under the style of Hiep Hoa. Publish this name among the people! May he who bears it be as virtuous as his predecessor and more fortunate. Beat a tattoo of mourning on gongs, drums and sounding stones! Let all festivities be suspended! Let everyone shed the customary tears and let the people pray to Heaven for the souls of their kings!'

The triumvirs at their meeting in Haiphong resolved that while General Bouet should proceed with the pacification of the Red River delta, Admiral Courbet and Dr Harmand would address their efforts against the capital itself. On August 16, 1883, a flotilla of seven ships, including two ironclads, and carrying a landing party of over a thousand men, assembled in the harbour of Danang. A boatload of mandarins, who came out to discover the purpose of the visit, were presented with an ultimatum to the Court of Hue, drawn up for the occasion by Harmand. It declared that the just grievances of the French were too many to enumerate. The Vietnamese had shamelessly violated treaties. They had hired into their service those infamous brigands the Black Flags, whose hands were stained with blood. They had even appealed to the government of China, a useless piece of treachery which they must now be bitterly regretting. The so-called complaints which they raised against the French, referred simply to the fact that the latter—who were it must be remembered in the position of Vietnam's creditors —having failed to get what was owing to them by friendly means had been compelled to take steps for the recovery of the indemnities due.

'We could [the document continued], for we have the means, destroy your dynasty from top to bottom, down to its very roots, and seize for ourselves all the kingdom, as we have done in Cochinchina. You will be perfectly aware that this would present no diffiulty to us. You are incapable of putting up a serious resistance to our armies. For a moment, you hoped to find help from a great empire on your borders, which has on several occasions posed as your suzerain, but even if such a suzerainty ever existed, whatever the consequence resulting from it, it can no longer have anything but an historical interest. . . . Now here is a fact which is quite certain: you are at our mercy. We have the power to seize and destroy your capital and to cause you all to die of starvation. You have to choose between war and peace. We do not wish to conquer you, but you must accept our protectorate. For your people it is a guarantee of peace and prosperity: it is also the only chance of survival for your Government and your Court. We give you forty-eight hours to accept or reject, in their entirety and without discussion, the terms which in our magnanimity we offer you. We are convinced that there is nothing in them dishonourable to you, and, if carried out with sincerity on both sides, they will bring happiness to the people of Vietnam. If you reject them, you must expect the greatest evils. Imagine the most frightful things conceivable, and you will still fall short of the truth. The Dynasty, its Princes and its Court will have pronounced sentence on themselves. The name of Vietnam will no longer exist in history.'

Two days later, having received no reply, the fleet steamed northwards up the coast and in a few hours anchored off the fortified entrance to the River of Perfumes. The tricolour was run up, and the ships' guns commenced to bombard the defence-works. Flashes along the battlements showed that the garrison was returning the fire, but the French were out of range of the antiquated cannon, and the balls splashed harmlessly into the sea. As night fell, the shore was lit up by the fires which the shells had started. Next day the bombardment was resumed until the defenders' guns were completely silenced. Early on August 20th, a landing party was put ashore and was soon in possession of the fort, which was discovered to be chockful of corpses, victims of the cannonade.

Among the French officers was Pierre Loti, an appropriate chronicler for such an exploit. The scene still lives in his pages:

the sailors, carefree and laughing, 'like great children'; a dying Vietnamese, whose jaw 'falls open with a noise like the opening of a box'. And then, after sundown, a line of junks appears through the gloom, lighted by a jet of flame in the front of one of them.

'Above this light was a white flag of truce. A voice, sounding very French, asks: Are you willing to receive a delegation from the Court of Hue, who are here to ask for peace? At the answer "Yes", the junks come alongside. We expected to see some important Asiatic personality, but the face is that of a European, and very pale. He is wearing a violet soutane, with a pastoral ring gleaming on his finger. "I am the missionary Bishop of Hue. I am with the truce delegation." [The following afternoon, the delegation passes through the camp again.] Their palanquins stayed shut, but His Lordship the Bishop half-opened the curtain of his to wave and tell us that the peace treaty has been accepted, including its stiffest clauses.'[27]

In fact Loti was slightly premature: what had just been concluded was an agreement for a truce. Harmand went on at once to Hue, and it was there on August 25th that the draft of a treaty proper was signed. It was intended to replace the one of 1874, and specified that Vietnam accepted a French protectorate with all the consequences entailed by such a relationship in European diplomatic usage, namely that France would control all communications between Vietnam and third powers, including China. Other clauses reinforced French authority in Tongking, providing for the withdrawal of Vietnamese troops from that region, and for the appointment to the chief cities of the various Tongkingese provinces of French residents to superintend the collection of taxes. France assumed the sole reponsibility for driving the Black Flags from Tongking, and of safeguarding the commerce of the Red River. The central portion of Vietnam was suffered, in contrast, to retain a certain automony, but under the overall control of a French Resident-General at Hue: besides, the area so indulged would be reduced by the annexation of the province of Binh-Thuan in the south to the French colony of Cochinchina, while the northern provinces would be reckoned as included in

Tongking. The fortifications at the entrance to the River of Perfumes were to be reconstructed and held by a French garrison.

While these developments were taking place at Hue, in Tongking General Bouet, contrary to his own cautious inclinations, was being pushed by the imperious will of Dr Harmand into an offensive against Sontay and the Black Flags. For this, he was able to employ about one thousand five hundred men, who marched out westwards from Hanoi at dawn on August 15, 1883. They were divided into three columns, whose task was to clear the Black Flags from Phu-Hoai and an adjacent village called Ve, after which they would converge and advance towards Sontay together. The column on the right hand, to whom Ve had been assigned as objective, very quickly ran into trouble, being harassed by sharpshooters and then brought to a complete standstill by a system of entrenchments dug around the village. Once halted, they seemed to be invaded by a kind of indefinable fear, in which recollections of the fate of Garnier and Rivière undoubtedly had a share. At all events it was with the greatest difficulty that they were induced to make a show of action, and when darkness fell, they bivouacked where they were. In the meantime, Bouet himself had been heartened to discover that Phu-Hoai was abandoned, but the enemy had left merely to occupy a stronger position in a town called Phong, some five miles away, where an elaborate set of earthworks had been erected. Here the Black Flags sustained all the fire-power that the French could employ, never themselves replying with a single shot until the attackers came within range, when they riposted so heavily that every attempt to advance was driven off in confusion. After some hours of this, completely demoralized—for his third column had fared no better—the General returned to Hanoi, where next morning he was rejoined by the first column, who had given up hope of taking Ve. Forty-two dead had been left on the field.

The news of the victory at Hue must have stimulated Bouet to a renewed effort, for on September 1st he marched out again, this time keeping his troops in a compact body. The expedition lasted only for two days. It failed in its purpose of capturing Sontay, for the troops got only half-way to that city. They did enter Ve, but probably for the same reason that was given for abandoning the march to Sontay, namely that the countryside was inundated. Floods at this time of year were common, but in 1883 they were so widespread that Liu Yung-fu (wrongly as it appears) swore that the French had breached the dykes. His own position at Phong was rendered precarious by the water, but what made him hang on all the more stubbornly was his fury at receiving word from Prince Hoang that in order to avoid too open an infringement of the recent treaty the Court of Hue insisted that the Black Flags must withdraw to Sontay. Only after reiterated instructions and a menacing rise in the level of the water did he reluctantly obey. To add to his ill-temper, appeals by T'ang Ching-sung for co-operation from Chinese troops had been answered very grudgingly: a small number of men from the Kwangsi provincial army stationed at Bac-Ninh and other towns in northern Tongking had at last been sent, not to the front at Phong, but to the rear at Sontay. As for the Yunnanese army, it had got no further than Laokay. Indeed, we hear that Liu in a fit of pique threatened loudly that he would leave so thankless a service, and it took all T'ang Ching-sung's diplomacy to pacify him.

On the French side, too, the triumvirate of command was being riven asunder. It is obvious from the tone of Harmand's ultimatum to the Court of Hue that he had fallen a prey to a specially perni-cious form of megalomania, and his exalted views of his own importance must have been even more extravagant after his success in obtaining the treaty. On his return to Hanoi early in September he made no attempt to conceal his disgust at Bouet's performance: for his part, Bouet was equally convinced that all blame for the lack of success was due to Harmand, who had pestered him, against his own better judgment, into undertaking a major compaign with insufficient forces and at the wrong time of year. Relations between the two reached the breaking-point, and on September 10th the General abruptly quitted his post, carrying his recriminations with him to Paris. Admiral Courbet assumed command of combined military and naval operations.

Another victim of Harmand's arrogance was Jean Dupuis, who now turned up in his old haunts, smacking his lips at the prospect of riches to come, and innocently anticipating a hero's welcome. In this frame of mind he presented himself to Harmand, only to have his high spirits dashed by the inquiry: 'And what are you doing here?' Caught by surprise, Dupuis mentioned his connections with the Tongkingese, the Chinese and the Montagnards. 'I must ask you to be careful with the Chinese at Hanoi,' snapped Harmand. 'Otherwise, I shall have to do something about it. The fact is, M. Dupuis, you are a good deal too Chinese yourself. It's you who caused all this trouble China is stirring up for us about her suzerainty.' When we remember the care with which Dupuis ten years earlier had claimed to represent a Chinese authority, the reproach seems justified. Dupuis himself admitted as much by reminding Harmand of his patriotism. 'You know perfectly well,' he said 'that I was master of the situation in Tongking, when I offered everything to my country.'

Within a few weeks Harmand's delusions of grandeur proved his undoing. Forgetting the very junior rank which he had occupied in his own naval days, he complained that the Admiral was not showing him sufficient respect. By now, though, Paris was apprised of the situation. At the end of October 1883, Harmand was curtly instructed not to interfere with the Admiral's operations, and a few weeks later he was recalled altogether.

CHAPTER FOURTEEN

The Rage of Liu Yung-fu

WHILE these events were taking place in Tongking, relations between China and France had not been static. On August 10, 1883, the French proclaimed that their navy was instituting a blockade of the Vietnamese ports in order to prevent the delivery of munitions of war. They justified this action by reference to the Treaty of 1874, and in fact it caused only the slightest of international repercussions. For China, this measure, even though it was directed particularly against her shipping, was put entirely in the shade by the surrender of the Court of Hue and the new France-Vietnamese agreement a few days later. Few observers, whether in Peking or elsewhere, believed after such a demonstration that an independent Vietnamese state was any longer viable. The only question was how much China could retrieve for herself from the wreckage. It was therefore with peculiar attention that the French government was heard to propose the creation of a buffer zone in Tongking to guarantee the security of the Chinese frontier. The actual terms of the proposal, contained in a memorandum of September 15, 1883, handed to the Marquis Tseng by the French Foreign Minister, were not of a kind to inspire enthusiasm, being far more restricted in scope than the abortive settlement reached between M. Bourée and Li Hung-chang a year previously. Then, as may be remembered, it was agreed that Chinese troops should occupy territory north of a line to be drawn midway between the Chinese frontier and the Red River. Now it was merely suggested that a strip of northern Tongking from the Chinese border to the 22nd parallel should be left as a neutral buffer under Vietnamese administration, while by implication the land further south passed without let or hindrance to the French. At the same time, the Yunnanese town of Manghao was to be opened to foreign trade, so that the French could exploit the Red River over its whole length.

For several weeks, in September and October 1883, the matter was argued from the Chinese point of view by the Marquis Tseng in a number of interviews in Paris, as well as by Li Hung-chang in conversations at Tientsin with M. Tricou. Even Li saw that the French terms as they stood had no chance of being accepted. However, it was Tseng was first stated a counter-proposal which would satisfy China. Even then, to save appearances, the Marquis declared that the ideal solution was for the French to restore Vietnam to the position it had held prior to 1873. Failing this, in the interests of peace, China *could* accept the creation of a neutral zone, provided that it extended from the southernmost boundary of Tongking to the 20th parallel. As for the Red River, the Chinese government was disposed to facilitate commerce by opening the waterway from the sea as far as Sontay, and establishing a trading station opposite that city on the northern bank. In other words, the whole of Tongking would have to be given to Chinese administration: the neutral zone would lie entirely beyond, in what was the central part of Vietnam. Within Tongking, only the delta of the Red River would be open to international shipping. China was, in fact, proposing the partition of Vietnam, in a manner that would nullify all French acquisitions and claims in the north.

In his dispatches home, Tseng gave evidence on many occasions of a remarkably cool insight into the political condition of France, interspersed with reflections on the Gallic character that he must have picked up from Macartney.

'The French [he wrote], are by nature inclined to bully the weak and to fear the strong. Although they are boastful and vainglorious, as soon as an enterprise become difficult they abandon it: they are better at starting things than at seeing them through. The more obviously China prepares for war, the easier it will be to reach a solution. On the other hand, if we prepare too slowly, France will already have seized her prey and it will be all the harder to make her disgorge. Remember too that the French aim is not limited to the annexation of Vietnam, which is no more than a springboard. What France is after are the coalfields on the Kwangtung border and the minerals of Yunnan. If we let go of our vassal kingdom, we shall be depriving ourselves of a defensive screen. The British are hankering after Tibet, and the Russians after Korea, and both of them are waiting to see how we are going to behave over Vietnam before they decide what steps to take. True, it is at sea that we have most cause to fear the French, and the places that would suffer in case of a war would not be Yunnan or Kwangsi, but the ports along our coastline. Yet if we go to war with France, even though Britain, Germany, Russia and America do nothing to help us, they will not permit the French to blockade the Chinese coast or to attack our ports. Seeing this, the French will back down and they will back down all the sooner if we stand firm now. France is rent asunder by party struggles: there is unanimity about nothing, least of all about adventures at the other end of the world. And to add to all this, she is without a single friend in Europe'.[28]

Li Hung-chang, aware that these arguments and others of the same way of thinking were increasingly in the ascendant, was meanwhile expressing his own opinion with disconcerting frankness. He had been instructed by Prince Kung at the Foreign Office that in further contacts with M. Tricou he must be careful not to give the impression of yielding on such points as the withdrawal of the Black Flags. It was only proper, too, he was told, that in view of his long connection with national defence he should now assume responsibility for military preparations to meet any eventuality. His reply was not encouraging.

'The country is far from having recovered [he said] from the floods and drought that have plagued so many provinces during recent years. In particular, owing to the vast length of our coast-line, there are many weaknesses in our defence system. If we should go to war over a perfectly useless tract of land in a vassal kingdom, we shall be fighting on behalf of Vietnam when the latter has already surrendered to France. We shall be disrupting our international trade to no purpose whatsoever, and what is worse we shall have started a war without any prospect of ending it on satisfactory terms. [He was specially insistent on the sanctity of treaties.] Although this new agreement reached in August at Hue was extorted by force, yet since Vietnam is a country, and its ruler and his ministers have acquiesced in the arrangement, how can China take it on herself to set it aside ? Does anybody seriously think we can dislodge the French from Hanoi or Saigon ?'

He used more or less the same tone to M. Tricou, so much that the envoy could not refrain from pointing out that these views were scarcely shared by the Chinese Foreign Office or by the Marquis Tseng. 'Oh, the Foreign Office,' snarled Li, 'the Foreign Office is living in the moon! And don't mention Tseng's name to me! I have nothing to do with what he says!' M. Tricou promptly cabled these remarks to Paris, with the result that Jules Ferry, who in spite of his oriental ambitions had only the woolliest notion of who was who in China, declared in a speech that the Marquis Tseng had been officially disavowed by his own government, a gaffe which resulted in a spate of embarrassed telegrams between Paris and Peking. [29]

One cannot help feeling a certain sympathy for Li Hung-chang when one looks at some of the suggestions put forward at this time by men in positions of trust and authority. A highly-placed mandarin, appointed to supervise the military installations in Kwangtung province, offered the following advice in all earnestness to the Court:

'According to one of my staff named Wang, a man called Cheng Kuan-ying went to sea in his youth and saw a lot of Vietnam and Siam. The king of Siam is Cantonese, and is also named Cheng. Not only that: all the officers in his army are Cantonese, and in talking to Cheng Kuan-ying about the war between Vietnam and France, they expressed the deepest concern. Siam is adjacent to Saigon, and they wanted to make a surprise attack on the latter city, thus catching the French leaders in their lair. Then there is a British colony called Singapore, a very rich place, with over a hundred thousand Cantonese residents. I suggest we should offer substantial rewards to attract able-bodied men both in Saigon and in Singapore secretly to join us, so that as soon as an army from

Siam arrives on the scene, they can rise in support, seizing warships and burning munitions. We ought to send Cheng Kuan-ying secretly to make the necessary contacts, and perhaps my Mr. Wang could go along with him in disguise. With Saigon lost, Hanoi and Haiphong would be untenable for the French, who would thus be driven out of Vietnam altogether.'

This was rather too much even for the Court of Peking:

'Siam is already hard-pressed enough [said an imperial rescript], hemmed in as she is by the British in Bengal and Singapore. She no longer sends us tribute: how in the world could she raise an army, since by so doing she would bring a strong enemy down upon her? Even though this Cheng Kuan-ying may be on friendly terms with the king because of his Cantonese origin, he would never be able to persuade him to take such a step. Saigon and Singapore are commercial ports, and merchants are extremely unreliable. Besides, think what a vast sum of money it would need to recruit such people into our service!'[30]

By the middle of November 1883 Paris was finally convinced that there was no prospect of a neutral zone acceptable to both parties. At the same time the virtual stalemate in Tongking after the failure of General Bouet's offensive was causing some anxiety among the French public, who were beginning to discern that the war might well be more troublesome than had been bargained for. To dispel all such doubts, and to restore confidence in the government, it was essential to defeat the Black Flags once and for all. If possible, however, it was still desirable that this should be done without coming into direct conflict with Chinese regular troops. On November 17th, Jules Ferry, who had now assumed charge of foreign affairs, wrote to inform the Marquis Tseng that orders had been sent for the French troops to occupy Sontay, Bac-Ninh and Hung-Hoa, the three most notable Chinese bases in Tongking. He added that it would seem a sensible precaution for the French and Chinese commanders on the spot to come to some arrangement for the demarcation of their respective positions. But the suggestion was still-born: the letter containing it crossed with a communication from Tseng notifying the French government (for the express purpose, he said, of avoiding a collision) that the places in question were actually occupied by Chinese forces, who had received orders to hold them. The exchange of messages found an echo in the Chamber of Deputies. More credits had to be voted, this time nine million francs; and there was a heated debate, during which the government, although it got its way, was denounced by its opponents —most eloquently by Clemenceau on the left—for leading the country into war with China.

At Hanoi, Admiral Courbet waited until the last moment before committing himself, for he had already seen in the case of Bouet the danger of acting prematurely. Yet the delay, necessary though it was, filled him with despondency. At the beginning of November, six weeks before he was able to take to the field, he wrote to a friend that he was already months too late: 'Sontay and Bac-Ninh have had time to get from China all the supplies they want in men, guns and ammunition.' If he had only known, his anxiety was excessive. True, the Chinese government, in spite of Li Hung-chang's prophecies of disaster, had given orders for the provincial armies of Kwangsi and Yunnan to cooperate to the fullest extent with the Black Flags, and the Kwangsi treasury had been directed to advance the sum of one hundred thousand silver dollars to Liu Yung-fu as a bounty for him and his men. Not a dollar had been paid, and any Kwangsi troops that advanced from the frontier towards Liu at Sontay, had been halted at Bac-Ninh; for the majority opinion in the Kwangsi command was that it was this northern town which was for geographical reasons the peculiar concern of their province, while Sontay, as a glance at the map would show, was the key to the defence of Yunnan from an attack by river. If enough Yunnanese soldiers had been available, things would not have been so bad: but in spite of Ts'en Yu-ying's willingness to participate in the struggle, he himself was still some distance away, and only a small portion of his forces had arrived in the vicinity. The result was that, apart from three thousand Black Flags, the only Chinese troops at Sontay were about a thousand Yunnanese, and rather less than five hundred Kwangsi men whom T'ang Ching-sung, by dint of frantic intercession, had contrived to transfer under his personal command to the threatened city. In other words, the Chinese garrison did not amount to more than four thousand five hundred men, to whom were added about five thousand Vietnamese of very dubious quality.

Liu was well aware that Courbet was building up his strength for the encounter. Reports reached Sontay of the exotic reinforcements arriving in Hanoi—Turcos in Arab dress, and foreign legionnaires in scarlet trousers. Unabashed, Liu dictated a letter of defiance, which Chinese historians treasure as a monument of the national spirit: to us, it is of interest as revealing the extent of Liu's information.

'You Frenchmen, [it says], have now been in Tongking for nineteen months. Your defeats have disgraced your country, while your people are being bled white to support your cost. And yet you show no sign of repentance. You stay in your lair, not daring to come out and fight, although your countrymen brag that you are going to attack Kwangtung province. You set black devils to plunder and ravage a defenceless population, more cruelly than the vilest of bandits. But today the mighty Emperor of China is moved to anger and pronounces your doom. I, Liu Yung-fu, have received instructions from the Governor of Kwangsi that an imperial edict orders us to retake the city of Hanoi. The people of Vietnam will come alive again. Saigon will follow Hanoi, and not one of you will be left on Vietnamese soil. The shameful fate of Napoleon III will be reenacted.'

At the beginning of December 1883, four thousand more French troops arrived in Tongking, and Admiral Courbet decided the time had come for him to strike, since to delay any longer would incur the risk of finding the level of the river too low to take the naval vessels he proposed to use. First of all he struck a blow against the enemy's morale by capturing a couple of Vietnamese magistrates whose seats of authority lay on the road to Sontay and taking them to Hanoi, where they were shot by a firing squad, on the grounds that they had continued their opposition to the French in defiance of the recent treaty. In considering this and similar exploits of Courbet, it is interesting to bear in mind that in 1848, during his student days, he had fought on the Paris barricades. In Peking in 1964, the Chinese Communist Minister of Foreign Affairs, Ch'en Yi, in a speech to students of French urged them, while acquiring the French language, to give French ideas a wide berth.'We don't want Liberty, Equality and Fraternity in China,' he said, and when we recollect what French republican principles, as exemplified by such men as Courbet, have done in Asia we can see what Ch'en was driving at.

The expedition moved out from Hanoi on December 11, 1883. There were five thousand five hundred troops, about half of them advancing overland, the rest on board a flotilla of boats which moved up the river to a point chosen for disembarkation, about six miles on the nearer side of Sontay. Here the two halves of the army assembled. They met in a beautiful landscape. Around them lay a vast plain richly cultivated with rice, sugar-cane and maize, and dotted with neat villages surrounded by groves of trees. Every now and then a graceful pagoda varied the scene.

In the distance they could discern the object of their campaign, and a formidable sight it was. The heart of it was a Vaubanesque citadel which put some of them in mind of Antibes. Clustered round the walls of this fortress was the town itself which the Black Flags had enclosed within an earthwork, nearly twenty feet high and fifteen feet thick, densely planted with bamboos. On the out-side of this earthwork there was a ditch filled with water. Along the river-bank, where the defenders expected the attack would come, a dyke was strongly fortified so as to constitute an extra rampart. But distrust had arisen in Liu Yung-fu's mind towards his Vietnamese allies, no doubt because of the ambivalent attitude towards the war now being shown by Prince Hoang after the capitulation of Hue, and he declined to permit other than Chinese forces to enter the town precincts. Throughout the engagement, indeed, the Vietnamese on Liu's side seem to have played a negligeable role, and might just as well not have been present. In contrast, useful service was performed for the French by militia from Cochinchina, and even by a freshly-formed company of Tongkingese auxiliaries, mostly Christians. It will be seen that if we consider the Chinese as the sole effective garrison—and this is no more than the plain truth—the attackers outnumbered the defen-ders by about one thousand men, and were besides incomparably better armed, having at their disposal a large number of field guns.

The action commenced on December 14th with an attack on the riverside dyke by the Foreign Legion and a body of Marines. The struggle was extraordinary bitter, but by the afternoon the dyke had changed hands. Then during the night the Black Flags launched a furious counter-attack which might well have succeeded had there not been a particularly bright moon—Chinese observers remarked that this was a rare phenomenon in Vietnam—which made every corner of the terrain clearly visible. Having withstood this onslaught, the French passed the next day in consolidating their position, which gave them the advantage, from the parapet of the dyke, of being on a level with the top of the earthwork around the town proper. It was apparent from the outset that any attempt to penetrate the thicket of bamboos would be suicidal: the sole feasible means of ingress was through a gate, and the one on the west side was chosen for the purpose. Artillery was brought up and the bombardment began on the morning of December 16th. Although overwhelmed by the superior French fire-power, Liu and his men held their ground, their Black Flags fluttering defiantly, until just before nightfall 'a human tempest', as a French officer puts it, stormed through the barrier, to discover that the defenders had withdrawn into the citadel itself. That night the besiegers slept on their arms, but when dawn broke on December 17th it was noticed that a gate of the fortress was ajar. The Chinese had retired under cover of darkness and were now well on the way to the old Black Flag stronghold of Hung-Hoa, up river.

The French losses amounted to eighty-three killed and three hundred and twenty wounded. The Chinese, on the most trustworthy calculation, had upwards of a thousand dead. When the news reached Peking, there was at first consternation, since it was supposed that Liu Yung-fu had been killed or made prisoner, and the relief to learn that he and most of his men were safe and sound was correspondingly keen. In the wave of patriotic feeling, even Li Hung-chang thought it prudent to express the view that it would be wrong to let the result of one battle influence policy, and that the defence of the southern frontier must be seen to. In fact, on the very day after the fall of Sontay, the Governor of Kwangsi province at the head of a numerous army crossed the Vietnamese border to Langson, from where he went on to inspect Bac-Ninh, recognized as the next target of French advance. The five hundred or so Kwangsi fugitives from Sontay, or as many of them as had made good their escape, decided not to dally down on the Red

River at Hung-Hoa, where they would no doubt have had to bear the rough edge of Liu's tongue, but fled to the by now more familiar surroundings of Bac-Ninh, which had become quite a home from home for them and their fellow provincials, so much so that there was already murmuring among the local population. For Liu and the Black Flags were not the only ones to be defrauded by the Kwangsi treasury. The stipend of the Kwangsi soldiers was badly in arrears, and they were living openly on the country, commandeering everything that took their fancy and spending most of their time in a perpetual haze of opium. The Governor was one of those Chinese mandarins who were the despair of Li Hung-chang—incapable of learning by experience and with a contempt for Europeans proportionate to his ignorance and stupidity. Worse still, his military commanders were at loggerheads among themselves, while the most senior of them, having left his own concubines behind in the safety of Kwangsi, complained so angrily to the Vietnamese authorities of their inhospitality in not providing him with company that a seraglio of thirty or forty young women was hastily assembled for his consolation. His example was followed, on a more modest scale, by practically the whole of his army. One begins to understand why Liu Yung-fu's appeals for help had fallen on deaf ears.

One ally, however, was now well on his way. Ts'en Yu-ying entered Laokay from Yunnan at the beginning of January 1884 at the head of twelve thousand men, and by the middle of the month was at Hung-Hoa to meet the Black Flags and their commander. At their first encounter, Ts'en and Liu more or less fell into each other's arms. They had indeed a great deal in common: early poverty, a congenital aptitude for violent adventure, and boundless credulity towards the peasant superstitions of their childhood, especially when these portended personal good-fortune. What was more to the point, the Yunnanese army had some military techniques which Liu and his officers found of interest—above all a skill in constructing dug-outs on a scale and with an elaboration of detail which astounded the Black Flags and which they were told had been learned from the miners who had taken part on both sides in the recent Muslim rebellion.

One of the hardest tasks confronting Ts'en Yu-ying was to

persuade his new friend not to break with the Kwangsi army; for, as may be imagined, Liu could not forgive the manner in which assistance had been witheld from him in his necessity at Sontay, and he pretended, in his anger, that even the miserable contingent which T'ang Ching-sung had added to the garrison had bolted in panic leaving him and his men to their fate. When Ts'en first raised the suggestion that the Black Flags ought to go north and reinforce the defence of Bac-Ninh, Liu refused point-blank. It was not Bac-Ninh that wanted helping, he said, but rather Sontay which with a proper effort could be snatched back out of French hands. It is unlikely that the counter-proposal was meant seriously or was intended as more than a manifestation of displeasure, and at length, about the beginning of March 1884, Liu did what he was told and led his men, who seem to have returned to their old strength of three thousand (probably by means of fresh recruitment —though of this we have no information), on the five days' march northward to Bac-Ninh.

It may appear strange that the French should have granted their enemy so long a respite, instead of at once following up their triumph at Sontay. But on their side, too, professional spite and jealousy had come to the boil. Scarcely had Sontay fallen when Courbet was relieved of his post as supreme commander and relegated to his original duties as head of the naval squadron, where there seemed little opportunity for an ambitious man to perform any outstanding exploits. He was justifiably furious and made no attempt to conceal his feelings. The change was a great blow to the missionaries, for Courbet, whatever the libertarian frolics of his student days, was now a model of Catholic piety: before setting out for Sontay, for instance, he had written to ask Bishop Puginier for his prayers. It was hinted that the demotion was due to anti-clerical intrigues. The true reason, however, was almost certainly less ideological. The French had been deeply impressed by the performance of the Black Flags, down to and including their fierce defence of Sontay. At this rate, it looked as if the total subjugation of Tongking would entail a compaign of considerable dimensions. Reinforcements were shipped from France to bring the number of troops to upwards of seventeen thousand. It was considered unfair that the prestige of leading an army of this size should be assigned to a naval officer: thus Admiral Courbet was compelled to make way for General Millot, who assumed the command in February 1884.

The so-called 'Mandarin Road', constructed eighty years earlier under Gia Long and running through the entire length of the country from Saigon to the Chinese frontier, joined Hanoi to Bac-Ninh and, further north still, to Langson. Rather naively, the Kwangsi forces had anticipated that the French offensive would keep to this highway, along which numerous strongpoints had been prepared for such a contingency. When Millot gave the word to move, about a month after his arrival, the attack was delivered in two columns which avoided these obstacles by going round on either side, and meeting at a spot just outside Bac-Ninh. The next day, March 12, 1884, the assault commenced.

The Black Flags had reached Bac-Ninh over a week earlier, to find the situation far worse than could have been feared. The Kwangsi men were quite well-armed, with a park of Krupp cannon, a circumstance not calculated to put Liu Yung-fu into a good humour when he remembered the desertion of Sontay. On a closer look, however, he became convinced that the gun crews were incapable of using their weapons properly. Years afterwards he remembered that the only sort of modern training he had noticed among the garrison of Bac-Ninh was an obsession with bugle-calls, which at the high command's instructions were being practised incessantly. The disposition of the troops offended the simplest rules: for instance, it had not been thought necessary to man the vantage-points overlooking the city. The pillage and lechery of the Chinese of all ranks had inspired among the Vietnamese a hatred which Liu, attuned to the mood of the country, could scent from afar; but in spite of his warning, as the French approached, weapons were issued indiscriminately to the local population for use against the common enemy.

Expecting the worst, Liu stationed his force in the hills outside the city and awaited developments. As he had foreseen, the French, finding the commanding heights unguarded, made sure of occupying them before turning their attention to Bac-Ninh itself. The Kwangsi army, seeing the tricolour waving on the slopes above them, panicked and fled pell-mell along the highway towards

Langson, carrying their women and their loot with them, while their Vietnamese allies fired on them from the rear. Ten brand-new Krupp cannon, having done harm to nobody, fell into French hands, as did a great deal of other military equipment. Chinese sources insist that in the confusion more than two hundred thousand silver dollars were left behind: the victors on the other hand, who as a rule had a keen nose for such matters, complained that the city had been stripped bare of money. One hopes as an explanation of the mystery that some Vietnamese husbands or fathers managed to compensate themselves for the rape of their women, but it sounds too good to be true.

'The resistance at Bac-Ninh,' wrote a French officer, 'bore not the faintest resemblance to what happened at Sontay. The Chinese aren't real fighters like the Black Flags.' The language is rather confused, but it is reasonable to assume that the writer was never aware that the Black Flags were only a mile or two away when the city fell, so completely had Liu washed his hands of the affair. In Liu's own accounts he tells us that the débâcle took him quite by surprise, so much so that on hearing the noise of the French attack he was at first convinced that the Kwangsi troops were coming out to give the foreigners battle. As things were it would have been folly for him, grossly outnumbered as he was, to do other than withdraw as discreetly as he could to the safety of Hung-Hoa.

There is little doubt that something of the panic of the Kwangsi army had communicated itself to the Black Flags, for there is mention in the Chinese books of massive plundering during their retreat, and it would be strange if the Vietnamese population did not hold them in equal detestation with their compatriots of the regular forces. Back in Hung-Hoa, they faced a delta which seemed irretrievably lost, while due north communications with Langson and Kwangsi were severed. Only to the northwest lay security, in the hills along the upper reaches of the Red River, and ultimately, if the worst came to the worst, in Yunnan itself. They were given the merest breathing-space before the French were upon them, deploying an encircling movement which threatened to cut their lifeline. To the Yunnanese soldiers Hung-Hoa meant little, and they removed themselves with alacrity to positions they had prepared in the more inaccessible terrain farther up the stream. But the Black Flags had been in the place for a decade and it went cruelly against the grain to say goodbye to it. At least they could deprive the French of the satisfaction of turning the old familiar huts and mess-halls into a peepshow. On their way out they set the buildings alight, and it was over an expanse of charred rubble that the tricolour was hoisted on April 12, 1884. Liu himself, leaving his followers in temporary security a few miles up river, returned to his favourite base of Laokay to take stock of the situation.

In China the first reaction to the news was one of rage. The provincial governors of Kwangsi and Yunnan were dismissed in disgrace; though, rather unfairly, Ts'en Yu-ying as Viceroy of Yunnan and Kweichow was untouched. The Commander of the Kwangsi army whose sexual appetites had been so unseasonable thought it prudent to evade the wrath to come by swallowing a lethal dose of poison: two of his subordinates, of less resolution, were beheaded in front of their troops. Stories like these, as they drifted down over the border were as balm to Liu's resentment. But along with them came other, less welcome, reports. Li Hun-chang and the faint-hearts seemed to be carrying the day at Peking.

CHAPTER FIFTEEN

Peace or War?

WE have seen in an earlier chapter that the Western Dowager Yehonala, upon the death of her son in 1875, in order to maintain her hold on the reins of power had insisted in defiance of the normal mode of succession that her infant nephew should be set upon the Dragon Throne. This certainly ensured that there should be a prolonged regency: the only drawback was that Yehonala still did not possess the monopoly of authority. Within the Palace, she was merely co-Regent, and had to share her status with the Eastern Dowager, who as a former Empress Consort was theoretically, though rather younger in age, superior in rank to Yehonala the ex-concubine. Outside, her brother-in-law Prince Kung remained chief minister of the Empire. The cameraderie which in 1861 had bound the three in an alliance which had seemed to promise well for the future of the dynasty had long since been turned to hatred by rivalries and intrigues: the Eastern Dowager and the Prince, neither of them alone a match for Yehonala, even in combination found it all they could do to preserve an uneasy equilibrium. It was true that for some years after getting her way over the succession she had tended to prefer her domestic pleasures to interference in public affairs, but this was scarcely an unmixed blessing, for China was soon buzzing from one end to the other with ribald accounts of what was passing inside the Forbidden City. One name was continually mentioned in the course of these stories, a name which was to be linked with Yehonala's for the rest of her life. No history of the Chinese nineteenth century would be complete without a mention of Li Lien-ying the eunuch—if indeed he could properly be so described, for rumour had it that no surgeon's knife had ever been near him and that Yehonala could testify, if she had a mind to, that he was as good a man as any within the Four Seas. Certainly the pair of them indulged in strange familiarities during the masques and revels which were the chief occupation of their days, until even the least censorious observers recalled the fate of earlier dynasties brought to ruin in just such a way, and began to wonder whether that model of matronly virtue the Eastern Dowager might at the eleventh hour be induced to assert her authority, if not on behalf of public morality at least to spare the imperial house further shame. There were signs that gave ground for hope. She had certainly uttered a bitter denunciation of the eunuch and, by implication, of his mistress. When therefore on a spring afternoon in 1881 the news swept round Peking that the Eastern Dowager was dead, mandarins who had heard her voice that morning through the audience curtain swore there must have been foul play, but precisely of what sort nobody could tell. Even today opinions are divided as to Yehonala's guilt, but whether in the course of nature or not, she had become sole Regent.

Now three years later the disasters at Sontay and Bac-Ninh gave her an occasion to get rid of her second enemy. On April 8, 1884, an imperial decree was promulgated which declared that Prince Kung and several of his colleagues, from poor health or advancing age, had not lived up to their early promise, but were stubbornly clinging to ideas which had been shown to be detrimental to the country. It was high time that they should be relieved of duties which were clearly beyond their capacity, and should be offered the chance of a peaceful retirement. Significantly, the man chosen in replacement to act as the coordinator between the imperial family and the Grand Council was Prince Ch'un, Prince Kung's brother, who was the father of the young Emperor by his marriage with Yehonala's sister, and whose attitude towards the problems of the day may be gauged from the fact that in a monent of Manchu conviviality he had been heard to say that if it was ever necessary to get rid of the Empire, he would sooner give it away to the foreign devils than return it to his Chinese slaves.

Among the European employees of the Chinese Customs was a

German named Detring who had spent years in Tientsin where he had enjoyed Li Hung-chang's confidence. At the end of March 1884, while in Hong Kong on his way to take up the post of Customs commissioner at Canton, he encountered an old acquaintance of his Tientsin days, a French naval captain named Fournier, who obligingly offered him a passage to his destination. Naturally enough their talk turned to the present crisis, and Fournier, who himself had somehow got into the good books of Li Hung-chang during his stay in the north, professed a total inability to understand the Chinese reluctance to face the facts of life, which were, according to him, that the French were inevitably on the point of becoming the masters of Tongking. If China persisted in her opposition to her new neighbours, she would find that they could turn very nasty indeed. It was all very fine to boast about the Black Flags, but everybody knew that these were nothing more than a gang of freebooters who, if the French thought it worth while to bribe them, would be only too glad to turn against their mother country for the sake of a few dollars. If the Black Flags went on the rampage in Kwangsi and Kwangtung, and Muslim troops from Algeria crossed into Yunnan to summon their co-religionists into another Holy War, the Chinese government would soon find out what a mistake it had made in not coming to terms. Fortunately it was still not too late to be sensible. The French were not unreasonable. The acceptance of three basic conditions would end the crisis overnight. These were: the recall of the Marquis Tseng, whose mission to Paris had plainly been a disaster; the withdrawal of Chinese troops from Tongking and the abandonment of all claims of Chinese suzerainty; and last, the payment by China of an adequate indemnity in respect of the military operations rendered necessary by her intervention. As to this final item, the earlier the negotiations began, the smaller would be the sum demanded.

Immediately on his arrival in Canton, Detring cabled an account of this conversation to Li Hung-chang. The speed of Li's reaction probably surprised him. Within a week he was summoned to Tientsin where he arrived on April 17th, and went at once to the Viceroy's headquarters. Here, besides confirming his cable he added a startling piece of information confided to him by Fournier at the moment the two had taken leave of each other; namely that, failing an early settlement of the dispute, the French fleet would seize a large Chinese port and hold it as security. All this Li at once wired to Peking. Meanwhile the tale was being corroborated by messages from the southern seaboard. Two French warships had passed Amoy steaming northwards. It was uncertain whether or not Fournier himself was the captain of one of them. He had told Detring he was due to go to Shanghai to join the squadron of Admiral Lespès, the second-in-command under Admiral Courbet of French naval forces in the Far East. There was no doubt at all that Fournier had put in at Keelung in Formosa, for his visit had been marked by a striking incident. His demand for coal having been refused, he informed the governor of the place that if his request was ignored any longer he would bombard the town there and then. Supplies of coal appeared as if by magic, and the governor called on the captain to explain that there must have been a tiresome misunderstanding.

Then, on April 19th, Li received a reply from Yehonala.

'For the last two years [it read], the question of France and Vietnam has been getting steadily more acute, in spite of Our repeated instructions to Our ministers. If Li Hung-chang at this juncture repeats his performance at Shanghai last summer and wastes time as an idle spectator, while opportunity of effective action is omitted, what excuse can he possibly allege? Now surely is the moment for energy and sincerity, to strengthen our ties with France and thus to stabilize the problem of Vietnam.'

The all-clear signal could not have been conveyed more unequivocally.

As it happened, the French Legation in Peking was then under the charge of a second secretary, the Vicomte de Semallé, the Minister, M. Tricou, having been recalled to his original post at Tokyo. A senior diplomat was to come out shortly as French representative, and in the meantime Paris did not make much effort to keep the Vicomte supplied with instructions, while the Chinese, sensing his junior rank, tended to ignore him. This state of affairs made it all the easier for Li to propose that talks should be started in an entirely new quarter. Also, he passed on to the

Foreign Office Fournier's opinion that, 'so long as the Marquis Tseng remained in Paris, it was impossible for France to negotiate the Vietnamese question with China'. On April 24, 1884, word came that the Marquis was still to be Chinese Minister, but from now on to London only. His room in Paris would be filled temporarily by one Li Feng-pao, at present stationed in Berlin, who, it was remarked, was beholden to the patronage of Li Hung-chang. Li Hung-chang then cabled to Admiral Lespès at Shanghai that he would be happy to confer in person with his old friend, Captain Fournier.

The news of what was being planned was passed from mouth to mouth among the mandarins of the capital, and the voice of protest began to be heard. It was pointed out that there was something odd in the fact that the French were so keen on seeking peace just when the military situation seemed to be going their way. Did it not suggest that they were discovering that the war in Tongking was costing more than they had bargained for? Or perhaps that they were afraid of getting embroiled with the rest of the western powers? These and similar objections were airily brushed aside by Prince Ch'un, and Li Hung-chang's manoeuvres proceeded smoothly and without interference.

Fournier reached Tientsin on the evening of May 5th, accompanied by Detring, who had gone to Chefoo to meet him, and he was ushered next morning into the viceregal presence. No time was wasted on preliminaries. The agenda had already been indicated in Fournier's original proposal, but there were some questions of nuance and emphasis. However one looked at things, China was being obliged to climb down, so it was only fair that in return every care should be taken to save her from excessive humiliation. It was decided that any agreement must begin with a solemn promise by France to respect and protect China's southern frontier. In return, China undertook to withdraw her troops from Tongking, but instead of a bald statement that she renounced her suzerainty—as Fournier had at first stipulated—she made a less embarrassing declaration that she recognized all existing and future treaties between France and Vietnam. Leaving aside altogether the treaty of 1874, it will be remembered that the agreement imposed on Hue in August 1883 expressly repudiated all

Chinese suzerainty. Then came the matter of financial indemnity. It appears that this item had been raised by Fournier in the first place merely as a bargaining point. The moment it was mentioned, Li exclaimed that such a thing was utterly impossible: no Chinese negotiator could accept such a clause, he said. For the sake of appearances, Fournier put up an argument, but at last allowed Li to have his way. As compensation, it was agreed that the Sino-Vietnamese frontier would be opened to French merchandise on the most favourable terms, to be fixed by a separate commercial agreement. The occasion was used to increase Li's influence by inserting a sentence to the effect that France waived the indemnity in homage to the patriotic wisdom of His Excellency Li Hung-chang. At Li's insistence there was a stipulation that in any future treaty with Vietnam France would abstain from any expressions injurious to Chinese prestige.

Having been cabled full powers by his government, Fournier, on May 11, 1884, signed a draft agreement, with Li as Chinese plenipotentiary. The ceremony was followed by a banquet at which, during the ritual exchange of toasts, Li raised his glass to the greatness and prosperity of France. During the next few days cordial messages passed between Paris and Tientsin, with predictions of a new era of friendship between the two countries.

The diplomatic world was aghast when it learned that negotiations of such importance had been successfully concluded by a mere naval captain; however, a career diplomat of adequate standing, M. Patenôtre, was even then at sea on his way to represent France at Peking. First, before beginning negotiations, he had to complete a different task. The treaty extorted from the Court of Hue a few months before by the vigorous M. Harmand had been found, on careful inspection at Paris, to have certain flaws—nor was this strange when we consider the boisterous manner in which it had been drafted. An alternative text had been drawn up on lines more acceptable to the Quai d'Orsay and M. Patenôtre had been instructed to take this to Hue for the King's signature before he continued his journey to Peking.

The throne of Vietnam in that summer of 1884 was no longer occupied by Tu Duc's brother Hiep Hoa, who had been reigning at the time of Harmand's terrifying visitation. At the end of

November there had occurred a *coup d'état* in the palace at Hue. The King, accused of some obscure offence against Confucian piety (very likely because of his suspected over-readiness to collaborate with the French), had been invited to choose his own style of demise by being confronted with a sword, a phial of opium, and a silken cord. He swallowed the drug and was carried in a dying condition out of the palace to what had formerly been his private residence. His place was taken by a nephew, and adopted son, of Tu Duc, an adolescent who assumed the regnal name of Kien Phuoc; while administration was in the hands of a pair of Regents, one of whom was the senior mandarin, Nguyen Van Thuong, who had interviewed, and disappointed, T'ang Ching-sung on the latter's passage through Hue a year before. Nguyen's influence was especially strong as his son had married a sister of the new sovereign.

The substitution of rulers was without doubt ,intended to inaugurate a fresh attempt at resistance to the French, but by ill luck it occurred on the very eve of Courbet's success at Sontay. This, followed in the spring of 1884 by the series of Chinese defeats in Tongking, had dashed the hopes of the patriots. Then, to crown everything, just as Patenôtre arrived off the River of Perfumes came the tidings of the latest agreement in Tientsin. Even without the substantial military escort which accompanied him, not to mention the deployment of a naval squadron at the mouth of the river, the French envoy would hardly at such a time have met with much difficulty. The new treaty which was signed on June 6, 1884 will not be described here: for our purpose the situation remained essentially as before. Only one circumstance attending the ceremony needs to be mentioned. The most important physical symbol of Chinese suzerainty was a seal presented eighty years ago to Gia Long, the founder of the dynasty, by his overlord the Emperor Chia Ch'ing. The French had decided that, so long as this token remained at Hue, the old link with China would survive in some form. The seal must be surrendered and sent to Paris. Browbeaten as they were, this was too much for the Regents to accept: they resisted so strenuously that Patenôtre finally had to content himself with a compromise, namely that the seal should be ceremonially destroyed in his presence. It was a silver plaque with gold plating, four and a half inches square and weighing thirteen pounds: it bore the carving of a sitting camel. A clay stove and a pair of bellows were fetched to the conference-room and the process began. 'A few minutes later,' said the correspondent of the Havas News Agency, 'the last palpable vestige of the long suzerainty claimed by China over Vietnam had become a shapeless lump of silver.'

Up in Tientsin, Captain Fournier was naturally all eagerness to return to Paris with the text of the Sino-French agreement and to enjoy the celebrity his endeavours had won for him. One practical detail, however, still remained to be dealt with: it was neces-sary to fix a date for the evacuation of Tongking by the Chinese troops, since any vagueness on this point was calculated to provoke a clash which might stultify everything that had been accomplished in the past few days. On May 17, 1884, the eve of his departure, Fournier raised the matter with Li in the course of a conversation. He suggested that the withdrawal should be carried out in two stages. The Kwangsi troops, in such places as Langson, should retire to their own province within twenty days, whereas the Yunnanese troops, who were farther away and needed more time for orders to arrive, would be given forty days. Li was inclined to demur, on the grounds that not enough time was being given, but on being reminded that telegraphic communication had been extended some distance into Kwangsi and that the French were similarly equipped in Tongking, he yielded the point, or at least gave Fournier the impression of doing so. To prevent any mis-understanding, Fournier tells us that he warned Li that he intended sending a wire to the French military authorities in Tongking to inform them that they could summarily expel all Chinese garrisons still on Vietnamese soil after the appointed interval of time; and, in fact, he did cable both General Millot and Admiral Courbet, mentioning the precise dates: June 6th for the Kwangsi troops and June 26th for the Yunnanese. Jules Ferry included the same information in his report to the Senate and the Chamber of Deputies on May 20th concerning the Tientsin treaty. He referred to Li as 'the eminent statesman who at present exerts a pre-ponderant influence on the destinies of China'.

Actually, Li had put himself in a very delicate position. The

agreement just concluded had been acquiesced in by the Dowager
with a marked lack of enthusiasm. The provision that the Chinese
frontier with Tongking would be opened on favourable terms to
French merchandise made necessary a further, commercial treaty,
and it was feared in certain Court circles that these fresh negotiations, when they came, would extend to a delimitation of the
frontier itself, almost certainly to China's detriment. Yehonala,
too, had to take cognizance of the numerous letters from mandarins calling for Li's impeachment. One eminent official who had
denounced the peace terms was favoured in secret early in June
with an imperial missive to assure him that the vigilance of himself
and his colleagues was still necessary to ensure that the French
would not try their old rascality again over the border trade.
Orders were sent from the Foreign Office that the Kwangsi and
Yunnanese troops should refrain from advancing more deeply
into Tongking, but should remain in their present positions until
further orders. In such an atmosphere, Li confessed that he did
not have the courage to tell Peking of Fournier's ultimatum about
the date of withdrawal. However, he sent personal messages to the
Kwangsi and Yunnanese commanders, informing them of what
had happened and giving them a broad hint that no harm would
be done by honouring the French, since 'the frontier country, all
mountain and jungles, is of small consequence, whether we hold
it or lose it'. From Li's notes and correspondence it can be gathered
that Fournier had particularly specified the Black Flags as the
Chinese whose presence could no longer be tolerated. Li himself
had done his best to persuade his countrymen along the same lines.
A couple of months earlier he had written: 'In their defeat, the
troops of Liu Yung-fu as they go through the countryside burning
and killing have emerged as the enemies of the people. No wonder
the French regard this undisciplined crew as a gang of brigands.'
He was aware, however, that such sentiments stuck in the throat
of nearly every ordinary Chinese—and particularly the Dowager.
It was now an article of faith that Liu Yung-fu and his men were
national heroes, and it would be rash in the extreme to deny such
a legend too ostentatiously. Nevertheless, in a confidential message
to Ts'en Yu-ying he tried to convince that hard-headed character
that if French patrols approached the vicinity of Laokay—a most

unlikely event in the malarial heat of summer—their purpose was merely to pursue the Black Flags, and Ts'en need not go out of his way to create an incident.

On the French side, General Millot permitted more than a week to go by after the expiry of the allotted period before he took steps to occupy Langson, and, whether relying on the agreement or out of some contempt for his enemy, he despatched only a column of eight hundred men under a Lt.-Col. Dugenne, with a baggage train of about the same number of coolies. Setting out along the 'Mandarin Road' from Bac-Ninh on June 15, 1884, the party soon ran into most atrocious weather. The heat was insupportable and floods had washed most of the road away: it was all they could do to struggle two or three miles a day knee-deep in mud. On June 19th they came to the hamlet of Bac-Le, about thirty miles from their destination, where they were held up for the next three days by a river in spate. Goaded into action by a sarcastic message from the General, on June 23rd they struggled across the stream, clinging desperately to their mules in order not to be swept away; but as soon as the advance party had set foot on the opposite bank they were greeted by rifle shots from a mound covered with bushes about three hundred yards off. Shortly afterwards an unarmed man approached, obviously a messenger, for he was carrying a letter at the end of a bamboo stick. He was blindfolded and led before Dugenne. The French had had the foresight to take an educated Vietnamese along with them to act as interpreter, but he had enormous difficulty in elucidating what had been written. Actually, the letter, which was drafted with notable courtesy, explained that the Chinese commanders were aware of the period of twenty days stipulated by Fournier for the withdrawal of the Kwangsi army, but were unable to retire without definite orders. They requested the French to wire to Peking on their behalf to press for instructions. The letter ended by stating that as the two countries were now at peace, they should not needlessly come to blows.

The request could easily have been complied with, or at least a message could have been sent by field-telegraph from the nearest outpost to Bac-Ninh or Hanoi: but Dugenne, anxious, perhaps, to make up for the delay which had annoyed the General, declared in a lordly manner that he would allow the Chinese one hour to clear the way, and then he would advance towards Langson. When the time was up the French marched forward, only to be halted by a punishing fire, for the Chinese were armed with Remington rifles. The invaders formed a square and dug themselves in for the night. Next morning, realizing their situation was desperate, they retreated across the river to the hamlet of Bac-Le. The name of this village, which was given to the engagement, was within a few hours echoing around the world. By itself, the repulse was not especially costly: the French had twenty-two dead and sixty wounded: but the war had irrevocably entered upon a new phase.

CHAPTER SIXTEEN

France : The Day of Glory

THE cry of the French was that the affair had been a deliberate trap, set to snare their unsuspecting troops. 'We had
full confidence in your word,' said Jules Ferry in a personal
cable to Li Hung-chang. What rankled especially with the Paris
government was the fact that arrangements were already being
made to reduce the number of soldiers in Tongking. Now not only
would all these plans have to be cancelled; it would be a miracle
if further supplies and expenditure were not required.

As early as June 28, 1884, the Vicomte de Semallé, French
Chargé d'Affaires, had protested to the Chinese Foreign Office,
making it clear that his government would demand an indemnity.
The Chinese rejected the protest, insisting instead that the French
had brought the disaster on themselves, and that if there had to be
any talk of indemnities, it was for the French to do the paying,
since China too had suffered casualties amounting to a total of
three hundred men killed and wounded. There was not a word in
the Tientsin treaty, they said, of any date for the evacuation of
Tongking. On the contrary, the question of commerce and the
frontier had been left to be settled by later negotiations, and until
then the Chinese garrisons had been ordered to remain in their
present positions. It will be remembered that the Chinese government had the month before informed some of its own mandarins
that it considered that the problem of Sino-French commerce via
the Tongking frontier called into question the demarcation of the
frontier itself.

It was in such an atmosphere that on July 1st M. Patenôtre, the

French Minister, arrived in Shanghai, where he was followed five days later by Admiral Courbet with his squadron. The two men found they were much of the same mind. Patenôtre had already represented his country in Peking, and prided himself on his expert knowledge of how to manage the natives: a few days in Shanghai, that Mecca of Old China Hands, were more than sufficient to give him the imperious manner proper to his mission. As for Courbet, his spirits had been badly dashed by the news of the Li-Fournier treaty which seemed to deny him the opportunity to advance his career by some resounding exploit worthy of the victor of Sontay. It will be understood, therefore, that he was in the best of humour at the latest turn of events. Diplomatic refinements, in his view, were wasted on orientals, who were impressed only by force. For the time being, the summer rains precluded any sizeable land operations in Tongking. The blow could be struck only by sea, and he would strike it at China herself.

To the Minister and the Admiral, as they deliberated in the humid Shanghai heat, the course to follow was plainly indicated. China must be presented with an ultimatum, requiring the recognition of the Tientsin treaty and a promise of the immediate evacuation of Tongking, the payment of an indemnity (which they assessed provisionally at two hundred and fifty million francs), and the surrender of the arsenals of Foochow and Nanking into French hands as security. If these conditions were not accepted within three days, the French Chargé d'Affaires would quit Peking and the French forces would seize the above-mentioned arsenals, and perhaps other such establishments. The consent of Paris would have to be obtained before an ultimatum of this nature could be presented, and at the same time permission would be sought for even more extensive action against bases in North China, for instance Port Arthur in Manchuria, and Weihaiwei in Shantung, at the Admiral's discretion.

However, the French government was not composed of Old China Hands, and the proposal excited more alarm than enthusiasm. To begin with, the northern bases—and, for that matter, Macartney's old establishment at Nanking—were the foundations on which had been constructed the power of Li Hung-chang, and

Ferry and his colleagues understood that it would be Li Hung-chang to whose collaboration they would have to look for the accomplishment of their purpose. Then again, an ultimatum couched in such brutal terms would quite certainly be rejected, and the action envisaged, especially that at Nanking, would commit the French to a campaign on the mainland with totally inadequate resources, not to mention the offence that would almost inevitably be given by damage inflicted on the commercial interests of neutral countries.

On the other hand, the seizure of Chinese property as security was in itself a perfectly sound idea. The port of Keelung, in the north of Formosa, and the coalfields in its vicinity, would constitute a splendid prize which might be acquired without much risk of unwelcome complications, and would prove particularly valuable if the affair developed into a regular war and other countries considered themselves bound by the rules of neutrality to deny refuelling facilities to French naval vessels. Of the arsenals mentioned, that at Foochow could be threatened without undue danger to foreign interests. Courbet, then, might detach units of his fleet to Keelung and Foochow, but he must on no account take military action until the receipt of specific orders. Furthermore, in presenting the French ultimatum, a delay of one week—not three days—must be granted for a reply. The revised list of demands was addressed to the Chinese government on July 12th: it required principally that Chinese troops should be ordered to quit Tongking without delay, and that payment of two hundred and fifty million francs should be made as indemnity. M. Patenôtre would wait in Shanghai to meet any Chinese plenipotentiary empowered to discuss the implementation of the Tientsin treaty.

During these days the emotions of the Dowager, on whom everything depended, were fluctuating violently. It seemed for a time that apart from the indemnity—the amount of which Paris was, in any case willing to reconsider—the French requirements would be met. A conciliatory message to that effect was forwarded to the Legation in Paris through Li Hung-chang, who had just been severely reprimanded for not having informed Peking of his verbal exchanges with Fournier concerning the date of troop withdrawal, but who (as was shown by this mark of confidence) had now been forgiven. Yet a day or two later, Yehonala's mood had veered once more and she was lending an ear to the sounds of protest that came in from every side. That she was capable of almost boundless credulity where claims of national power were concerned was to be demonstrated sixteen years later in her assessment of the Boxers. Compared with the boasts of those fanatics, the xenophobes of 1884 sounded reasonable enough, though in fact their versions of what was going on were often the wildest inventions. The Kwangsi field commander, for instance, assured the government that 'several thousand' Frenchmen had perished at Bac-Le, and although a report from the Legation in Paris gave the lie to this absurdity it is doubtful how far Yehonala was willing to listen to the truth. On July 19th, Tseng Kuo-ch'uan, the uncle of the Marquis Tseng, who until recently had been Viceroy at Canton, but now held an identical post at Nanking, was given plenipotentiary status to treat with Patenôtre at Shanghai. Tseng's very name was enough to satisfy the enemies of appeasement, and his instructions lacked nothing in firmness.

'You must on no account give way on the question of indemnity [he was told]. Reply that you are referring the point to Us. The most important thing is that the King of Vietnam should continue to be enfeoffed by Us and to pay Us tribute. If they mention Liu Yung-fu and his army, say that it is a matter for China to deal with. In delimiting the frontier, an area should be left as no-man's land on the Vietnam side of the boundary. If the negotiations break down, go straight back to Nanking. In no circumstances must you go on board a French ship, for you would be putting yourself in their hands.'

To a foreigner, it seemed hopeless for Li Hung-chang to try and dilute the severity of this programme, but he was not the man to be easily discouraged. 'If there is no other course open to you,' he cabled to Tseng on July 23rd, 'whatever the rights or the wrongs of the case, it would not damage our prestige to give a few hundred thousand dollars as compensation for the killed and wounded French soldiers.'[31]

In face of the Chinese willingness to treat, the French had extended the time limit of their ultimatum to August 1st, and it was July 29th when Tseng and Patenôtre began their talks in Shanghai. From the start it was plain that too great a distance separated their positions for there to be any real hope of a compromise. Nevertheless, Tseng was so intimidated by the Frenchman's stern and implacable demeanour that he offered five hundred thousand dollars as compensation. Patenôtre coldly pointed out that this amounted only to the derisory sum of three million three hundred thousand francs. Such a proposal could not be entertained for a moment. Nor was that all: sensing the admiration in which by now nearly every Chinese held the Black Flags, he insisted that the government at Peking must publicly strip Liu Yung-fu of his commission and dissociate itself from him and his followers. As the exchanges continued, August 1st came and went: the French resolved upon action.

In the middle of July Courbet had moved his ships so as to be ready to meet all eventualities. He himself with the bulk of his force had steamed due south along the coast as far as Foochow. On August 1st, with the expiry of the time limit, orders arrived to seize the port and mines of Keelung in Formosa, and Courbet's second-in-command Admiral Lespès sailed for that destination with the armoured vessel and a gun boat. One cruiser was already lying off the place. On August 5th, the governor was summoned to surrender and when he refused the French opened fire against the fortifications until the Chinese guns were silenced. A landing party was then put ashore, to find the garrison had fled leaving many dead behind them. So far only two Frenchmen had been killed and ten wounded, but now he was on the spot, Lespès recognized that his forces were insufficient to make any attempt on the coalfields. For a little while, however, he imagined it would be possible to hold the port itself, until even this ceased to be feasible on the apparition up in the hills of a Chinese army judged to comprise at least fifteen thousand men. Cursing the faulty information with which he had been furnished, Lespès brought back all his men on board, and decided to rest content with blockading the harbour.

To the Chinese the incident was most readily interpreted as a setback for the French, especially since the latter not only persevered with diplomatic negotiations, but began to lower their terms. On August 19th, yet another ultimatum was served, reducing the amount of the indemnity to eighty million francs and allowing two days for a reply. What the foreigners did not know was that a few days previously Tseng Kuo-ch'uan had received a stinging rebuke from Yehonala.

'We hear you have promised to pay the French five hundred thousand dollars as compensation, [she said]. We realize that you took this step in order to hasten the conclusion of peace, but its sole effect has been to make China ridiculous. The French envoy declares that he is bound to obey the head of his government. When a Chinese minister makes promises so lightly, it is clear that he lacks a proper grasp of the situation.'

With such ideas in favour in the Forbidden City, the new proposal had no better chance of acceptance than the old. This time, the refusal was taken at its face value. On August 21, 1884, the French Chargé d'Affaires in Peking hauled down the tricolour from his Legation flagstaff in sign that his mission was at an end. In reply, China cabled to Li Feng-pao, who had stepped into the Marquis Tseng's shoes at Paris, to return at once to his original post at Berlin.

The French ultimatum of August 19th concluded with these words: 'Admiral Courbet will immediately take whatever steps seem to him necessary to secure for the French government the reparations to which it is entitled.' In spite of this, however, the plan which was being followed was in several respects divergent from Courbet's personal views. He had never, for instance, been enthusiastic over the Keelung project, which he thought was a wretched substitute for the heroic onslaught against the mainland bases, including those in the north, which he would have preferred. The Formosan adventure had been the pet idea of Lespès and Captain Fournier which a pusillanimous government had adopted as less dangerous. Lespès had obviously got himself into a mess, but orders were orders and the business would have to be followed up. Since the middle of July Courbet's squadron had been stationed about twelve miles up the Min river, near the city of Foochow, at a place called Pagoda Anchorage, opposite the famous Arsenal, itself built by French advisers and the home base for what was esteemed the most formidable of China's fleets. This the Admiral was now able to inspect at his leisure, for it was drawn up in the river nearby. It consisted of eleven ships, nine of them wooden, amounting to almost six thousand five hundred tons and carrying forty-five guns, only a few of these being of large calibre. Besides these vessels there were a dozen junks equipped with guns and a number of armed rowing boats. The French, in contrast, had eight ships, two of them armoured, totalling over fourteen thousand tons, and a couple of torpedo boats. They carried seventy-seven cannon, not to mention a large number of machine guns of the most modern type. Communication with the outside world could be maintained through the telegraph on shore, though for most of the time messages for greater security were sent from the maritime cable station at the mouth of the river.

The news from Keelung made it imperative that Courbet's force should be withdrawn to that theatre of action, but in his opinion it would be disastrous to retire from Foochow without striking a blow. In any event, it was doubtful if the Chinese would permit them to leave in peace, since between Pagoda Anchorage and the sea there were a number of fortified positions from which their passage could be intercepted. It ought to be added that in the French view the destruction of the Chinese fleet and of naval installations would not be an act of war, for which the Constitution of the Third Republic required the approval of Parliament, but would form merely a case of reprisal. Nevertheless it was a step of such gravity that Jules Ferry decided he had better unburden himself to the Chamber of Deputies, which he proceeded to do in a debate on August 14th concerning the grant of another credit of thirty-eight million francs for operations in Tongking. As might have been anticipated he did not have things all his own way.

'We are now [said Ferry] in front of the arsenal at Foochow, containing all the military and naval resources of China. We could destroy this arsenal, but we remain in a state of peace. Before going further, it was our duty to ask the consent of this Chamber. I have shown you how China is irresolute, waiting, Waiting for what? Waiting for your vote, gentlemen.'

At this, both from the right and from the left, protests were heard that the country was being ineluctably committed to a war with China. There were those who went so far as to suggest that

Peking was quite blameless in the Bac-Le affair. But finally, by a hundred and seventy three votes to fifty, the Chamber adopted a motion of confidence 'in the firmness with which the government will compel respect for the treaty of Tientsin'.

For some months, Peking had been keenly aware of the danger which threatened both Foochow and Formosa and had given orders for defensive preparations to be set in motion. This was the true explanation for the rapid assembly of the army which rescued Keelung early in August. Foochow had been specially alerted, but the measures taken there were ludicrously inept. The one which made the deepest impression on the population was a decree that the entrance to every side-street and alleyway in the town should be barred by the erection of a wooden palisade with a gate in it. It is worth mentioning that precisely the same order was issued by the Nationalist authorities in Shanghai on the approach of the Communists in the spring of 1949. Indeed, in Shanghai the precaution was carried even further, and a wooden fence was constructed around the perimeter of the city. In this latter case, however, there was method in the apparent madness, for it was an open secret that a Nationalist commander had bought up all available stocks of timber which he was thus enabled to sell back to the municipality at a handsome profit, and one may incline to think that a similar transaction may have occurred at Foochow.[31]

The great question is why in the world Courbet should have been allowed to sail unmolested up twelve miles of river. To be sure, he came wearing a mask of friendship, and the charade was kept up so scrupulously that as late as August 16th, ten days after the attack on Keelung, the French ships were dressed overall to celebrate the Emperor of China's birthday. One eminent authority, H. B. Morse, in his *International Relations of the Chinese Empire* says:

'The Chinese were helpless in his [Courbet's] presence; not so much because their force was less, as because, in dealing with questions of international law, they were as tyros in the presence of masters—like amateurs playing with chess champions. Had they wished to order him out of port, they would not have known how to do it.—Even if the Chinese had been willing to lay themselves open to the charge of a treacherous breach of hospitality, and had wished to attack the French ships, they would have required a skill which they did not possess to avoid inflicting serious damage on the neutral war-ships and merchant-ships lying in close proximity to the French.'[33]

Yet the Viceroy of Chekiang and Fukien, who was in the city, and the Director of Coastal Defence both had some reputation for being knowledgeable in military affairs, and the latter in particular was well known as a partisan of firmness. In July they had sent a memorandum to Peking asking that the ships of Li Hung-chang's northern fleet should come down and join them, but Li pointed out that his vessels were no match for the enemy, and that in any event the defence of the north, because of its proximity to the capital, was more important than that of the south. So gloomy was he concerning China's chances in a war at sea that he privately transferred the ownership of his China Merchants' cargo vessels to an American company on the understanding that he could redeem them after hostilities had endered. Before Courbet's arrival at Foochow, the best advice Li could give to the fleet there was to scatter for safety. When this counsel was no longer feasible he recommended giving way as far as was humanly possible, a course which was followed beyond the limits of prudence.

Behind the screen of official courtesy Courbet was burning for action; he could not forgive Paris for its lethargy. At last, on the afternoon of August 22nd, there was received the long-expected authorization to open fire. Next morning, the Director of the Arsenal was officially notified that hostilities would shortly commence. He passed the word to the Viceroy and his colleague in charge of Coastal Defence, and according to a story current at Foochow the three of them put their heads together and decided to write to Courbet saying that they were not yet ready and asking him if he would be so kind as to postpone his attack till the next day. It is quite conceivable, such was their naivety and confusion, that the tale is true. Certainly a Chinese official carrying a message of some kind attempted to go on board Courbet's flagship, but was brusquely sent away. It seems that the higher mandarins, however, did not take their subordinates into their confidence, and when the cannonade began, just before two o'clock in the afternoon, the crews of the Chinese ships were still largely unprepared: in fact ammunition had still to be issued in most of them. The Chinese flagship was torpedoed and sunk in little more than a minute. Within an hour all the Chinese vessels were either sunk or drifting in flames. At two-thirty the dock was blown up. The Director of the Arsenal, as well as the mandarin charged with Coastal Defence, bolted almost at the first shot and fled on foot through a storm of torrential summer rain out into the country where they finally sought shelter in a Buddhist monastery.

During the next three days Courbet's squadron made their way down river to the sea, methodically destroying the forts along the banks. This task was rendered all the easier since the Chinese guns, like the British cannon at Singapore in 1942, were directed seawards and were useless against an enemy who attacked from the rear. Their mission accomplished, the French fleet anchored off the island of Matsu, famous in our own day with its sister Quemoy as an outpost of Nationalist China, while Courbet himself crossed the straits to take a look at Keelung, the next item on his agenda. Before leaving, in his report to Paris he expressed his pride in the conduct of all under his command during 'the brilliant day of August 23rd'. All the ships were safe, but 'we have cruel losses: ten killed, including one officer, and forty-eight wounded, including six officers. As for the Chinese, it is impossible to make a precise estimate. The fantastic figure put out in the first shock of terror has now been replaced by a very likely number of between two and three thousand killed or wounded.'

Back in Foochow, the people were busy dragging the river for the bodies of the dead, most of whom were natives of the district. Relatives flocked into the town to search among the corpses laid out for inspection in a temple, but these were so mangled that few of them were recognizable. They were buried in a mass grave on the side of a hill and a monument erected over them.

In Peking the events at Foochow had proved the last straw, and on August 27th an imperial decree proclaimed that China was in a state of war with France. Liu Yung-fu was formally named as having the rank of general and was enjoined to recover the territory lost in Tongking. French ships of war were to be attacked wherever they made an appearance. At Canton, the Viceroy renewed the proclamation in a more traditional manner by offering rewards to whoever brought him the head of a Frenchman. The same zealous official shortly afterwards extended the scope of his bounty to encourage Chinese living in such places as Singapore to poison any Frenchmen among their fellow-residents, a notion which elicited a scandalized protest from the British Minister.

The French, for their part, were in no hurry to acknowledge that they were formally at war, since for their own convenience they were anxious to use neutral ports such as Hong Kong for as long as possible. They continued, therefore, to maintain the pretence that at Formosa and elsewhere they were engaged not in acts of war but in 'reprisals'. It was some considerable time before the fiction was rejected by third parties, and meanwhile the French enjoyed coaling and other facilities unhampered by the laws of neutrality. In China itself French missionaries and other civilians even outside the foreign settlements were in general unmolested, French consuls remained at their posts in such places as Tientsin and Shanghai, and at the latter city M. Patenôtre continued to reside in the French Concession.

CHAPTER SEVENTEEN

Formosa and Tongking

ADMIRAL Courbet, on reconnoitring Keelung from the sea, felt all his original uneasiness at the prospect of a Formosan adventure confirmed by what he found. The harbour was restricted in extent, and even then did not afford an adequate shelter from the constant heavy ground-swell which would become worse with the monsoon. It was true that there were coalfields adjacent to the port, but the loss of these would be no hardship to the Chinese, while the coal to be got from them was of such poor quality that it would make a most unsatisfactory substitute for what was now being burned. Then there was the great distance of Formosa from the seat of government in Peking, which meant that whatever happened there would not have much influence on Chinese policy. Any serious operations would demand more troops than he had at present. Besides, he had no sympathy with this perpetual dithering on the skirts of the problem. In his view what was required was an outright declaration of war on China and the occupation of northern harbours such as Weihaiwei and Port Arthur, from where pressure could be brought to bear on Peking by blockading the Gulf of Pechili and intercepting the supply of rice from the south.

Paris had once already rejected the idea of an assault on the north. Still, it was undeniable that the bombardment of Foochow had in no way weakened the Chinese will to resist, and without doubt a blow nearer home would be more effectual. Jules Ferry was ready this time to give the Admiral more liberty of action. The trouble was that Courbet did not conceal his belief that a mere cannonade of the northern ports would be insufficient. That had been done to Foochow, and no sooner had the French retired than the local commanders were blatantly pretending that they had repelled the enemy. Weihaiwei and Port Arthur would have to be occupied. Paris had just consented to divert two thousand men from Tongking for the Formosan undertaking: why not use them in the north instead? This was too much for the government to admit: if Courbet had his way, they would be dragged into a large-scale campaign on the Chinese mainland, which was the last thing in the world they wanted. Besides, the rice shipments for the year had already been sent. In a few weeks winter would be at hand and the northern harbours would be sealed by ice. A blockade of the Gulf of Pechili would be of little use before the coming of spring. No, all things considered, the original plan of seizing Keelung and its neighbourhood was the safest. On September 18, 1884, this cable went to the Admiral: 'Begin by occupying Keelung, which the government is most anxious to have as security.'

The rendezvous for the expedition was the island of Matsu, where at the end of September the promised reinforcement of two thousand men from Tongking joined the flotilla, which appeared in front of Keelung at daybreak on October 1st. Keeping close inshore the ships opened fire on the hill-top forts overlooking the town, while the troops were landed at a spot from which they could make a detour and scale the heights from the rear. The climb was formidable, and was made even more difficult in places by almost impenetrable thickets of stunted trees. The soldiers' packs were loaded to the full, but not a drop of drink had been issued and the hillside was parched and waterless. Hours passed, until at midday those in front emerged on a peak behind the Chinese defence-works; the Chinese garrison, seeing their line of retreat threatened, began to withdraw. Even then it needed another couple of hours for the invaders to struggle to their goal, and they arrived there so dry that they threw themselves on some large jars of water left by the Chinese. Only when they had slaked their thirst did it occur to them that the water might have been poisoned, but mercifully the enemy had not had the presence of mind to take so obvious a step.

Also on the northern coast of Formosa, and a mere twenty miles westward of Keelung, lay another harbour, that of Tamsui, which in certain respects was a more valuable prize still, for it was an open port and in consequence the international gateway to Formosa. To capture the customs-house there would certainly inflict a painful injury on China, but the matter required the most careful handling, since there was an acute danger of damaging property as well. Yet the prospect was too tempting even for the caution of Paris, and Courbet had been empowered to carry out this additional operation, which he delegated to Lespès, his second-in-command, for it seemed a sound move to divide the Chinese forces by a double attack. On October 2nd Lespès silenced the coastal batteries near Tamsui, but discovered the river entrance barred by a line of submerged junks. A landing-party of about six hundred men was thereupon put ashore, only to be confronted by four times as many Chinese, well-armed with quick-firing rifles, whom no efforts could dislodge. Finding the situation desperate, after some hours the French retreated to their ships, and decided, for the time being at least, to satisfy themselves with a simple blockade.

This setback, which obviously was going to be represented by Peking as a resounding Chinese triumph, cast a gloom over the victors of Keelung. Nor was it long before other events occured to lower their spirits. Towards the middle of October the monsoon broke, bringing with it the rain, which fell incessantly, turning the ground on which the French were encamped into a foul stinking morass. It is astonishing to learn that despite their national reputation they had come so wretchedly supplied with victuals that they were compelled to eke out their ration of mouldy biscuits with handfuls of sweet-potatoes grubbed up from the fields around them. Soon these fields were being put to another use, that of burying the dead, for men were falling ill and succumbing in the space of a few hours. At one of these funerals, at the beginning of November, Courbet said in the course of a graveside address, 'We have found here an enemy we were not counting upon'. The enemy was disguised as far as possible under a cloak of officialese but the soldiers, seeing it face to face, recognized it plainly for what it was —the cholera. In one month, the landing force of eighteen hundred men had been reduced by a third, and was tightly hemmed in by a Chinese army of many thousands. So wide were the intervals between the French outposts that night after night the enemy would slip through to exhume and decapitate the bodies of the dead, for the mandarins were offering fifty dollars' reward for any such trophy.

At the end of October, in the hope of retrieving the situation, the French proclaimed a blockade of Formosa, and gave neutral shipping three days' notice to quit the island. This had the effect of doubling the price of imported articles, but French naval strength in those waters was not sufficient for the task, especially at the peak of the monsoon, and reinforcements of Chinese troops continued to find entry. By the last days of December, twenty thousand well-equipped soldiers confronted a mere six hundred Europeans, capable of bearing arms, but in a deplorable condition with every kind of affliction from anemia to tapeworm. French books refer to the 'calvary of Keelung', and it was obviously from the Chinese point of view sounder policy to let the affair drag on, rather than pay the price which the guns of Courbet's ships could have exacted in order simply to put the invaders out of their misery by driving them into the sea.

In Vietnam itself things were not standing still. The royal palace at Hue again witnessed a mysterious death, but one which to certain seasoned observers did not come altogether as a surprise. When King Kien-Phuoc signed the treaty with M. Patenôtre in June, it was whispered that in spite of his youth he would not long survive such a gesture of abnegation. It seemed as if the French reverse at Bac-Le precipitated events, for on July 31, 1884 the King died, exactly how from that day to this has never been fully explained, though few doubted that poison administered by the Regents was the cause. His second brother, a lad of fourteen, was elevated in his place under the style of Nam-Nghi, and the significance of what had happened was emphasized by the ostentatious omission of the Regents not only to seek the approval of the French but even to give them prior warning of the choice of sovereign. To let such impertinence pass unnoticed, it was felt in Paris, would be to invite insubordination in the future. The challenge was therefore accepted. On August 12th, the Chief of Staff of the French expeditionary force arrived in Hue with a battalion of troops and a battery of artillery, and immediately presented the Regents with an ultimatum: they were curtly told that they were required to make an application in due and proper form soliciting the assent of France to the nomination of the new monarch. Faced with this firmness, the courage of the mandarins evaporated. The petition was submitted and granted, and on August 17th the French Resident, with the Chief of Staff, made a ceremonial entrance into the Palace by the self-same door through which in former years had passed the envoys of Peking, and witnessed the enthronement.

Throughout July Chinese troops in increasing numbers had been moving south to the Tongking border. The new Governor of Kwangsi—it may be remembered that the previous incumbent had committed sucide after the loss of Bac-Ninh—manifested a striking reluctance to risk his provincial forces in battle, alleging, which was true, that malaria was very prevalent in Vietnam at that time of year, and that it would be folly to expose his men to the risk of contagion. He urged that until the autumn season was well advanced all active campaigning should be relegated to the Black Flags who had lived in the country so long that they were completely immune. However, we know that the Governor was under the patronage of Li Hung-chang, and from this circumstance the Communist historians deduce that Li's influence was ulti-mately responsible for the extreme deliberation, not to say lethargy, of the Kwangsi command at this juncture. Be that as it may, an order did reach Liu Yung-fu from Peking directing him to take the field. For a while, the idea that the brunt of the fighting was again to be left to him failed signally to arouse his enthusiasm, and he stayed aloof, sulking in his quarters as he had done a couple of years before. In the long run, though, the appeals of Ts'en Yu-ying, who was amassing a numerous army at Laokay, had their effect; and the Black Flags with a substantial contingent of Yunnanese troops marched against the walled town of Tuyen-Quang, situated on the Clear River (the northern tributary of the Red River), and in French hands since May 1884. The siege began in the middle of October 1884 and lasted intermittently for the better part of five months. In November the siege was raised for a brief period and a fresh garrison of about six hundred men put into the place, but then the circle was drawn round it again. As could have been expected from an action in which Liu Yung-fu played a leading role, the besiegers displayed remarkable pertinacity. The presence of the Yunnanese troops contributed to the technical side of the operation, both in the laying of mines against the town-walls, and in the construction of a system of entrenchments to hold a relieving force at bay. By February 1885, the garrison was in a desperate position and was appealing frantically for help by means of letters enclosed in bottles or bamboo tubes and thrown into the river in the hope that such of them as escaped the notice of the Chinese would be carried far enough by the current to fall into French hands.

The previous winter, immediately after the victory at Sontay, jealousy on the part of the army had resulted in Admiral Courbet's replacement, as head of combined operations, by General Millot. This arrangement in its turn was proving intolerable to the navy, and had led to a series of incidents described by a Paris newspaper as being almost without precedent.[34] The naval captain in charge of the flotilla attached to the Tongking expeditionary force was mortified to discover that orders were being issued from headquarters directly to gunboat commanders instead of being transmitted through him, as courtesy required. Moreover, when he ventured, in respectful terms, to draw General Millot's attention to this unusual state of affairs, he was promptly placed under arrest. The same punishment was meted out to the chief naval doctor for refusing to obey an order of an army colleague, even though the latter was his inferior in rank. At length the outcry became so loud that Millot whose health, undermined by the climate, had not been improved by the shock of Bac-Le, was relieved of command at his own request, and was succeeded early in September 1884 by General Brière de l'Isle, an infantry officer who had already for some months been campaigning in Tongking.

During that same month of September it became evident that in spite of the dilatory attitude of the Kwangsi authorities there was a considerable build-up of Chinese forces south of Langson, extending in places as far as the periphery of the Delta. In the first days of October the French launched an offensive aimed at clearing the country between Bac-Ninh and Langson, and in the middle of the month encountered strong Chinese resistance at points a little to the south of Bac-Le. This proved, however, an untypical performance by the Kwangsi army, for once overcome they fell back in such disorder that if the French had decided to drive forward Langson would very likely have been taken there and then. As it was, past experience, the prior claim of Tuyen-Quang, of which the first relief was organized at that time, and the fact that General Campenon, Minister of War in Paris, was for limiting operations to the Delta, postponed this exploit for several months; and it was not until the end of January 1885, after Campenon had resigned, that the advance towards the Chinese frontier was resumed. For a fortnight the newspapers of Paris regaled their readers with stories of victory at places with unpronounceable names. Then on February 13, 1885, the tricolour waved over the fortress of Langson, abandoned the day before by its Chinese garrison. The road to China lay open, as the Kwangsi troops poured back in confusion over their own border.

Yet there were other Chinese soldiers of different calibre. While this undignified route was in progress in the northern portion of Tongking, Liu Yung-fu, further west, had reimposed his stranglehold on Tuyen-Quang, and messages, floating downstream in their bottles, spoke of a breach in the walls. It was vexatious, but Brière de l'Isle had no choice but to forgo the pleasure of battering on the doors of the Celestial Empire, to use a favourite journalistic expression of the day: the appeal from Tuyen-Quang was irresistible. Yet he had no wish to be a spoilsport, and as he marched off along the path of duty, he delegated the honour of baiting the dragon in its lair to his second-in-command, General de Négrier, a strutting martinet whose hour-glass figure bore witness that whoever made his stays did not stint the whalebone, and whose frantic exhortations to his men to be up and doing had earned him the nickname of General Man-len, from a Vietnamese word meaning 'quick'. On February 23rd, this fire-brand accomplished what was no doubt the crowning exploit of his career by the capture of Chennankuan, called by foreigners, with good reason, 'the Gate of China', for on the line of the frontier as it traversed a narrow valley, had been erected a wall with a fortified gateway, which the conquerors now proceeded to demolish.

As he looked through the ruins at the prospect of Kwangsi, stretched tantalizingly before him, General de Négrier must have been amused by the ludicrous measures to which the Chinese were resorting in their panic. In the last engagement, the Governor of Kwangsi had to some extent salvaged his honour by receiving a wound, but this was insufficient to atone for the unbroken list of disasters attributable to his mismanagement, and it hardly came as a surprise to learn that he had been deprived of his post. The desperation to which the Chinese had been reduced could be seen in the recall to the colours of the veteran General Feng Tzu-ts'ai, whom we met during the 1870s in charge of bandit-suppression in Tongking and who for several years had been enjoying a well-deserved retirement, for he was by now a septuagenarian. The title of the appointment was fully as grotesque as the choice of appointee: General Feng was named commander of Kwangsi forces beyond the frontier, a body of troops which was no longer in existence. One can imagine the guffaws in the French officers' mess at this latest example of oriental face-saving. To add to the high spirits, there came word from Tuyen-Quang that Brière de l'Isle had finally rescued that much harassed fortress from the clutches of the Black Flags. To be sure, it was announced even at that early stage that French losses had been grievous. There was talk of five hundred casualties incurred in continual assaults against the Chinese entrenchments. For the moment, however, nothing could compare with the splendour of the triumph, and the heroes of Tuyen-Quang were celebrated for months afterwards by the ballad-makers of Paris.

Out in the China Sea, too, the war was entering upon a new stage. So far no third power had felt that the hostilities required formal acknowledgment. It was known that with the blessing of the Marquis Tseng a bureau had opened in London to recruit soldiers of fortune under the Chinese flag. On January 23, 1885 the British government, by invoking the Foreign Enlistment Act, put a stop to this activity and recognized that a state of belligerency existed between China and France. The immediate consequence was that neither side could thenceforward use such ports as Hong Kong and Singapore for replenishing its naval vessels, an eventuality which the French had tried to avert as long as possible by refraining from a declaration of war. Yet the inconvenience was mitigated by the fact that Admiral Courbet at last had his hands freed to use the rights of a combattant in warning neutral ships that they carried contraband to China at their own risk and peril. Early in February it was reported that some units of the Chinese fleet were sailing out from the Yangtze, and Courbet at once went off in search of them. When sighted off the coast south of Shanghai on February 15th, which happened to be Chinese New Year's Day, the chief members of the squadron, three cruisers—two of them of German manufacture—succeeded in escaping into the harbour of Ningpo, where they remained for the rest of the war. A frigate and a corvette, hotly pursued, were obliged to take refuge nearer at hand in an anchorage on the coast of Chekiang province where they would be covered by coastal batteries. During the night, a couple of tiny French boats went in and torpedoed the frigate, while the corvette was sent to the bottom by the misdirected fire of the artillery on land. Occurring as it did about the same time as the capture of Langson, the exploit helped to console Courbet for the miseries of Keeling, which were still dragging on with no end in view.

At last the melting of the ice along the northern coast heralded the arrival of the ships from the south, bearing rice to refill the storehouses of the capital after the consumption of the winter months. This was the very moment the Admiral had been waiting for, when a really formidable blow could be struck where it would hurt most. To seal the passage through the straits, it was decided to occupy the chain of islands called the Pescadores, which extend between the southern tip of Formosa and the mainland, and on March 31st, at the cost of only trifling losses, the port of Makung fell into French hands. All in all, the Chinese situation looked hopeless. Yet at that very moment, both in Tongking and in Paris, events took a surprising turn.

⚜ CHAPTER EIGHTEEN

Catastrophe

ALTHOUGH the conflict had been watched with varying emotions by third parties, it was only in recent months that diplomatic etiquette allowed cognizance to be taken of the confrontation between China and France. Before the end of 1883, for instance, Peking had never officially acknowledged that imperial troops participated in the fighting in Tongking, nor on the French side was there any disposition to force the Chinese into admitting their intervention. From the middle of 1884, however, such a conspiracy of silence was no longer maintained, and Britain, Germany and the United States could openly assess the consequences to their own interests of the changed situation. Their immediate reaction, of course, was anxiety at the threat to commerce which a war would bring in its train, and in consequence a certain inclination to look askance at French aggression. This was especially true of the British, whom the founders of French Indochina had to a man regarded as their supreme enemy. Public opinion in London was not unfairly represented by such books as *Tonkin, or France in the Far East* by C. B. Norman, an officer in the Indian army, who seems to have devoted all his waking hours to the detection of the anti-British machinations of the Paris government. In this work, published in 1884, it was suggested that Britain and China might well have to become allies to suppress the nuisance once and for all, and the author made no secret of his conviction that every red-blooded Englishman would prefer a Chink to a Frog any day of the week. However, once the conflict was joined, these ideas were seen as so much schoolboyish naivety, and Britain and the other powers recognized that whatever the divisions between them they would be compelled to present a united front to the Chinese. The matter was put in a nutshell by M. Billot, a high official at the Quai d'Orsay who has given us the fullest account of the diplomatic side of the affair. The western nations, he says:

'are trying together to open to themselves this vast market of four hundred million consumers, which traditional policy is determined to keep shut against them. They act together to consolidate the concessions they have already won and to obtain fresh ones. There exists between them a solidarity which they could not break without weakening themselves. Not one of them gets an advantage from which the rest do not benefit. On the contrary, when one of them suffers some reverse in its dealings with the Celestial Empire, they are all affected. It is in their common interest therefore to lend one another mutual assistance. . . . Applying these principles to the situation created by the French action in Tongking, we can see that the Powers had a two-fold motive for concern. On the one hand, the interests of their commerce and of their nationals were bound to lead them to localize the conflict as far as possible, to prevent a breakdown of relations, and in case of war to hasten its end. On the other hand, the political solidarity we have just mentioned did not allow them to be absolutely disinterested as to the settlement of the dispute. Their prestige and authority in Chinese eyes would have suffered by a solution which Peking could regard as a check inflicted on one member of the European group. This was sufficient to override any secondary considerations which might have disposed certain governments to show themselves unfavourable to our plans in Vietnam.'[35]

The justice of these words is illustrated by the various attempts at mediation which began in the summer of 1884. First in the field was the United States, in the Chinese view then the most benevolent of the foreign powers. The Sino-American treaty of 1858 provided that 'if any other nations should commit an act of injustice or oppression, the United States, on being informed of the fact, will lend their good offices with the purpose of bringing about an amicable solution of the problem'. On July 18, 1884, the Chinese Foreign Office reminded the American Minister in Peking of this undertaking and formally requested Washington's mediation in the dispute. To a preliminary American inquiry a few days later Jules Ferry replied in effect that so long as China accepted in principle the duty of paying an indemnity for the injury caused to France at Bac-Le, he would welcome America's good offices. The U.S. representative in Peking, however, advised the Chinese that it was inconceivable that Washington, when properly acquainted with the facts, could for a moment hold China responsible for what had occurred at Bac-Le, and taking the hint the Chinese Foreign Office suggested that as this was the basic ground of disagreement the President of the United States should arbitrate on the question. This proposal was duly transmitted to Paris on August 1, 1884, the very day on which the French ultimatum to the Chinese expired, and Ferry interpreted it as simply a Chinese attempt to play for time. Besides, in his opinion, the question affected French national interests and prestige too closely to permit of arbitration by an outsider. The offer was accordingly rejected, but America was unwilling to abandon her efforts entirely and raised the subject again in September and October. This time Washington had made a considerable advance towards the French point of view and suggested to Paris that over and above the implementation of the Li-Fournier agreement, China should pay an indemnity, either of five million francs, the mode of payment to be fixed by American arbitration, or of a sum itself to be calculated by the same intermediary. Since the proposal still included the arbitration clause it remained unacceptable to France.

Meanwhile, on October 11, 1884, M. Patenôtre, who had not quitted Shanghai, was authorized to inform Li Hung-chang, who had been making discreet inquiries, that negotiations could be resumed without mention of the obnoxious indemnity provided that, in addition to carrying out the Li-Fournier pact at once, China agreed to French occupation of the mines at Keelung and of the customs-station at Tamsui for a period to be determined by mediation. These terms, which for some months represented the minimum French demands, were rejected by Peking, where anger over the bombardment of Foochow combined with the reassurance imparted to national pride by the unbroken resistance in Formosa to keep warlike views in the ascendant. The mood of intransigence was encouraged by the steady flow of dispatches from the Marquis Tseng, who, snug in his vantage point in London, was scrutinizing every facet of the French scene and noting with satisfaction the mounting opposition to the ever-increasing cost in men and money which Ferry's policy was exacting. In November 1884 the stiffening of China's attitude had an embarrassing diplomatic consequence. Lord Granville, then the British Foreign Secretary, having offered his own good offices to bring the parties together, was handed by Tseng a list of the Chinese terms. From this it appeared that Peking required the annulment of the Li-Fournier agreement, the demarcation of the Chinese frontier south of Langson, and the maintenance of Chinese suzerainty over Vietnam. As a gesture of magnanimity China would be prepared to waive the claim for the large indemnity which she had every reason to demand. Shocked to the heart, Lord Granville exclaimed that these were the conditions a victor in war would impose on the vanquished and declined utterly to forward them to the French.

However, while international mediation of the normal diplomatic sort had scarcely begun, foreign intervention made itself felt by another channel. A German employee of the Customs Service, Herr Detring, had as we have seen been the prime begetter of the ill-fated Li-Fournier agreement, and now the British head of the same Service was about to take a page from his subordinate's book.

Sir Robert Hart, an Ulsterman of forty-seven, had held that vital charge since 1863, and under his management a powerful organization had grown up, staffed by five hundred Europeans, who manned all the key positions, and upwards of two thousand Chinese. The memory of this particular aspect of foreign domination is naturally infuriating to Chinese of every shade of political opinion, who point out that the Customs Service so constituted was one of the most effective instruments which kept China for so many decades as a semi-colony. The system with its British Inspector-General lasted till 1942, and there is no reason to doubt that it would be with us still, if it had not been for the Pacific War. Some day an impartial Chinese historian, giving credit where credit is due, will acknowledge that it took Japanese bombs on Pearl Harbour to liberate China from a century of unequal treaties.

In the beginning Hart not only shared in the universal disapprobation entertained by third parties towards the French aggression, he supposed that Chinese resistance could well prove to be effective. For example, in a letter of August 31, 1884, a week after Courbet's bombardment of Foochow, he declared: 'If China will only have "the stay" and "the pluck" to hold out—and today it really looks as if she will have both—China may win in the end.'[36] Before long however, the considerations mentioned by Billot were clearly influencing his mind, for, in addition to the general threat to foreign commercial interests, the form the hostilities had assumed created particular difficulties for the Customs Service. Hart was responsible, among other things, for the upkeep of lighthouses along the China coast, a duty which the activities of Courbet were rendering increasingly hard to perform. Furthermore, a steamer belonging to the Customs had been seized by Courbet during the blockade of Formosa. There was every reason why Hart should seek to come to some arrangement with the French authorities concerning these awkward problems. As it happened, he had as his agent in London a Scotsman named James Duncan Campbell who seemed peculiarly fitted to serve as go-between, being well acquainted with Paris, where he had organized the Chinese section at the Universal Exhibition of 1878, an achievement which had earned him the Cross of the Legion of Honour. With these distinctions to recommend him, he was received personally on January 11, 1885, by Jules Ferry, who showed himself so amiable and so disposed to comply with all reasonable requests that it was inevitable the conversation should have ranged far beyond its original purpose. Indeed Mr Campbell ventured to speak of the satisfaction it would give to his employer if the parties to this unfortunate dispute could be brought sensibly together. Nothing would suit France better, said Ferry, if only her protectorate over Vietnam were recognized. The news of this friendly reception, conveyed to Hart by cipher telegram, encouraged him to keep Campbell in Paris, where at intervals during the next two and a half months he transmitted messages to and from Peking. It was soon established that Hart was speaking on behalf of the Chinese Foreign Office, and that his claim to be the only man so empowered to speak was not far from the truth, even though his insistence that no word of the conversation should be divulged to a living soul apart from the handful of persons in the know was made to look rather foolish when it became obvious that Li Hung-chang was certainly being kept abreast of events.

At first, the voice of the Inspector-General merely echoed the already familiar tones of the Peking government. The Li-Fournier agreement, he said, was not unacceptable if two extra provisions were added to it, namely, that Vietnam must be permitted, if it so desired, to continue to be a tributary of China and that the frontier should be drawn somewhere south of Langson. The first of these points was immediately rejected as being quite out of the question, and was not again referred to. As for the readjustment of the frontier, Ferry was inclined to be more accommodating, provided always that there was no dispute about Laokay. That haunt of the Black Flags must be ceded to France without more ado. But the Black Flags were a sore point with Peking, and it seemed impossible that any Chinese government could stomach the indignity of having to betray the men who were being acclaimed as heroes from one corner of China to the other. Yet as February yielded to March in that early spring of 1885, every day brought word of fresh Chinese defeats. Langson had gone, the French were on the frontier itself and were expected to arrive on Chinese soil from one day to the next: even the Black Flags seemed to have been routed. The counsellors who had been calling most loudly for war were becoming abashed in the face of these events, while Li Hung-chang could point to his disregarded warnings. There was scant willingness in Peking to make a stand over either Langson or Laokay.

Yet odd though it might seem, the attitude of the French government, so far from being stiffened by the uninterrupted succession of victories, was showing a remarkable degree of flexibility. This was evidenced especially in the matter of the indemnity. Earlier, this had been the great stumbling block in the way of all negotiations: even when the absolute requirement of a designated sum had been dropped, some form of compensation had been provided for by the stipulation that the Keelung mines and the Tamsui customs must be kept in French hands for a fixed period. Now even this condition no longer seemed essential. It looked more and more as if France would be contented with the revival of the Li-Fournier agreement, though as a guarantee that this time the Chinese would actually withdraw from Tongking, French troops would remain at Keelung and the French fleet would hold on to the Pescadores until such withdrawal had taken place.

What was the reason for this notable readiness to compromise? The fact was that the Marquis Tseng, in the words of a most trustworthy witness, M. Billot himself, was 'a clear-sighted observer, who took stock of the national state of mind in France'. For years now he had dinned it into the ears of the Peking authorities that China must not give way in Vietnam, and that a war would in the long run be disastrous to France. Just as the Second Empire had received a lethal wound from the Mexican Expedition, so would a full-scale conflict with China ruin the Third Republic, riddled as it was with Bonapartist and Royalist intrigue. These views, formed so soon after Tseng's arrival in Europe, can scarcely be the fruit of his unaided reflexions; it is only reasonable to impute a major responsiblity to the advice of Halliday Macartney; but however we apportion the credit, the judgment was being proved correct by the development of events.

To go no farther back than May 1884, Jules Ferry, by his conduct, had been playing into the hands of his enemies. Already under constant attack in Parliament and in the press for his overseas adventures, he had in that month by-passed his own Foreign Office experts and empowered a naval officer, totally lacking in diplomatic experience, to conclude an agreement with the most wily of Chinese politicians. No attempt was made to compare the French and Chinese texts, and some of the most important clauses of the pact, the alleged breach of which was to provoke the crisis, were not included in a formal draft at all, and had never been communicated to the Chinese government. After the incident at Bac-Le, France had made herself a laughing-stock by demanding on July 12th a grotesquely huge indemnity of 'at least' two hundred and fifty million francs, which on July 19th had been reduced to one hundred million. The height of absurdity was reached on August 3rd, when, just as M. Patenôtre was cabling Paris that he had presented a 'final demand' for eighty million, he received instructions from Ferry to give Peking the choice: 'fifty million francs or war'. No wonder that when the poor bewildered Fournier returned home in the middle of this hullaba-loo, one prominent journalist taxed him with having invented the whole story of the pact with Li Hung-chang, an insult which in turn led to a duel and even more shouts of laughter from the Anglo-Saxons.

Then there was the mess in Formosa. Admiral Courbet had let it be known very clearly that he blamed government pusillanimity for keeping him and his fleet in this squalid trap, instead of setting him free to carry the war to the seat of enemy power. Ferry clung to the pitiful pretence that France was not at war with China, yet in an unguarded moment he had exclaimed in the Chamber of Deputies that the opposition must not expect 'in the middle of a war' to browbeat the government into revealing its plan of cam-paign. At this, it was interjected that if there was a war, Ferry had violated the constitution, which required parliamentary approval before such a step could be taken. Elections were approaching, and there was widespread dissatisfaction, especially among the peasantry, at the constant drain of resources for the sake of Tongking.

For a couple of months the Ferry-Hart negotiations were at Hart's insistence kept from the knowledge of Patenôtre, who in spite of the rupture of normal diplomatic relations, continued to watch the Chinese scene from the security of Shanghai. At last things had advanced so far that it was considered safe to let him into the secret, though no doubt he must already have had a shrewd suspicion of what was happening behind his back. On March 23, 1885, Patenôtre confirmed that the imperial assent had been given to the principal articles of an agreement, and the business looked as good as settled. Hart, however, said peremptorily that no public statement was to be made until after the pact had been concluded, arguing that the warmongers in Peking were still powerful enough to frustrate the grand design if they got wind of what was being contrived. The danger was emphasized just at that moment by a somewhat confused report from Tongking that on March 23rd General de Négrier, having decided 'to treat himself to a little fresh air'—a phrase which after the fate of poor Rivière one might have thought no French commander in Vietnam would have had the temerity to use again—had finally marched across the frontier into Kwangsi, only to encounter Chinese forces in such overwhelming numbers that he had been obliged to break off the engagement and fall back on Langson. The possible effect of such news in Peking could well be imagined. In the Chamber of Deputies it caused the attacks of the opposition to double in fury, and even moderates no longer felt able to support the government. Ferry insisted that undue importance was being attached to the report, and that the French forces were, and would remain, in control of Langson, but it was observed that few of his colleagues had much confidence in his assurances.

Then the thunderbolt fell. The evening papers of March 29th carried the following telegram from Brière de l'Isle, commander-in-chief in Tongking, sent from Hanoi the night before:

'Grieved to announce General de Négrier seriously wounded and Langson evacuated. Mass of Chinese furiously attacked our forward positions. Overwhelmed by enormously superior numbers, Colonel Herbinger, short of munitions and worn out by series of earlier battles, tells me position untenable and he is forced to retreat—Enemy strength growing, looks as if we have against us whole Chinese army, trained in European methods and apparently following well conceived plan. Whatever happens, hope to be able to hold Delta, but Government must send reinforcements (men, munitions, animals) urgently.'

Other messages, from private sources, declared that on the Red River itself, the Black Flags and their Yunnanese allies, who a week or two earlier had been described as fleeing in disorder after the relief of Tuyen-Quang, were now massing to threaten Hung-Hoa. Everywhere in France the cry was of a catastrophe, of another Sedan. As for the Parliament: 'I don't believe', remarked one eye-witness, 'that Waterloo itself can have produced such a panic.'[37]

What had really happened in Tongking during that last week of March 1885 ? The Chinese accounts are plain and straightforward and, when allowance is made for pardonable exaltation, very largely credible. It seems that the seventy-year old General Feng Tzu-ts'ai had been warned by a Vietnamese informant that the French were planning to invade Kwangsi in order to cut off his line of retreat and had decided to catch them napping instead. He accordingly set an ambush, the result of which exceeded all expectations by throwing the French in confusion back over the frontier towards Langson. Then on March 23rd General de Négrier brought up all his available troops and advanced against the so-called Gate of China in three columns. Feng Tzu-ts'ai administered a solemn oath to his men, pledging them to keep the foreigner off Chinese soil, and the old fire-eater with his two sons beside him played an active part in the subsequent battle which lasted for two days and ended in a French defeat. The attack on Langson began on March 28th, and the city fell the following day. The next goal of the Kwangsi army was their familiar stronghold of Bac-Ninh, but while General Feng was organizing the twenty thousand Vietnamese volunteers who now flocked to his banner, the news of an armistice intervened.[38]

As for the Black Flags, even the French version of the story, though very naturally stressing the relief of Tuyen-Quang, makes it clear that this exploit was achieved only after the most savage fighting and at the price of numerous casualties. The Chinese books described Liu Yung-fu and his men as having retired in good order, and as continuing to offer such heavy resistance when the French started to move in the direction of Laokay, that, considering the Tuyen-Quang campaign as a whole, although the relief of the town was a pyrrhic victory for France, the total bill amounted to a French defeat on a large scale. Ts'en Yu-ying, whose Yunnanese troops fought side by side with the Black Flags, reported to Peking: 'The French have never been dealt such a blow since they invaded Vietnam: the past victories of the Black Flags were nothing to this.' He added that Vietnamese volunteers were streaming in from the country round Hung-Hoa and Sontay. Here again, the Chinese were halted in their tracks by word of the armistice.[39]

273

In comparison, the usual French explanation of their retreat from Langson imposes in parts a severe strain on our credulity. It should be mentioned that, less than a week after his message of doom, Brière de l'Isle had second thoughts and sent another cable to say that the precipitate withdrawal had been due to a gross error of judgment in the officer temporarily in charge after the incapacitation of General de Négrier. This is still the official French version. To support it, statements are produced by survivors of the affair, which allege that Colonel Herbinger, who took over the command, was obsessed with notions of classical western strategy which were inapplicable to Vietnamese conditions. He had felt in the first place that the advance to Langson and beyond had been undertaken with too little care for the necessity of adequate lines of communication. These ideas, combined with an enfeebled state of health, had produced in his mind a nightmare vision of being cut off by the swarms of Chinese he thought were in control of the country around him. In fact, General Feng, having made one attack on Langson, had been ignominiously routed, and there was no danger to the city when Herbinger ordered the garrison to abandon it. Strange anecdotes were quoted as evidence, notably the adventure of the six foreign legionnaires who got drunk and were left behind. Next day, on emerging from their stupor, they set off southwards along the 'Mandarin Road', and when they caught up with their comrades a good twenty-four hours afterwards they swore that all along the way they had had not a glimpse of an enemy. The same panic which had inspired the evacuation of Langson turned the retreat into a flight. Herbinger, ignoring the expostulations of his brother-officers, insisted that all baggage, regardless of value, should be thrown away so as not to encumber the march. What particularly infuriated the soldiers was learning that even regimental funds worth six hundred thousand francs, which might surely have been distributed among them without an unendurable increase of burden, had been flung into a river. Artillery, field telegraphs, everything was thrown away, while in agitated tones the colonel advised all within hearing to be sure and keep one cartridge intact for the job of blowing out their own brains to spare themselves Chinese tortures.[40]

The trouble with this story, apart from its basic improbability,

is that some of the circumstantial reports on which it is based are
glaringly self-contradictory. One witness, for instance, after
alleging that the Chinese were themselves in full flight northwards
at the time, concludes that the French situation was 'difficult but
by no means hopeless' without apparently noticing the absurdity.
It is a pity that poor Herbinger did not live long enough to give us
his version. Criticized by a commission of inquiry for unjustifiable
conduct, he died in 1886 a broken man.

The storm burst inside and outside the Chamber of Deputies on
March 30, 1885. Ferry, accepting that French troops in Tongking
were now fighting a defensive action merely to maintain themselves
in the Delta, asked the Chamber for an extraordinary credit of two
hundred million francs for the purpose of the war with China.
Reinforcements were to leave at once for the Far East. Interrupted
continually, he was driven to declare that for the sake of national
unity he was asking not for a vote of confidence in the government,
but simply for the means of carrying on the war. Clemenceau, who
had a personal grievance against Ferry arising from antipathies
going back to the tragic events of 1870, denounced him as a traitor.
When Ferry tried to brush off the stream of abuse with a disdainful
smile, there were shouts of: 'Look at the wretch! He's grinning!
They're not grinning in Tongking!' Hemmed in from right and left
with equal malevolence and vituperation Ferry lost the motion by
three hundred and six votes to one hundred and forty-nine, and announced his resignation. To avoid the mob which was yelling in the
street for his blood, he had to leave the building by a secret passage.
Throughout his career as empire-builder he had been influenced
by English models, and now at the supreme moment he preserved a
truly Anglo-Saxon phlegm. While his fellow deputies were loading
him with abuse for having dragged them into war with China, he
knew that at that very hour Peking was ready to accept peace
terms. But he had solemnly promised Campbell to reveal nothing
until the signatures were on the paper, and he stoically kept silence.
Besides, as he afterwards admitted, even if he had proclaimed the
truth, not a soul in the assembly would have believed him.
Historians of French imperialism have made a shamefaced
comparison between the hysteria of Paris in 1885, and the Roman
gravity with which the British House of Commons, shortly

afterwards, heard the news of the death of Gordon and fall of Khartoum.[41]

The departure of Ferry and his ministry did not affect the peace negotiations, since Grevy, then President of the Republic, authorized M. Billot of the Quai d'Orsay to act in the name of France. China was represented by Mr Campbell. The document signed by the two on April 4, 1885 provided in effect for the execution of the Li-Fournier agreement, and for the cessation of hostilities. France consented to lift the blockade of Formosa and to send an envoy to Tientsin or Peking to draw up a detailed treaty. As for the evacuation of Tongking by the Chinese, it was to be completed on April 30th by the troops east of Tuyen-Quang, and on May 30th by those to the west of that city. Meanwhile, on the conclusion of a formal treaty, French naval vessels would discontinue the blockade, and Chinese ports would be opened to French ships. Letters exchanged between the parties stipulated that pending the ratification of such a treaty, France would continue to regard rice as contraband of war. There was, of course, an outcry from the Marquis Tseng and the other partisans of residence. The Viceroy at Canton protested:

'An armistice is well and good, but a withdrawal of our troops, especially a withdrawal as far as the frontier, is quite impermissible. In Tongking the military situation is in our favour: indeed things have never looked brighter for us since the present hostilities began. If we let ourselves be tricked into retreating now, we shall regret our stupidity when it is too late'.

But Li Hung-chang had the last word: 'So long as Liu Yung-fu stays in Laokay, the French will never quit the Pescadores.'[42] The recalcitrance was confined to grumbling: both the regular forces and the Black Flags retired, sullenly it is true, behind the Chinese border, and on June 11, 1885, a formal treaty was signed in Tientsin between Li Hung-chang and M. Patenôtre.

The French, too, had their malcontents. Admiral Courbet in particular was loud in his anger at finding that China was to escape so easily. The exploits and sufferings of himself and his men during the past twelve months had, he declared, been quite in vain.

Not only had the demand for an indemnity been dropped; but a project especially dear to his heart, which was that the Pescadores should be kept and turned into a French Hong Kong, or, as he himself put it, into 'the Gibraltar of the China Sea', had been rejected out of hand by the cowards in Paris. Yet fate spared him the final insult of having to lead the retreat in person. It was in the Pescadores, on board his flagship in the harbour of Makung, that he breathed his last on June 11, 1885. His body was carried to Paris and given a magnificent funeral in the Invalides.

⚜ CHAPTER NINETEEN

The Aftermath

WITH China's renunciation of her ancient suzerainty over Vietnam our story has come to an end, but in Vietnam itself the French conquest was still far from complete. In July 1885, a month after Li Hung-chang in Tientsin had signed the treaty which formally recognized the French protectorate, the Court of Hue, having done nothing to cooperate with China when such action might well have been effectual, at last exploded into a hopeless revolt. The French garrison easily repelled an attack on the Legation, and stormed into the Palace, while the young King Ham-Nghi, with a suite of elephants bearing his treasury, fled into the mountains. At the news that its sovereign was in arms against the invader, the country took fresh heart and rose to defend itself. The French reacted with the most atrocious severity, which will always be remembered as a disgrace to their national honour, but it was not until the turn of the century that the military suppression could be said to be completed. King Ham-Nghi with a price on his head stayed at large until November 1888, when he was betrayed by an informer, seized and deported. After his flight, the French had replaced him on the throne by an adopted son of Tu Duc, who was content to serve as their puppet. It seemed that the name of Vietnam had disappeared for ever from the face of the earth. The country itself, on the principle 'divide and conquer', was cut in three, each part provided with its separate laws and institutions, in the hope that the inhabitants instead of thinking of themselves as Vietnamese would grow used to being citizens of Tongking, of Annam (for that old title was retained for the central region) or of Cochinchina. In Annam, a phantom monarchy was preserved as a marionette-show at Hue. Together with Laos and Cambodia, the country so butchered was stitched up to form that geopolitical monstrosity, French Indo-china.

In China Li Hung-chang had emerged triumphant. For the next ten years he was at the peak of his power and influence. A close working alliance existed between him and the Dowager, and he well understood the best way of keeping in favour. The des-struction of the fleet at Foochow had shown incontrovertibly the need for an adequate naval establishment, and the responsibility for creating such a force was naturally put on the shoulders which seemed best able to support it, i.e. Li's. From then on, Port Arthur and Weihaiwei were the undisputed centres of Chinese naval aspirations, and copious funds were dedicated to the im-pressive programme of construction which was set under way. However, as chance would have it, the Dowager was pining after that pleasure-ground of her youth, the Round Bright Garden, barbarously put to the flames by the British in 1860; and nothing would satisfy her but that a new Summer Palace should be contrived hard by the ruins of the old, a few miles to the west of Peking. It was noticed that the Grand Eunuch was on remarkably affable terms with Li, even to the extent on one occasion of taking part in an inspection of the northern dockyard, but the true significance of the friendship was not appreciated for some years. Then, in 1894, China's suzerainty over Korea was threatened by Japanese aggression, and in the face of such an outrage on his own doorstep even Li Hung-chang could not keep his beloved army and navy in cold storage. When war broke out, nobody in the world, barring the Japanese themselves, had the slightest doubt of a resounding Chinese victory. The mortification was all the greater when the island dwarfs swept the seas clear of Chinese ships, sent an army across the Yalu River into Manchuria, disembarked a landing force to seize Port Arthur, and finally stormed Weihaiwei, obliging the remnants of the Chinese fleet to surrender. In April, 1895, Li Hung-chang, the only negotiator the Japanese would accept, signed the humiliating peace of Shimonoseki. Apart from the payment of a huge indemnity, the suzerainty over Korea had to

279

be given up, and worse still Formosa and the Pescadores were ceded to Japan.

For ten years, Li's enemies had been obliged to contain their resentment, but now they were able to give free expression to their pent-up hatred. The Marquis Tseng had died in 1890, but his ghost must have been more than appeased by the spectacle of what was passing. From one end of the Empire to the other, there was a great cry for vengeance. Respectable mandarins addressed memorials to the Throne in which they declared the satisfaction it would give them to dine upon Li Hung-chang's flesh; a figure of speech, no doubt, but an uncomfortable thing to have to listen to. If it had not been for the protection of the Dowager Li would almost certainly have lost his head. She herself was by all accounts not less guilty than the Viceroy—it was now said openly, what had only been hinted at before, that naval funds had been mis-appropriated in order to pay for her pleasure garden, and to this day visitors to the Summer Palace, now a People's Park, are shown a marble boat in a lake as evidence of the corruption and folly of the imperial regime. As it was, Li not only survived but even continued to play a role in political life, though with his beloved army in ruins and its sister navy no longer in existence, he retained merely a shadow of his former greatness. Only at the very end of his life did he return to the limelight. In 1900, the Dowager and some of the most ignorant of her courtiers were induced to throw in their lot with the group of anti-foreign fanatics known as 'Boxers'. In the resultant outbreak Christian missions in the northern provinces were attacked and for some weeks the foreign legations in Peking were besieged. Of course these events led to a massive intervention by the Powers and an allied expeditionary force marched on Peking to rescue the diplomats and wreak vengeance on China. The Court fled into the far interior, and in its absence, Li Hung-chang once again mounted the international stage as the Chinese statesman with whom the outside world prefer-red to do business. The terms of the settlement were severe, but by the time Li died, in November 1901, it was clear that he had at least saved the dynasty, though the threatened doom was averted for only ten years. The formidable Dowager died in 1908, and the Manchus abdicated at the beginning of 1912.

Meanwhile, in 1895 there was one supreme ignominy which Li's enemies were determined he must endure. The odious task of handing over Formosa to the Japanese was assigned to his eldest son. The poor devil arrived in Keelung harbour on June 1, 1895, but refused point-blank to go ashore. Instead, the next day he boarded a Japanese warship and there signed the instrument of surrender. One can scarcely blame him: the following is a specimen of the sort of placard which was being posted up in all the towns of the island:

'We, the people of Formosa, swear not to live under the same sky with Li Hung-chang. If we meet him, his sons or grandsons, or any of his kin, whether passing in a vehicle on the street, or within an inn or a government office, we shall slaughter them on the spot, in the name of Heaven and Earth and of our Ancestors, to avenge the injury Li Hung-chang has done to the graves of our parents and the lives and property of our families!'

Shortly before the war with Japan, Formosa, until then administered as part of the province of Fukien, just across the Straits, from which the dominant part of the population was drawn, had been created a province on its own; and the Governor at this time was no other than our old acquaintance T'ang Ching-sung, the mandarin adviser of Liu Yung-fu, who together with his hero had returned discomfited to China from Tongking after the armistice in 1885. For the last ten years, while T'ang had been climbing the official ladder, Liu had been basking in the admiration of his countrymen. Granted the honour of an audience with the Dowager, his commission as General had been confirmed and he was now installed in a military post in Kwangtung province.

On the approach of the Japanese war, T'ang had taken steps to reinforce the garrison by arranging for the transfer of soldiers from the mainland, and it was only natural that Liu should have been among those who answered the call. Accordingly in the summer of 1895 he was stationed in the city of Tainan in the southern part of the island, while T'ang remained in Taipei, the provincial capital in the north. There T'ang received orders from Peking to terminate his activities and return to the mainland, and it may be surmised there was nothing he would have liked to do better. The only trouble was that the Formosans would not let him go, and as their passions had reached great heights, it would have been decidedly rash to mention such a proposal to them.

Enthusiastic patriots though they were, the islanders still realized that China could do little to help them. They looked elsewhere, for any alternative seemed preferable to being swallowed up in a Japanese Empire. Their first thought was that perhaps Britain, which seemed bent on extending its control over as large a portion of the earth's surface as possible, might be induced to take Formosa under its protection, with China still holding the residual sovereignty. When London shied away in alarm, a similar suggestion was made to France with no greater success. Then, at their wits' end, the Formosans declared themselves a republic, and compelled the Governor, T'ang Ching-sung, to assume the style of President. In his proclamations the new Head of State made it clear that the separation was looked upon as a mere temporary measure, and that pending an eventual return to the mother-country the island would be in the position of a vassal of Peking. Privately he informed the Manchu authorities that he was staying in Formosa under duress and hinted that he would seize the first opportunity to escape. In fact he need not have worried. Within twelve days his 'capital', Taipei, had fallen to the Japanese, and he had fled to Amoy.

Down in the south, however, the fight went on. Liu Yung-fu, who condemned T'ang as a coward, announced that, being nearly sixty years old, he for one had lived quite long enough and would face death with equanimity. Indeed, for a couple of months this seemed more than a piece of bravado. The Black Flags did wonders in stiffening the resistance, until at length the Japanese superiority in equipment and numbers began to tell. Already in September it appears that Liu was toying with the idea of surrender, but was thwarted by his troops. In the middle of October the position had become so hopeless that he took passage for the mainland and left his followers to shift for themselves. By the end of the month, the Japanese were able to report that the 'pacification' of Formosa was completed.

It is not always thought necessary, either in China or elsewhere, for a general to stay with his troops, and it is only in our own day, and by Communist historians, that Liu's defection has been represented in a discreditable light. Even the Communists are not too severe on him: they are inclined to overlook this single fall from grace in consideration of his otherwise blameless record. At the time, his escape was treated as a romantic adventure, and for the rest of his life he enjoyed an added esteem from his Formosan exploits. He continued until the closing years of the dynasty in the employment of the Kwangtung provincial administration, and is said to have been a notable suppressor of bandits and a pacifier of clan feuds, those twin curses of the south China countryside. The advent of the Republic in 1912 found him in retirement, listening with interest to the news of public affairs as others related it to him from the papers, for he himself had never learned to read. Most of the time, though, his mind dwelt in the past. He would take out Garnier's watch and show the picture of the young wife inside the cover. He would tell of his challenge to Rivière and describe the battle at Paper Bridge. But he soon wearied of the incomprehensible foreign devils, and turned instead to what for him had been beyond comparison the most serious business of his life. The talk would then be all of the Black and the Yellow Flags, and of the long years of feuds and hatreds in the steaming malarial jungle and on the silent reaches of the great river. His published memoirs, for his reminiscences were reverently taken down in writing, have as their main theme the story of this interminable vendetta between expatriate Chinese. But when he died, in January 1917, it was as the scourge of a foreign enemy, the hero whose achievements were nullified by the cowardice of his own government, that he was mourned by his countrymen, and that is the way they still remember him.

For we must not be surprised that Liu Yung-fu and his Black Flags are present with unusual urgency in Chinese minds today, when once again such names as Hanoi and Bac-Ninh and Namdinh dominate the news, and bombs are falling within earshot of the Kwangsi border. It is recalled that the French conquest of Vietnam began, in 1858, as an episode of an Anglo-French war against China proper and that the purpose of the conquest was twofold. Over and above the colonial exploitation of Vietnam itself,

France aimed at using the territory as a base for the commercial penetration of southern and western China. This becomes abundantly clear when we remember the first establishment at Saigon, and the dream of opening navigation up the Mekong to Yunnan. No sooner had this project been demonstrated to be impracticable than attention was called to the Red River, and the doom of Tongking was sealed.

For centuries China had abjured all interference in Vietnamese affairs, and was content with a token acknowledgment of her suzerainty. Her action in 1788 against the Tayson, superficially an exception, in reality is strong evidence to prove the rule, for a humiliating military setback was immediately overlooked, once the enemy offered a theoretical submission. Only when it became plain, in the 1870s, that British and French designs on Burma and Vietnam were directed ultimately towards herself did she begin to take alarm and even then, had it not been for the accidental presence of the Black Flags in Tongking and their victories over Garnier and Rivière which captured the public imagination, it is doubtful how far a policy of intervention could have been carried against the wishes of Li Hung-chang. As for the circumstances of the direct Sino-French confrontation of 1884-5 it is impossible to reconcile the reports given by the two sides. No doubt the Chinese are prone to exaggerate their successes, but then only an excessively gullible person would accept the French accounts at their face value. One thing at least is certain. The war-party in China were often muddle-headed and ignorant, and made a poor showing in argument against the cautious, unenthusiastic Li Hung-chang. Yet they were right in believing that by protracted resistance China could exact a price which no French government could ask its people to pay. Even at the very height of the French victories in February 1885, the domestic situation was such that Jules Ferry had greatly modified his original peace terms. We may give less than total credence to the Chinese stories about the French reverses at Langson and elsewhere, but the fact remains that the first reports from the French commander in the field were what brought down Ferry's administration in ruins. It is quite inconceivable that after Ferry's collapse any French government would have been voted the enormous increase in expenditure that would have been considered neccessary for a full-scale war with China. In this respect, at any rate, Halliday Macartney and the Marquis Tseng displayed a perspicacity which unfortunately was wasted in the service of the Court of Peking. Regarding the conditions of the peace, it was pointed out by Li's opponents then, as by Communist historians today, that the British negotiators who were acting on China's behalf took no advantage whatsoever of the changed situation, but were satisfied with the selfsame terms that Ferry had offered in his season of triumph. True, Li Hung-chang is not without his admirers, mostly, as one might expect, now in exile on Formosa, but it is hard not to agree with the Communist judgment on him as a saboteur of Chinese national interests.

It is instructive, too, if we glance for a moment at the effect on China of the French presence in Tongking. There was first and foremost a French economic invasion of Kwangsi and especially of Yunnan by the construction of the Kunming-Hanoi railway. When the Manchu Dynasty fell, and the resultant Chinese Republic passed into the era of the warlords, this influence meant that France was able to give backing in those provinces to local militarist regimes independent of Peking, just as British concern for Hong Kong led London to prop up a similar separatist administration in Canton. In the long run these imperial intrigues had an unlooked for consequence. In 1917, Sun Yat-sen, the Father of Chinese Nationalism, disgusted at the betrayal of his principles in Peking, took refuge at Canton with some of his followers whom he organized into a body which claimed to be the legitimate government of China. It tickled the fancy of the local warlord to have such a movement under his control, though his patronage was precarious in the extreme, and poor Sun was frequently sent packing to Hong Kong and Shanghai. However, when in 1923 Soviet Russia decided to support Sun, and an alliance was formed between Chinese Communists and Nationalists, the situation changed decisively. By 1924, the new combination was in control at Canton, and its army, trained by Chiang Kai-shek, proceeded to exert its military superiority to bring the Kwangsi warlords into the fold. In 1926, a year after Sun's death, a great force composed of all these elements set out for the north to achieve the Chinese Revolution. The warlord regime of Peking was overthrown and a

National Government established at Nanking, but in the course of these events the united front broke down, the Communists were driven into the wilderness, and the Kwangsi militarists with French and Japanese encouragement turned against Chiang once more. In the summer of 1936, a war of the south against the centre was narrowly averted. Then the Japanese invasion of 1937, which brought a temporary truce between the Chinese factions, gave Vietnam a new and sinister importance. After the surrender of France in 1940, the Vichy government agreed to allow Japan to use airfields in Tongking for the bombing of Chinese cities.

At the end of the Pacific War, the ghosts of Liu Yung-fu and of the Marquis Tseng must have been consoled to see Chinese troops once more in Vietnam, for by allied agreement Chiang Kai-shek's forces were given the task of accepting the Japanese surrender in the northern half of the country. Only then, in 1945, as an episode of this operation, did the Chinese central government finally impose its control over the local warlord of Yunnan. Meanwhile the Kwangsi clique, although forming part of the Nationalist Army, still retained much of their old antipathy, as was demonstrated in 1966 when their chief survivor, General Li Tsung-jen, Vice-President of the Republic of China, after spending years of exile in the United States rather than live in Formosa with Chiang Kai-shek, made his peace with the Communists and went to Peking.

If there is one lesson for China to draw from the events of the last century and a quarter it is that military weakness on her part constitutes an irresistible invitation to aggression from abroad, and that Vietnam, under the control of a potential enemy, must always form a peculiarly lethal threat to her national security.

Principal Sources

IN CHINESE

Chung-Fa chan-cheng, 7 vols., Shanghai, 1955.
Chung-Fa Yueh-nan chiao-she tang, 7 vols., Taipei, 1962.
Ch'ien Hsing-ts'un (Ah Ying) ed. *Chung-Fa chan-cheng wen-hsueh chi*, Shanghai, 1957.
Lo Hsiang-lin, ed. *Liu Yung-fu li-shih ts'ao*, Taipei, 1957.
Li Wei. *Liu Yung-fu chuan*, Changsha, 1940.
Ho Hui-ch'ing. *Yuan-Yueh k'ang-Fa kuang-jung shih* (5 instalments in Shanghai fortnightly *I-ching*, Nos. 31–5, June 5–August 5, 1937).
Kuo T'ing-i and others. *Chung-Yueh wen-hua lun-chi*, 2 vols., Taipei, 1956.

IN WESTERN LANGUAGES

L'affaire du Tonkin, par un diplomate (i.e., A. Billot), Paris, no date.
Blue Book—China No. 1, 1886, London, 1886.
Boulger, D. *The Life of Sir Halliday Macartney*, London, 1908.
Buttinger, J. *The Smaller Dragon*, New York, 1958.
Cady, J. T. *The Roots of French Imperialism in Eastern Asia*, Ithaca, New York, 1954.
Chaigneau, M. D. *Souvenirs de Hue*, Paris, 1867.
Chassigneux, E. *L'Indochine*, in *Histoire des colonies françaises* (edited by G. Hanotaux and A. Martineau), Paris, 1932, vol. 5, pp. 311–583.
Chesneaux, J. *Contribution à l'histoire de la nation vietnamienne*, Paris, 1955.
Cho Huan Lai, *Les origines du conflit franco-chinois à propos du Tonkin jusqu'en 1883*, Paris, 1935.
Cordier, H. *Histoire des relations de la Chine avec les puissances occidentales*, vol. 2, Paris, 1902.
Deveria, G. *Histoire des relations de la Chine avec l'Annam-Vietnam du XVIe au XIXe siècle*, Paris, 1880.
Documents diplomatiques français (1871–1914). Première série, vols. 2, 3, 4, and 5, Paris, Ministère des Affaires Etrangères, 1930–3.

287

Dupuis, J. *Le Tonkin de 1872 à 1886*, Paris, 1910. *Les origines de la question du Tong-kin*, Paris, 1896.

Ferry, J. F. C. *Le Tonkin et la mère patrie*, Paris, 1890.

Gaultier, M. *Minh-Mang*, Paris, 1935.

Gosselin, Ch. *L'empire d'Annam*, Paris, 1904.

Huard, P. and Durand, M. *Connaissance du Vietnam*, Paris–Hanoi, 1954.

Kiernan, E. V. G. *British Diplomacy in China 1880 to 1885*, Cambridge, 1939.

Le Thanh Khoi, *Le Viet-Nam*, vol. 1, Paris, 1955.

Louvet, E. *Vie de Mgr Puginier*, Hanoi, 1894. *Monseigneur d'Adran*, Saigon, 1896.

Masson, J. *Souvenirs de l'Annam et du Tonkin*, Paris, 1892.

Maybon, Ch. B. *Histoire moderne du pays d'Annam*, Paris, 1920.

Norman, C. B. *Tonkin, or France in the Far East*, London, 1884.

Pouvourville, A. de, *Francis Garnier*, Paris, 1931.

Rocher, E. *La province chinoise du Yunnan*, 2 vols., Paris, 1879–80.

Romanet du Caillaud, F. *Histoire de l'intervention française au Tong-king de 1872 à 1874*, Paris, 1880.

Taboulet, G. *La geste française en Indochine*, 2 vols., Paris, 1955–6.

Notes

(1) A. E. Grantham, *A Manchu Monarch*, London, 1934, pp. 217–19.
(2) *Ch'ing-chien i-chih lu*, Shanghai, 1931, Chia-ch'ing 7.
(3) J. Chesneaux, *Contribution à l'histoire de la nation vietnamienne*, p. 45.
(4) H. Cordier, *Histoire des relations de la Chine avec les puissances occidentales*, Vol. 2, p. 330.
(5) G. H. Fontanier, *Une mission chinoise en Annam*, T'oung Pao, 2nd ser. 4 (1903), pp. 127–45.
(6) Michel Duc Chaigneau, *Souvenirs de Hue*, pp. 110–12.
(7) Chaigneau, *op. cit.*, pp. 217–19.
(8) E. Alabaster, *Notes and Commentaries on Chinese Criminal Law*, London, 1899, p. 58.
(9) Albert de Pouvourville, *Francis Garnier*, p. 84.
(10) Y. Ogaeri, ed, *Dōchi matsu-nen ryū-En nikki*, in quarterly *Ronshū*, Vol. 3, No. 1, p. 38 (published by Tokyo Joshi Daigaku, Nov. 1957).
(11) Liu Yung-fu's memoirs (entitled *Liu Yung-fu li-shih ts'ao*) are included in the first volume of *Chung-Fa chan-cheng*. A separate edition with useful notes by Lo Hsiang-lin was published at Taipei in 1957. I have also consulted the biography by Li Wei, *Liu Yung-fu chuan*, Changsha, 1940.
(12) E. Louvet, *Vie de Mgr Puginier*, pp. 278–9.
(13) J. Dupuis, *Le Tonkin de 1872 à 1886*, p. 73.
(14) F. Romanet du Caillaud, *Histoire de l'ntervention française au Tong-king de 1872 à 1874*, p. 96; de Pouvourville, *op. cit.*, p. 205.
(15) Louvet, *op. cit.*, p. 239.
(16) Romanet du Caillaud, *op. cit.*, pp. 238–9.
(17) Cf. C. B. Norman, *Tonkin, or France in the Far East*, pp. 141–7.

(18) For the Margary affair, I have followed the account of Ma Tzu-hua, published in the fortnightly *I-ching*, Shanghai, June 20, 1937, pp. 34–5.

(19) Hu Ping, *Mai-kuo-tsei Li Hung-chang*, Shanghai, 1955, p. 49.

(20) *Chung-Fa chan cheng*, vol. 4, p. 20.

(21) Cordier, *op. cit.*, p. 281, n.l.

(22) T'ang Ching-sung's own account, entitled *Ch'ing-ying jih-chi*, is included in *Chung-Fa chan-cheng*, vol. 2, as well as in *Chung-Fa chan-cheng wen-hsueh chi*.

(23) C. Gosselin, *L'empire d'Annam*, pp. 289–90, 367–8.

(24) Louvet, *op. cit.*, pp. 440–3.

(25) Gosselin, *op. cit.*, 179.

(26) *Chung-Fa chan-cheng*, vol. 4, pp. 40, 49, 51. Li Shou-k'ung, *Chung-kuo chin-tai shih*, Taipei, 1961, pp. 374–5.

(27) G. Taboulet, *La geste française en Indochine*, vol. 2, pp. 803–5.

(28) *Chung-Fa chan-cheng*, vol. 4, pp. 268–9.

(29) Cordier, *op. cit.*, p. 409.

(30) Li Shou-k'ung, *op. cit.*, p. 378.

(31) Li Shou-k'ung, *op. cit.*, p. 388.

(32) Some interesting reminiscences by a Chinese resident of Foochow are to be found in *Chung-Fa chan-cheng*, vol. 3, pp. 127–39.

(33) H. B. Morse, *International Relations of the Chinese Empire*, London, 1918, vol. 2, p. 358.

(34) *Le Temps*, July 20, 1884, *quoted in* Dupuis, *op. cit.*, pp. 505–6.

(35) *L'affaire du Tonkin, par un diplomate*, pp. 298–9.

(36) Hart-Campbell correspondence, manuscript in library of the School of Oriental and African Studies, University of London.

(37) Taboulet, *op. cit.*, p. 852.

(38) Li Shou-k'ung, *op. cit.*, pp. 390–1.

(39) Li Shou-k'ung, *op. cit.*, p. 391.

(40) Taboulet, *op. cit.*, pp. 846–51.

(41) Taboulet, *op. cit.*, p. 856, n. 2.

(42) Li Shou-k'ung, *op. cit.*, pp. 393–4.

Index

Adran, Bishop of, *see* Pegneau
Amoy, 282
Anglo-French expedition against China (1856–60), 79, 88, 91, 92, 117, 147
Annam, 16–17, 278–9

Bac-Le, 242–3
Bac-Ninh, 171, 202, 208, 217, 223, 224, 227, 228, 229, 230, 231, 234, 242, 273
Bain, Lieut., 137–8, 140
Balny, Lieut., 136–7
Basilan, 62
Bengal, 57
Bienhoa, French capture of, 76
Billot, M., 265, 268, 270, 276
Binh-Thuan, 215
Bouet, General, 211, 213, 216, 217, 223, 224
Black Flags, the, 96, 99, 105ff., 188, 194, 196, 223, 235, 283; at Hanoi, 135–7, 138–9, 216; at Red River, 165, 167–8, 171, 189, 215, 221; and Rivière, 190, 203–6, 284; and Hoang, 199, 202; and T'ang, 208; at Sontay, 216, 217, 224, 226–7, 228, 284; at Bac-Ninh, 230; at Hung-Hoa, 231–2; claim to Vietnam, 259, 273; and Yunnanese, 272, 273; and Japanese, 282
Bourayne, the ship, 114–15
Bourée, M., 186, 196, 198, 199, 210, 219
'Boxers', 280
Brière de l'Isle, General, 260, 261, 262, 272, 274
British East India Co., 34
Browne, Colonel, 155–6, 158–9
Buddhism, 32
Burma, 79, 80, 155, 162, 163–4, 284

Cambodia, 24, 28, 80, 279
Campbell, James Duncan, 268, 269, 275, 267

Campenon, General, 261
Canh, Prince, 37, 41, 47
Canton, 18, 21, 54, 55, 58, 71; and second opium war, 68; missionaries in, 60; Dupuis at, 94
Cantonese merchants; at Hanoi, 116–17, 131; at Manghao, 95
Cap St Jacques, 74
Cécille, Captain, 59
Chaigneau, 45–6, 47ff.
Champa, 24
Chasseloup Laubat, Marquis de, 80
Chefoo, 163, 237; Convention of (1876), 163–4
Chennankuan, 261
Ch'en Yi, 225–6
Chia Ch'ing, Emperor, 15–16, 17–18, 41, 239
Chiang Kai-shek, 285
Ch'ien Lung, Emperor, 29ff.
Ch'in First Emperor, 18
China; Communist, 58–9; courtesy of, 154–5; Customs Service, 267–8; defence of, 244; Foreign Office, 149, 222; legation in London, 174; legation in Paris, 174; maritime customs, 161-2, 234; Merchants Shipping Co., 152, 195, 252; navy of, 152; religion of, 32, 84–5 (and *see* Confucius); Republic of 1912, 283; Revolution of, 285–6
Cholon, 79
Christian settlements, 143, 145
Ch'un, Prince, 234, 237
Chunghow and the Russians, 172–3, 180
Chungking, 93, 126, 163
Clear River, 108, 259
Clemenceau, Georges, 224, 275
Cochinchina, 37–8, 39, 123, 189, 194, 215, 279; recognition of, 279
Commerce, Sino-French, 244
Confucius, 31–3, 42–3, 56, 64, 67, 149
Conway, Comte de, 38–9

291

INDEX

Haiphong, 129, 131, 144
Haishenwei, 69
Hakkas, the, 99
Han Dynasty, 18, 19
Ham Nghi, King, 278
Hankow, 65, 69, 91, 94
Hanoi, 24, 26, 28; Dutch at, 34, 35; British at, 34, 35; French at, 35, 37, 41, 44, 83; reached by Dupuis, 116, 117, 119, 121; Dupuis headquarters at, 122–3, 124, 125, 127–8; falls to Garnier, 132–4, 144, 171
Hanyang, 91
Harmand, Dr, 212, 213, 215, 216, 217–18, 238
Hart, Sir Robert; and Margary affair, 161–3, 173–4, 267; and French, 268, 269, 271
Hayang, 108, 111, 168
Herbinger, Col., 272, 274, 275
Hiep Hoa, 213, 238
Hoang, Prince, 134–5, 137, 139, 192, 198, 217, 226
Holland, merchants of, 30, 34, 35
Hongay, 199
Hong Kong, 58, 62, 72, 114–15, 124; and Foreign Enlistment Act, 262; gaol of, 178; and Shanghai Bank, 125
Hoti River, 83, 93
Hsien Feng, Emperor, 147
Huang Ch'ung-ying, 108–11, 167–70
Huc, Father, 71–2, 91, 92
Hue, 39, 41, 44, 185; and French, 73, 74; Dupuis at, 113–14; capitulation, 213–18, 226; Bishop of, 215; court of, 219, 278; agreement of 1883, 237; royal palace, 258
Hunan, 66
Hunan group, 152–4, 174, 177, 180, 182
Hung-Hoa, 119, 134, 223, 227, 228, 231, 272–3
Hung Hsiu-ch'uan, 63–6, 67, 69, 99

Ili, 154, 172
India, 155

Japan, 30–1, 48, 152, 207, 208; war with China, 279–82; war with Formosa, 281
Jaureguiberry, Admiral, 182, 190
Jesuits, 31, 33, 34, 35, 82

Kansu, 93
Keelung, 236, 246, 253, 281; battle at, 248–50, 255, 256; occupation of, 266, 270

Khoi, 49
Kien Phuoc, King, 239, 258
Kleber, 48
Korea, 207, 208; and China, 279–80
Kowloon, 69
Krupp cannon, 230, 231
Kuang Hsü, Emperor, 160, 212
Kublai Khan, 26
Kung, Prince, 148, 149, 150, 156, 160, 161, 165–6, 167, 187, 233, 234
Kunming, 86, 88, 89; Garnier at, 90; Dupuis at, 93, 120, 121
Kunming–Hanoi railway, 285
Kuo, Mr, 175, 177–8
Kwangsi province, 18, 63, 65, 83, 95, 98–9, 103, 104, 105, 108, 110, 193, 224; treasury of, 224; governor, 227, 232, 259, 262; army, 224, 229, 230–1, 240, 241, 244–7, 260, 261, 273; frontier, 272; French economic invasion, 285; militarists, 286
Kwangtung and Kwangsi, Viceroy of, see Tseng Kuo-ch'uan
Kwangtung province, 18, 83, 94, 95, 98, 99, 188, 281, 283

Langson, 198, 227, 240, 242, 261, 263, 273; evacuation, 272; French retreat from, 274, 284
Laokay, 95–6, 107–9, 111, 197, 198; battle of, 109–10; and Dupuis, 119; and Black Flags, 121 (and see Liu), 192 232
Laos, 26, 82, 91, 279
Later Le Dynasty, 25, 26, 27, 28–9, 74 76, 77
Lespès, Admiral, 236, 237, 248, 249, 257
Le Tuan, 115–16
Le Van Duyet, Marshal, 49
Li, Col., 158, 163–4
Li-Fournier agreement, see Sino-French Treaty at Tientsin
Li Hung-chang; and Taiping rebellion, 69, 148, 151; on Chinese policy, 149, 151; and Nien, 151–2; and Hunan group, 152–3; on Sinkiang rebellion, 154, 173; supports Yehonala, 160; and Margary affair, 161–3; and Macartney, 176, 177, 179–80; and Treaty of 1874, 186; and Bourée, 196, 219; and French, 207, 246, 247, 276; and 1883 agreement, 220, 221–2; and Tongking, 210–12, 227, 236, 238, 240–1, 244; and Germany, 235, 237; power of, 245–6; navy of, 252; influence of, 259; pact with Fournier,

293

INDEX

Pigneau, Father Pierre (called Pigneau de Béhaine), 36–41, 62
Pnompenh, 80
Pondicherry, 36, 38
Pope Hennessy, Sir John, 179
Port Arthur, 245, 255, 256, 279; seizure, 279
Portugal, 30, 34, 35, 55
Pothiau, Vice Admiral, 113–14
Poulo Condore, 38, 62, 76, 190
Protestant missionaries, 60–1, 63, 68
Puginier, Mgr Paul, 117–19, 122, 133, 135, 137–8, 140, 142–3, 145, 205, 229

Quinhon, 39–40, 41, 144

Railway, first in China, 152
Rangoon, 89
Red River, 19, 20, 25, 83, 93, 94, 108, 111, 113–16, 128, 131, 144, 165, 183, 186, 213, 215, 220, 272, 284
Rheinhart, M., 206
Rhodes, Alexandre de, 34–5
Rivière, Capt. Henri Laurent, 189–90, 191, 198; and Tongking, 191–2; occupation of Hongay, 199; attack on Nam-Dinh, 199–201; and Black Flags, 190, 203–6, 284
Russia; and China, 56–7; and second opium war, 69; intervention in Sinkiang, 154, 161, 171–4, 180; Soviet, 285

Saigon, Treaty of 1874, 143–4
Saigon, 24–5, 39, 40, 49, 284; and Tayson, 28, 29; and French intervention, 74–6; Treaty of, 76, 77; and Garnier, 79, 80; and Dupuis, 114, 123, 124
Semallé, Vicomte de, 236, 244
Senez, Captain, 115
Shanghai, 58, 61, 69, 72, 114, 194–5; arsenal at, 152, 161
Shensi, Muslim rebellion in, 153
Siam, 26, 49
Shimonoseki, 279
Sinkiang, 84; Muslim rebellion in, 84, 153, 155; Treaty of Livadia, 172, 173, 180
Singapore, 262
Sino-American Treaty (1858), 265–6
Sino-French Treaty (1844), 60, 61, 62
Sino-French Treaty at Tientsin (1884), 238, 239, 240, 266, 267, 269, 270, 284; fight over acceptance, 244–51; execution of, 276; final Treaty of 1885, 276–7
Sino-Japanese war, 279–82
Social habits of Vietnamese, 44–5

Sontay, 106, 107, 117, 119, 133–4, 216, 217, 223–6, 229, 234, 239, 273
Soochow, arsenal at, 152
Soult, Marshal, 48, 54
Spain; missionaries, 30, 35; navigators, 55; and French intervention, 73; missionaries and Garnier, 129, 142
Summer Palace, 279, 280
Sung Dynasty, 20, 21, 22
Sun Yat-sen, 285
Szechwan, 80, 93

Tainan, 281
Taipei, 281, 282
Taiping rebellion, 65–9, 83–4, 86, 88, 92, 99, 103–4, 105, 111, 148
Tali, 83, 86, 88, 91, 120; Sultan of (Tu Wen-hsiu), 89, 90, 91, 120, 155
Tamsui, 256–7, 266, 270
T'ang Ching-sung, 193, 194, 195, 197, 198, 201, 202, 208, 217, 224, 229, 239; and Japanese war, 281, 282
T'ang Dynasty, 20, 21
Tayson, 284; revolt of, 28, 29, 30, 36, 39, 40–1, 50
Telegraph office, Chinese, 152
Thai people, 26
Thaibinh, 131
Than-Hoa, 197
Thieu Tri, 62–3, 70
Thomson, M., 199
Tibet, 71
Tientsin, agreement of, 198; Treaty of 1884, 238, 239, 240, 244–51; Treaty of 1885, 278; second opium war, 68–9
Tongking, Kingdom of, 37, 73–4, 76, 83, 110, 117, 124, 127–8, 133, 140, 180, 197; and French, 115, 165, 181ff., 207, 211, 215, 285; evacuation of, 240–1, 276; campaign of (1884–5), 258–63; and Vietnamese citizens, 278–9
Treaty of 1787, 37–8, 72
Treaty of 1874, 183, 184, 185, 187, 190, 199, 219, 237
Tricou, M., 210, 211, 212, 220, 222, 236
Trinh family, 26, 27, 28
Tseng Chi-tse, Marquis, 174, 176–7, 179–80, 181, 183, 184, 193, 210, 285; and Tongking, 186, 187–8, 219; and French, 220, 222, 223, 235, 237, 270, 276; and British Government, 262; and Formosa, 267; death, 280
Tseng Kuo-ch'uan, 193, 195, 247, 248, 249
Tseng Kuo-fan, 67–8, 69, 75, 148, 151; his Hunan army, 151; and Nien, 151–2; death, 152; and Macartney, 176–7

295